AF411585

ANNA EHRENSTEIN

SALIOU BA / DONKAFELE / NYAMWATHI GICHAU
LYDIA LIKIBI / AWA SECK

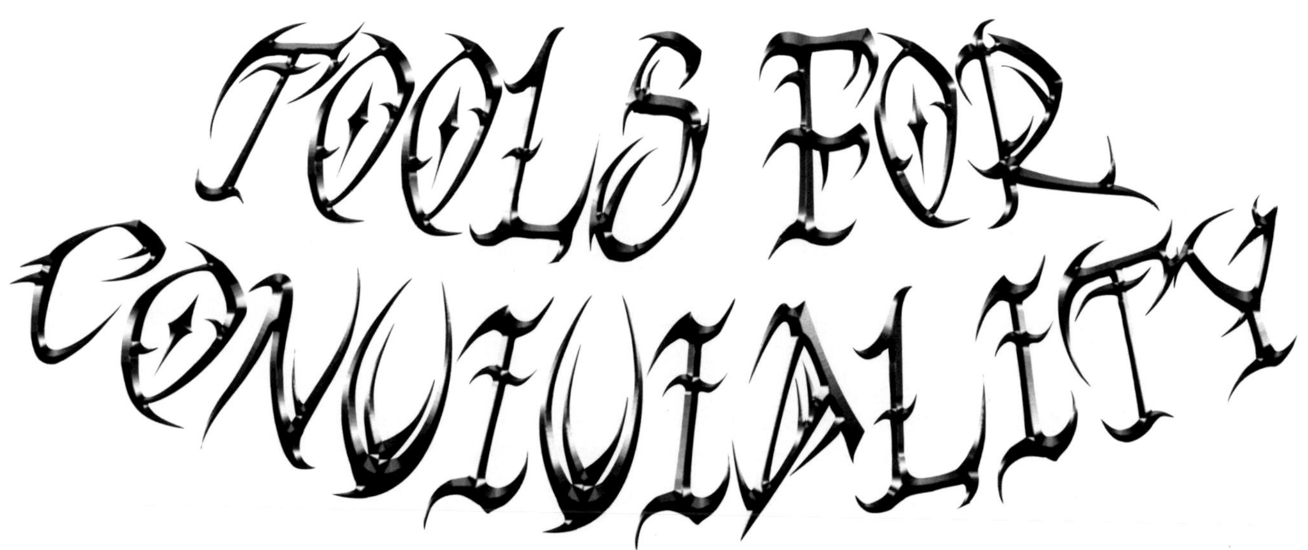

TEXT VON / BY
EMILY WATLINGTON

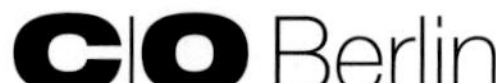 C|O Berlin   SPECTOR BOOKS

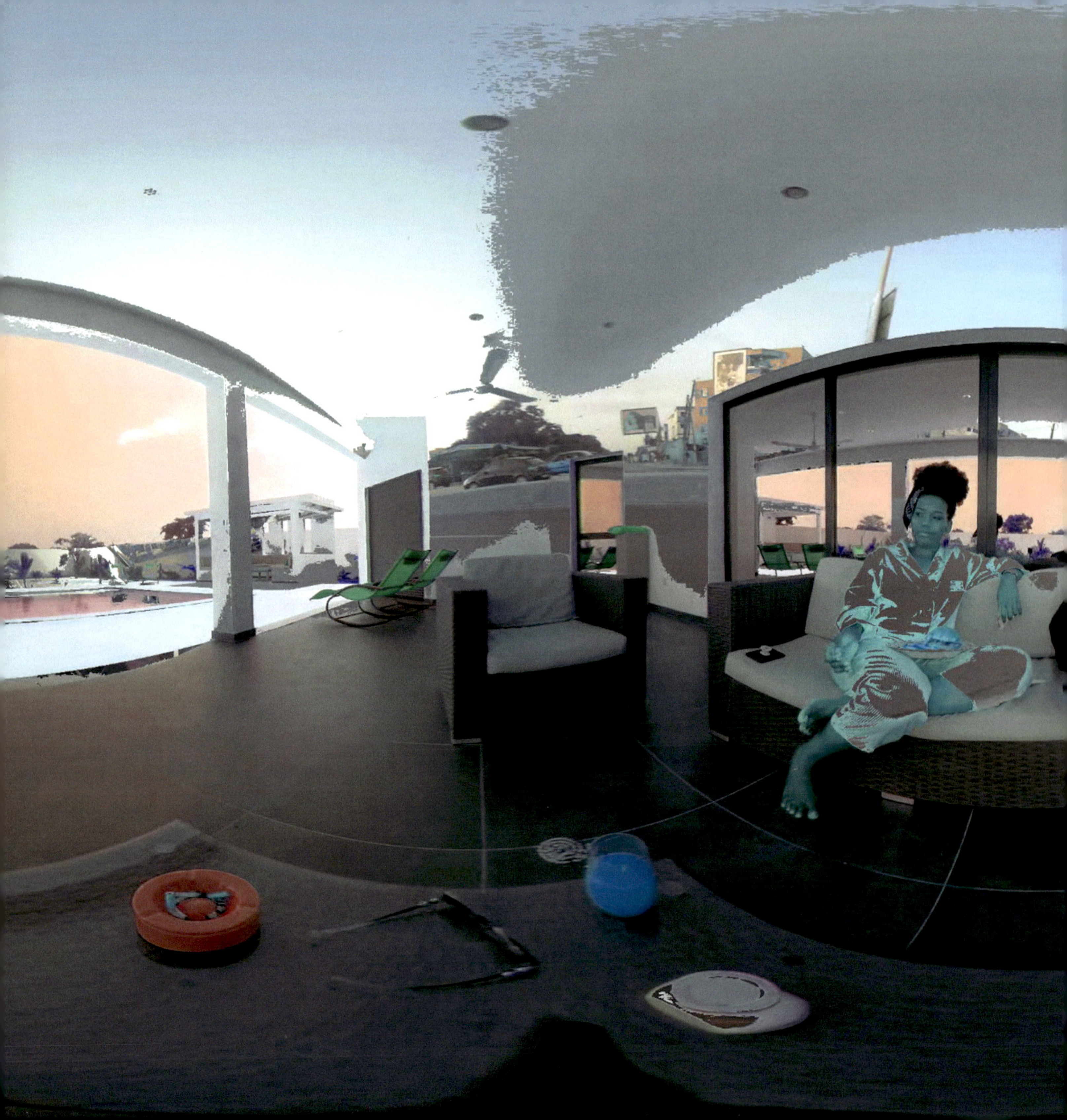

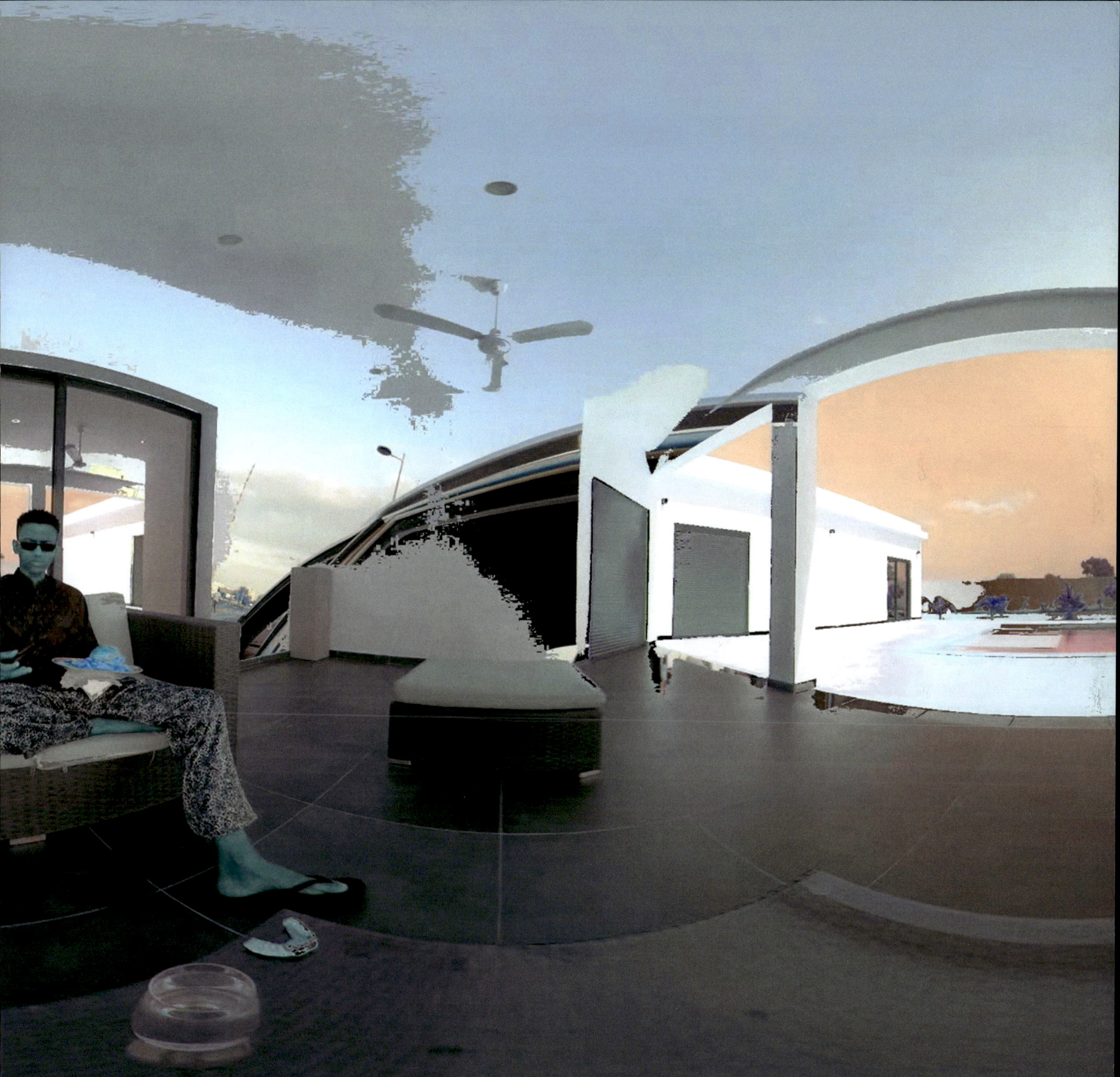

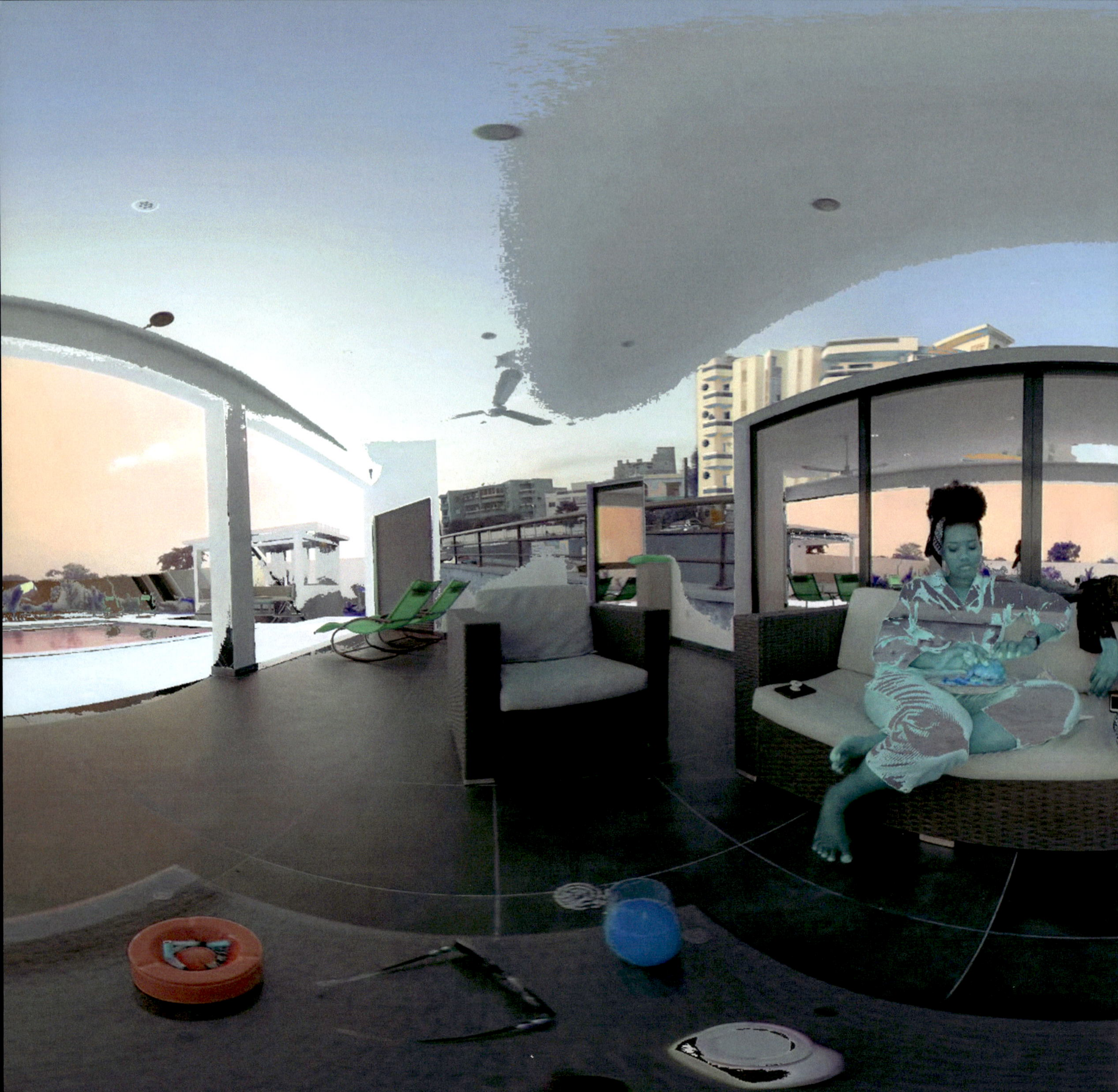

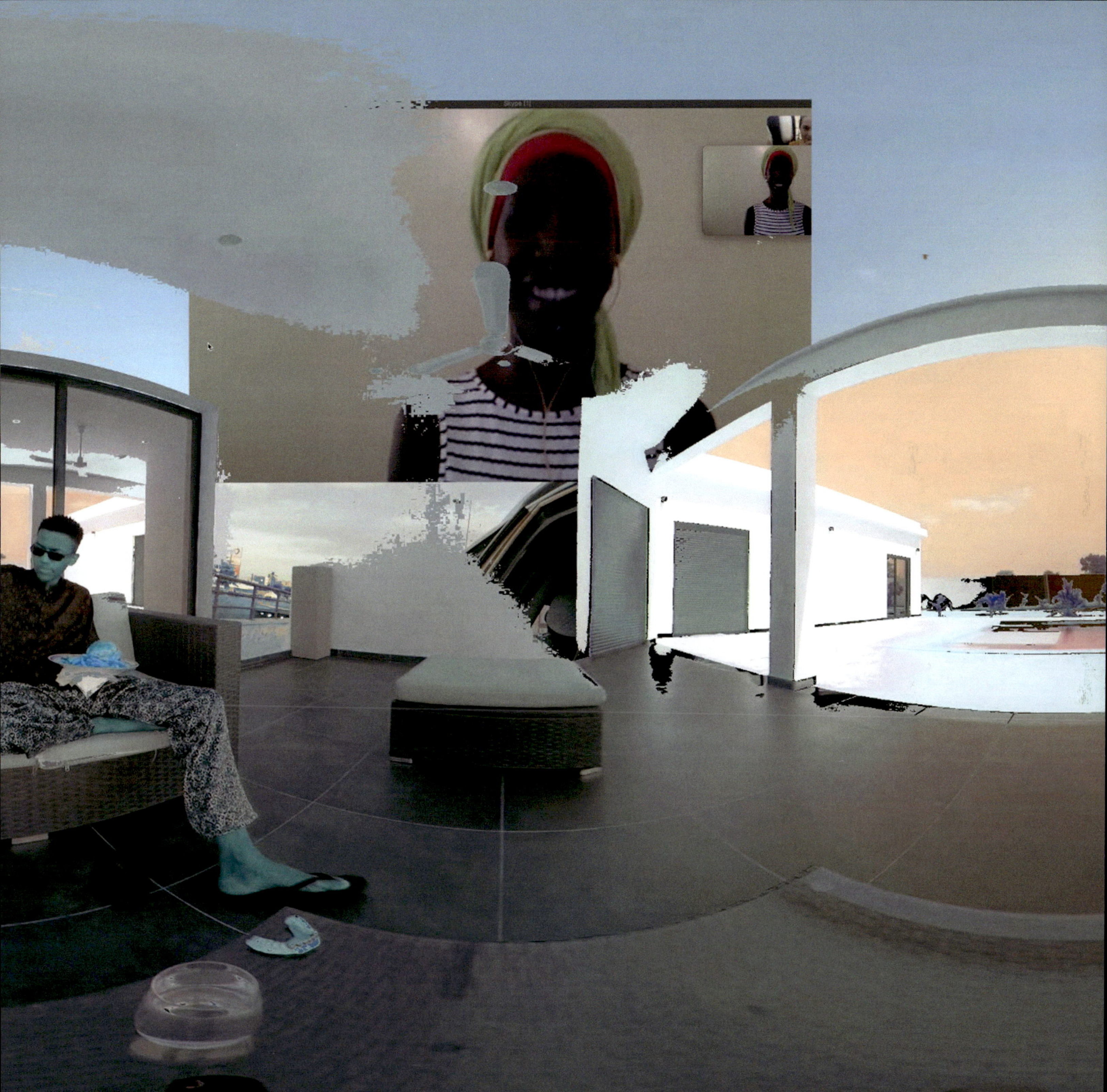

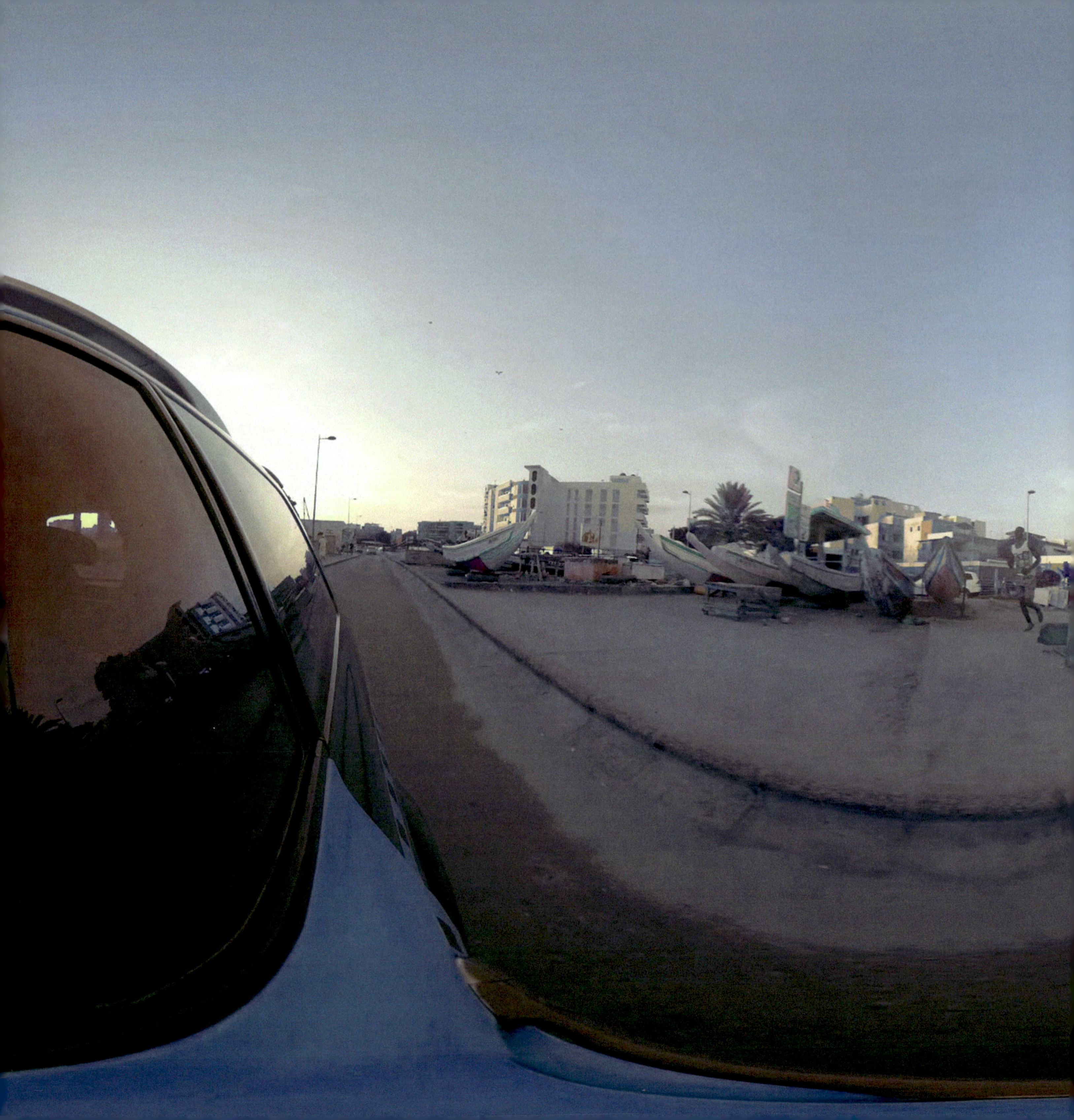

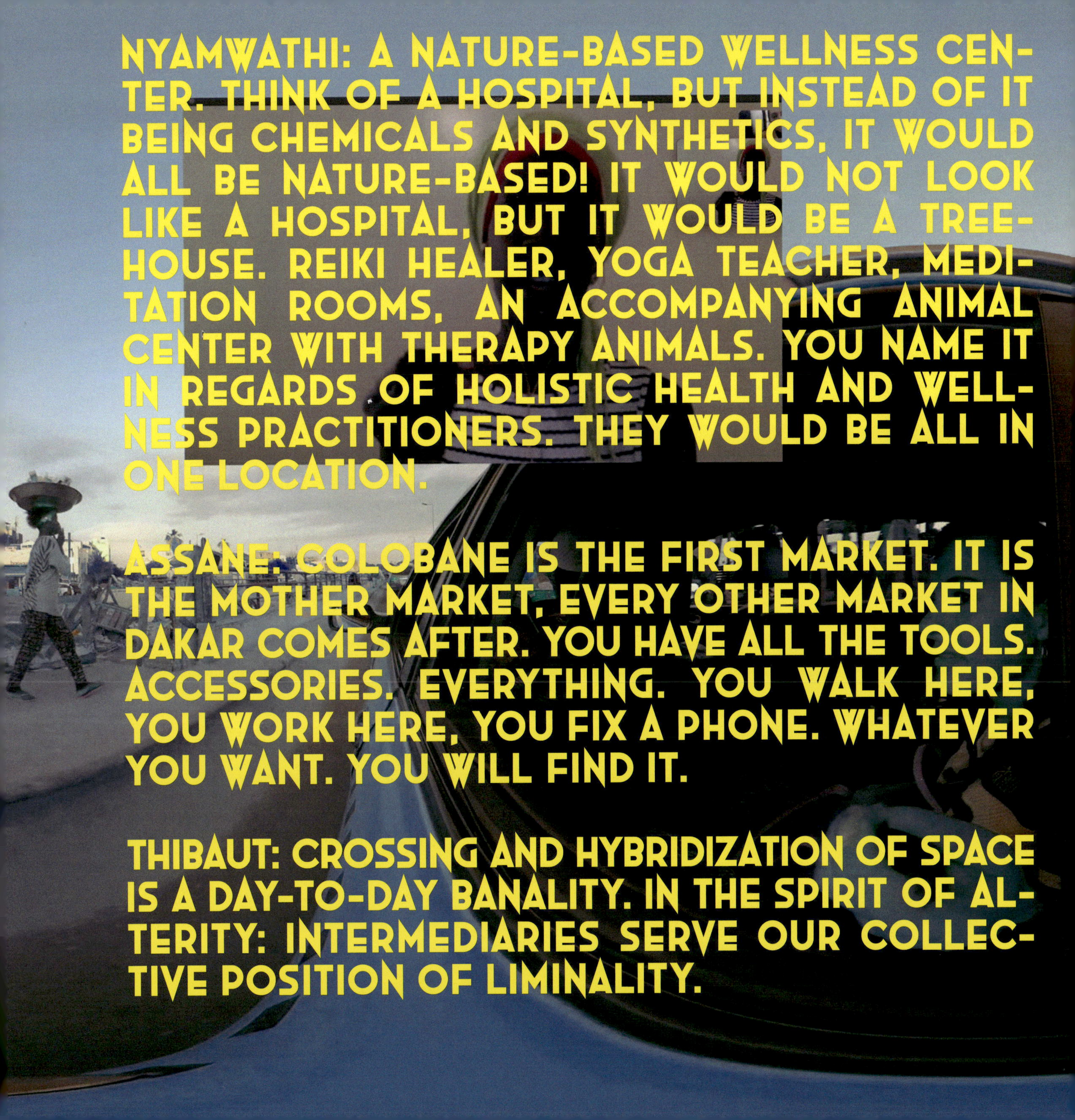

NYAMWATHI: A NATURE-BASED WELLNESS CENTER. THINK OF A HOSPITAL, BUT INSTEAD OF IT BEING CHEMICALS AND SYNTHETICS, IT WOULD ALL BE NATURE-BASED! IT WOULD NOT LOOK LIKE A HOSPITAL, BUT IT WOULD BE A TREEHOUSE. REIKI HEALER, YOGA TEACHER, MEDITATION ROOMS, AN ACCOMPANYING ANIMAL CENTER WITH THERAPY ANIMALS. YOU NAME IT IN REGARDS OF HOLISTIC HEALTH AND WELLNESS PRACTITIONERS. THEY WOULD BE ALL IN ONE LOCATION.

ASSANE: COLOBANE IS THE FIRST MARKET. IT IS THE MOTHER MARKET, EVERY OTHER MARKET IN DAKAR COMES AFTER. YOU HAVE ALL THE TOOLS. ACCESSORIES. EVERYTHING. YOU WALK HERE, YOU WORK HERE, YOU FIX A PHONE. WHATEVER YOU WANT. YOU WILL FIND IT.

THIBAUT: CROSSING AND HYBRIDIZATION OF SPACE IS A DAY-TO-DAY BANALITY. IN THE SPIRIT OF ALTERITY: INTERMEDIARIES SERVE OUR COLLECTIVE POSITION OF LIMINALITY.

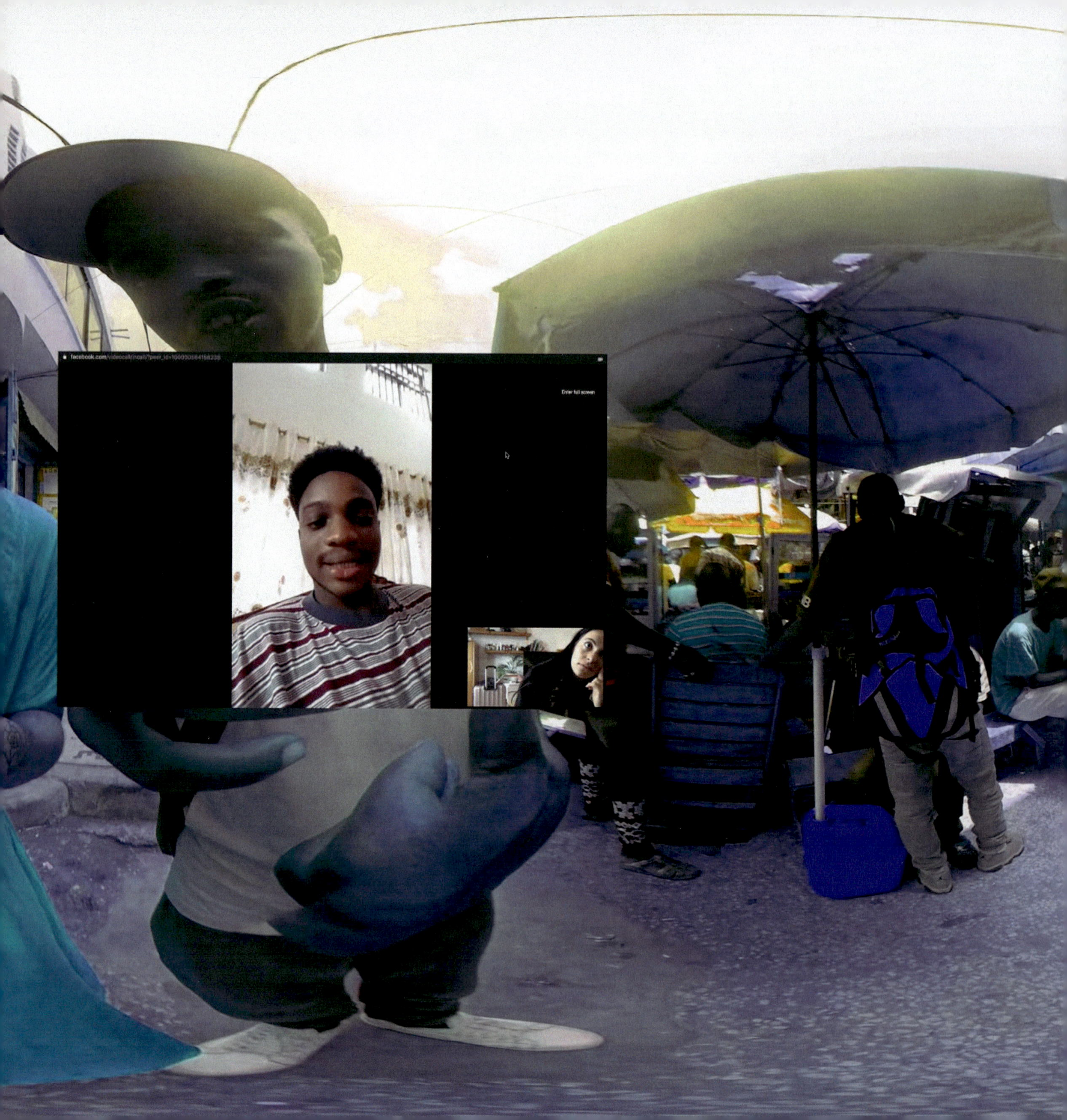

facebook.com/videocall/noah/?peer_id=100000564198238
Enter full screen

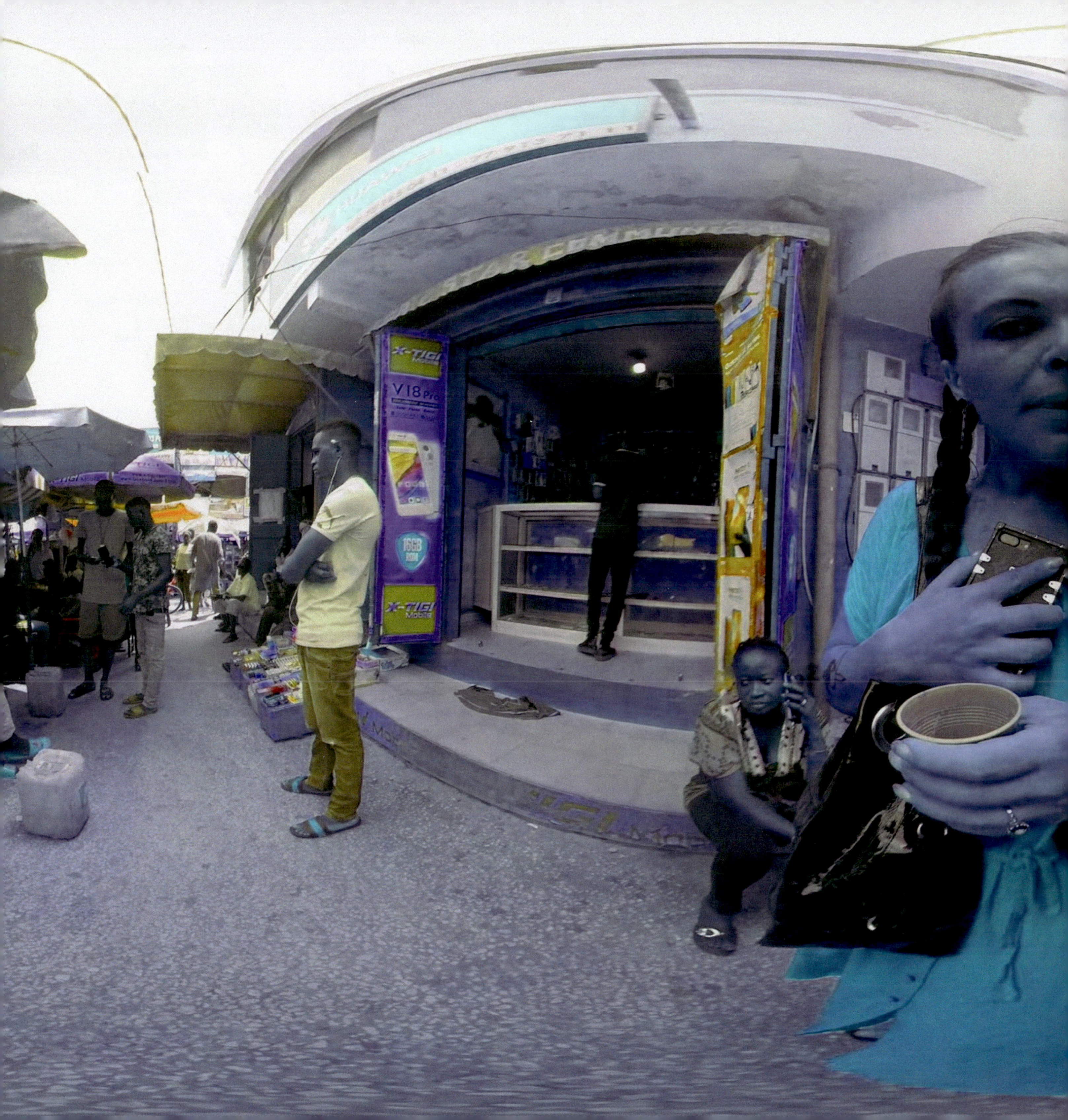
X-TIGI
Mobile
V18 Pro
16GB ROM
X-TIGI
Mobile

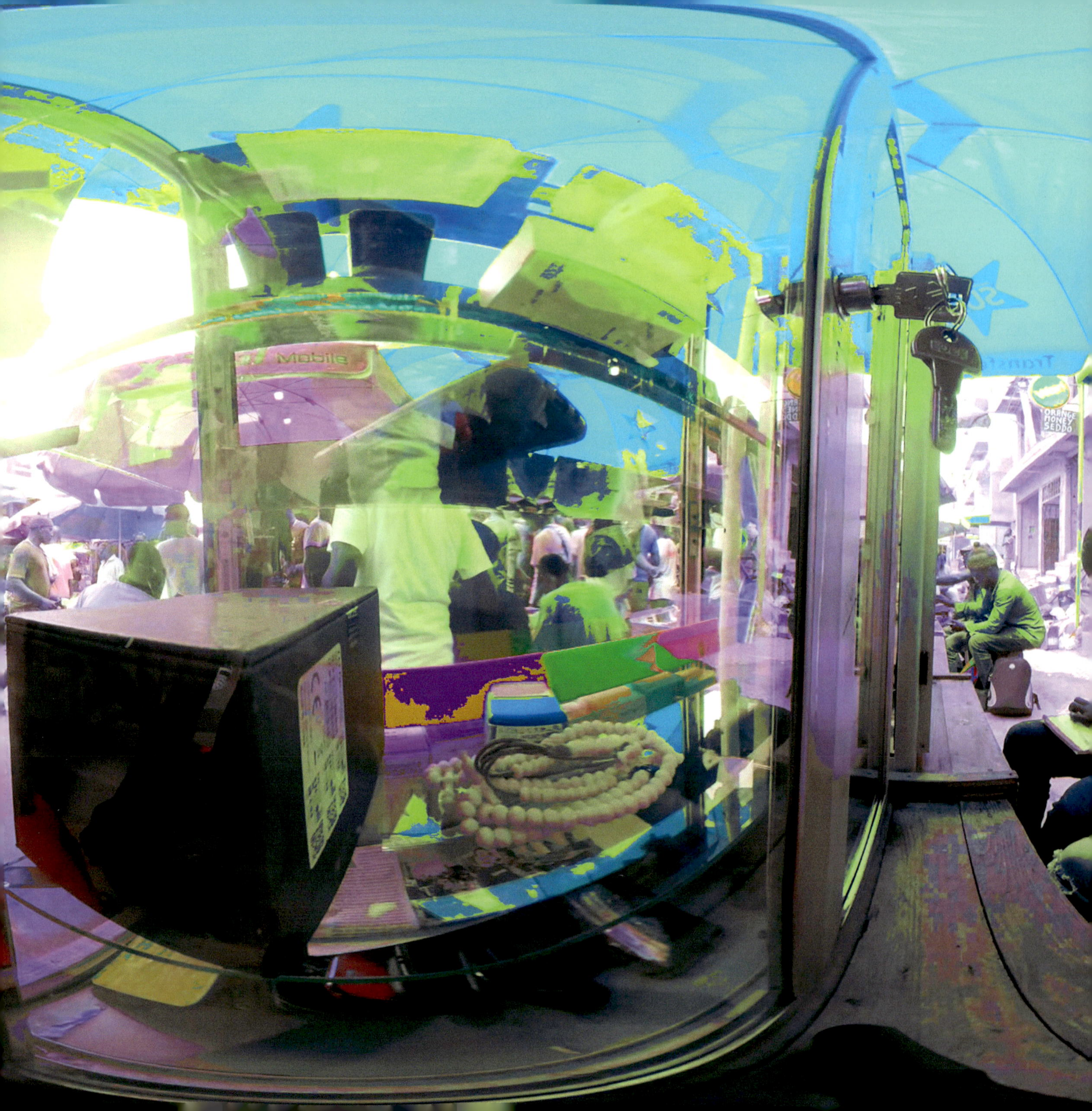

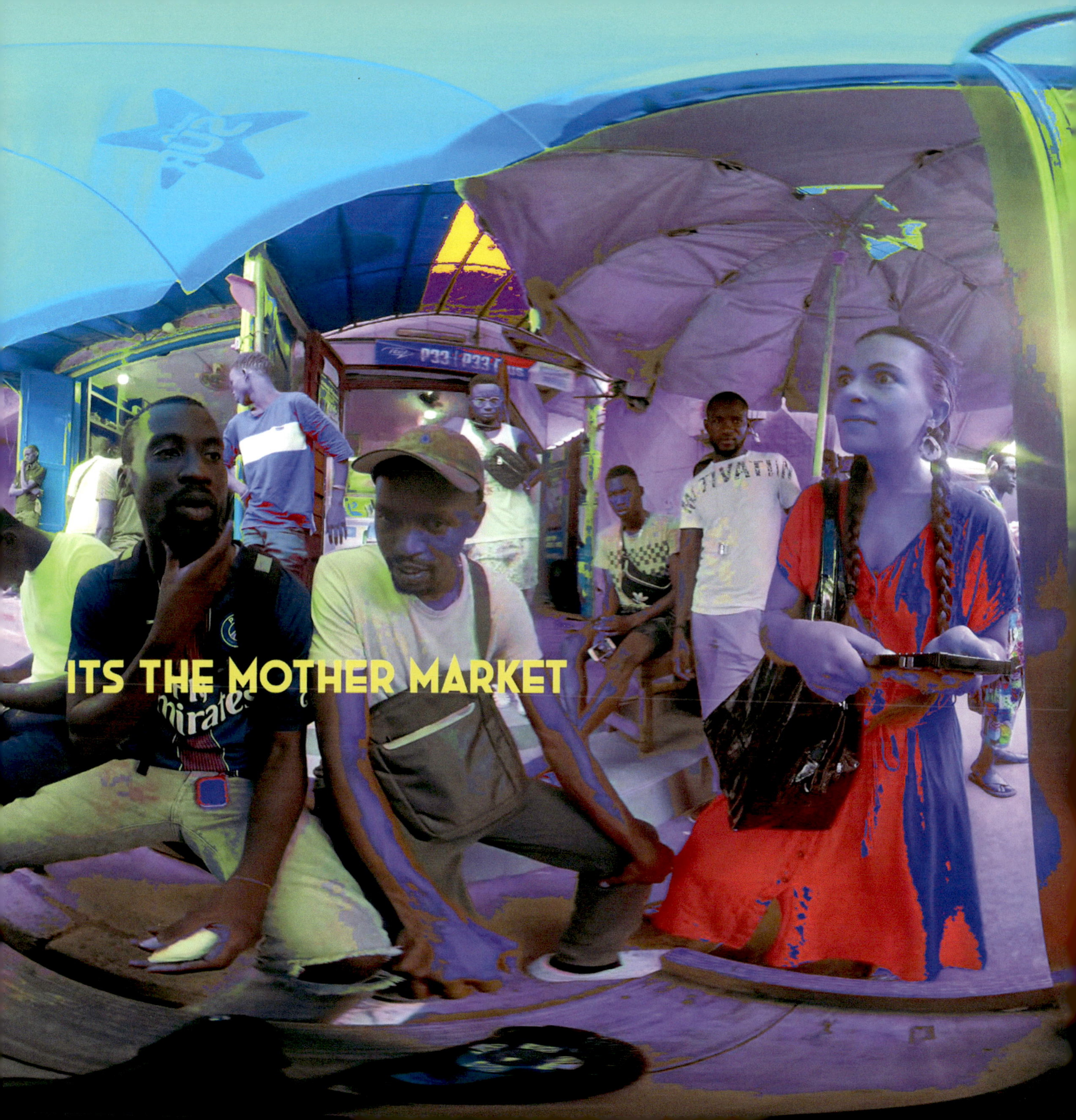
ITS THE MOTHER MARKET

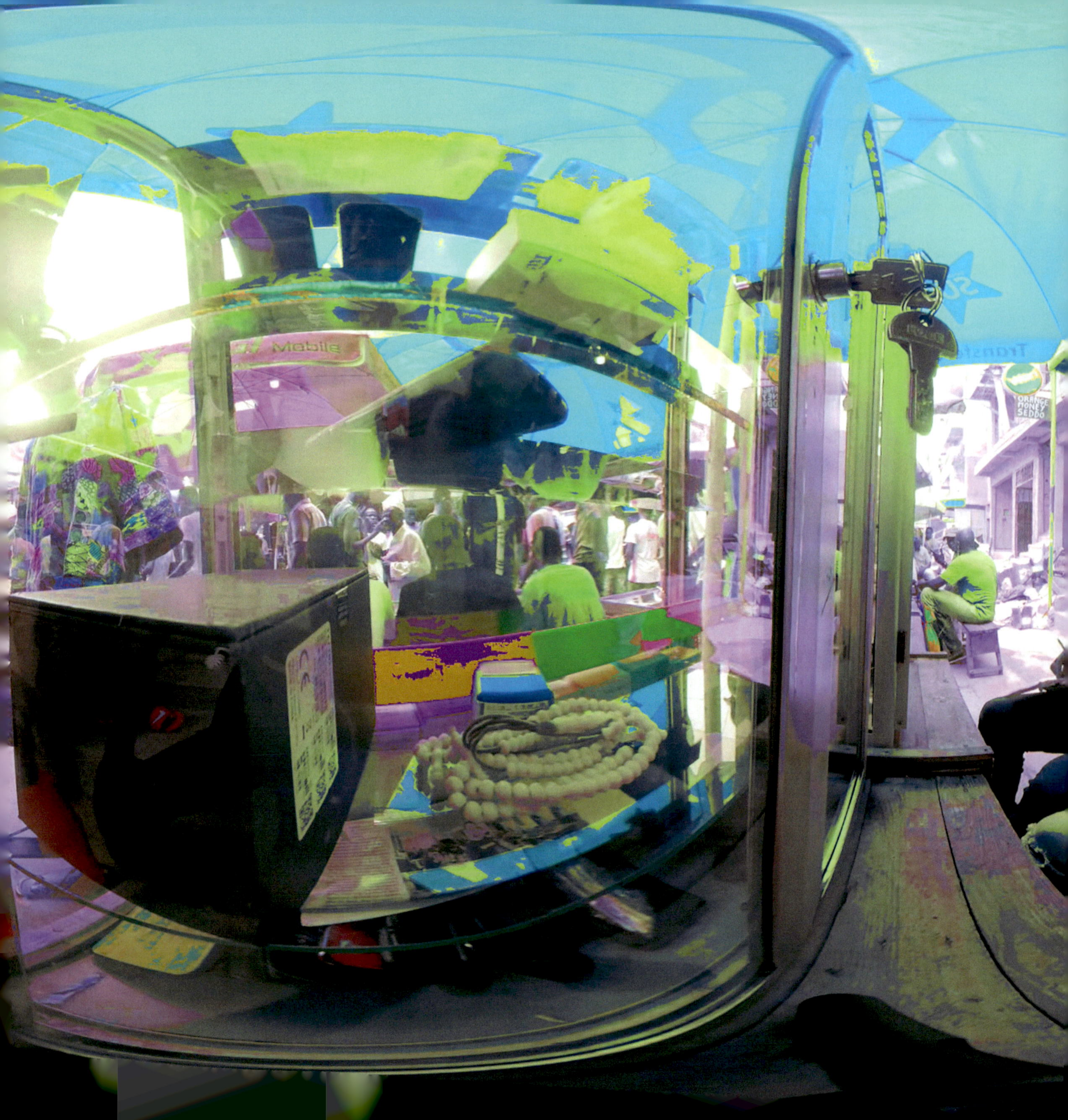

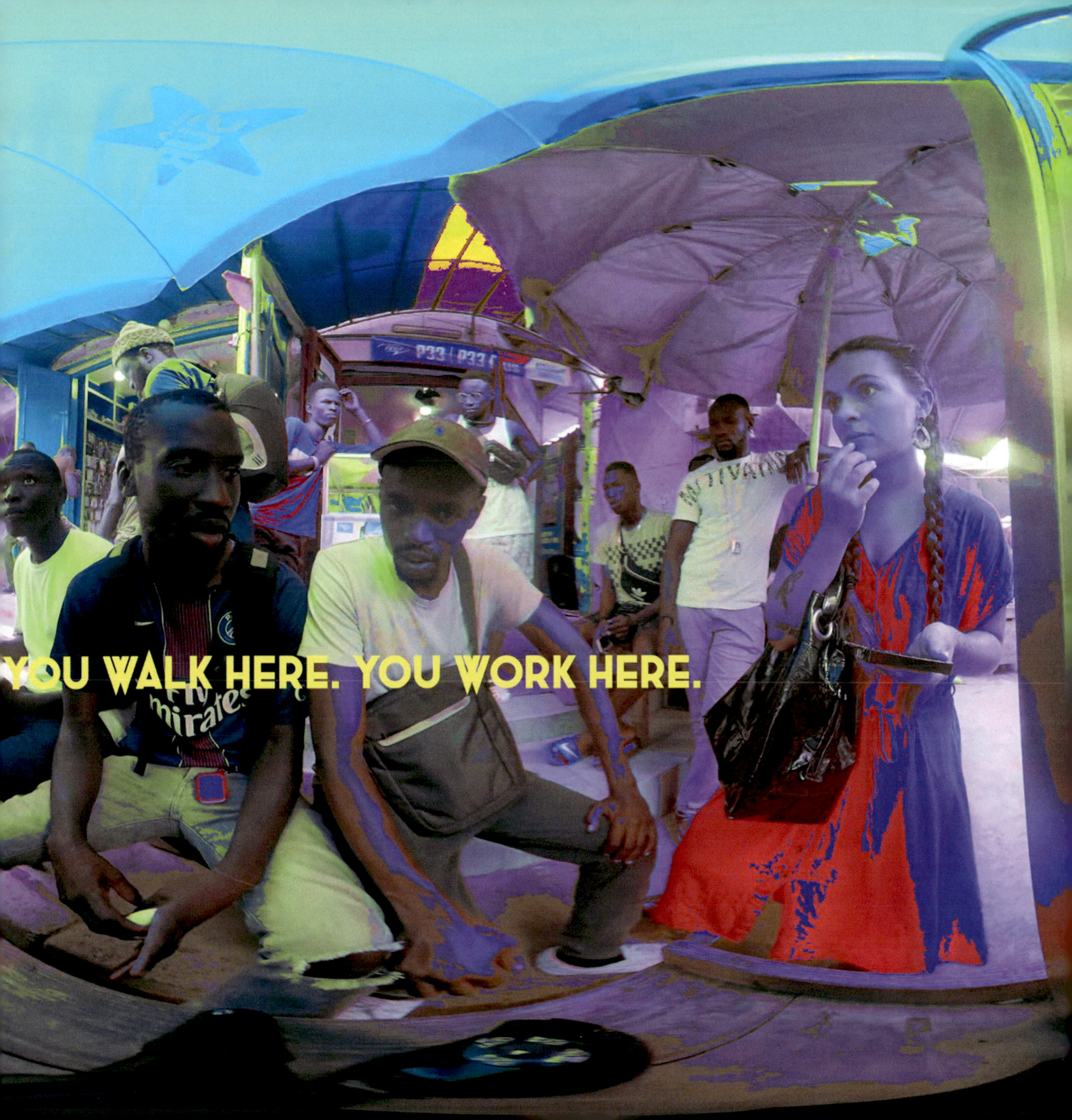
YOU WALK HERE. YOU WORK HERE.

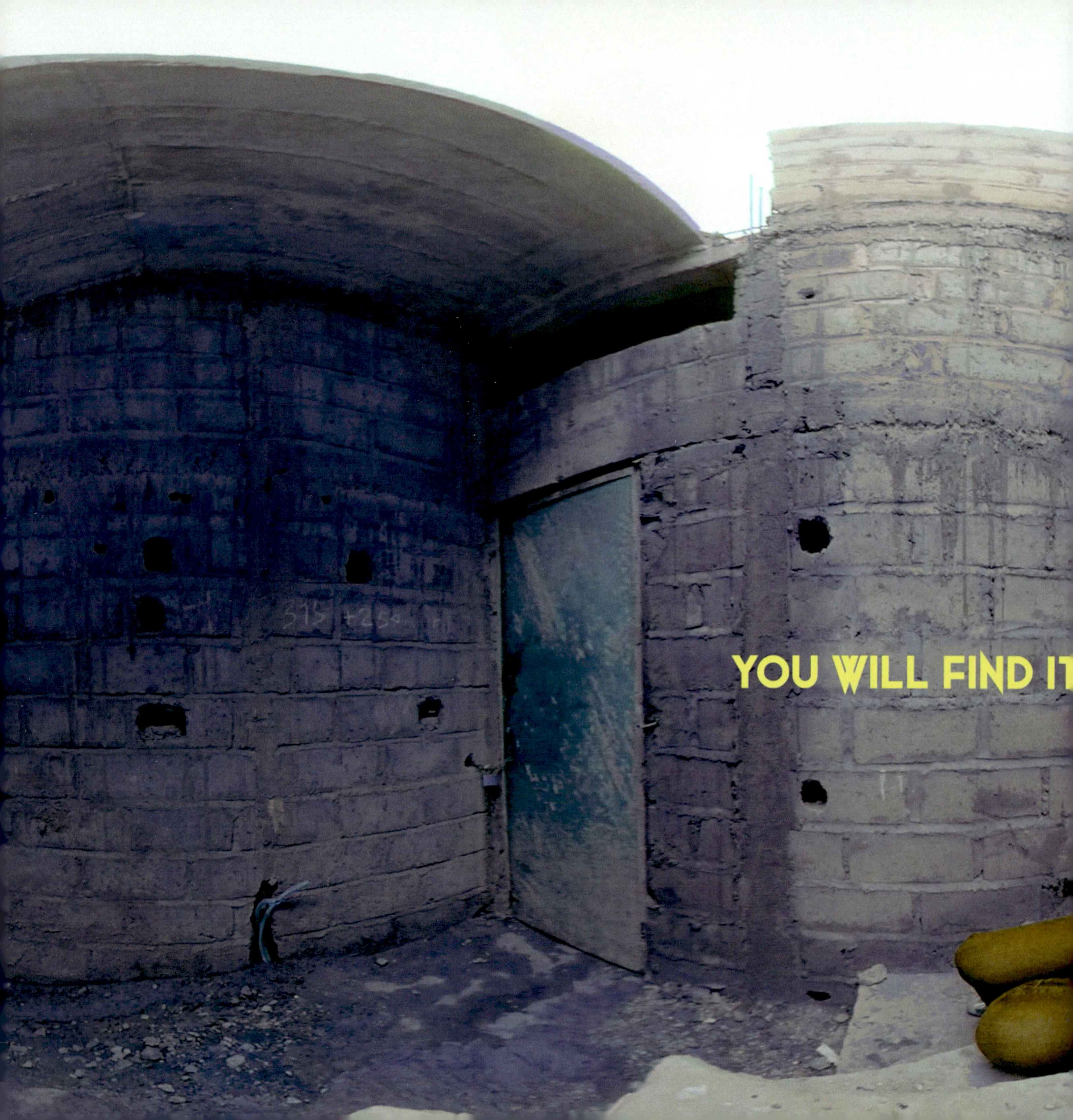

YOU WILL FIND IT

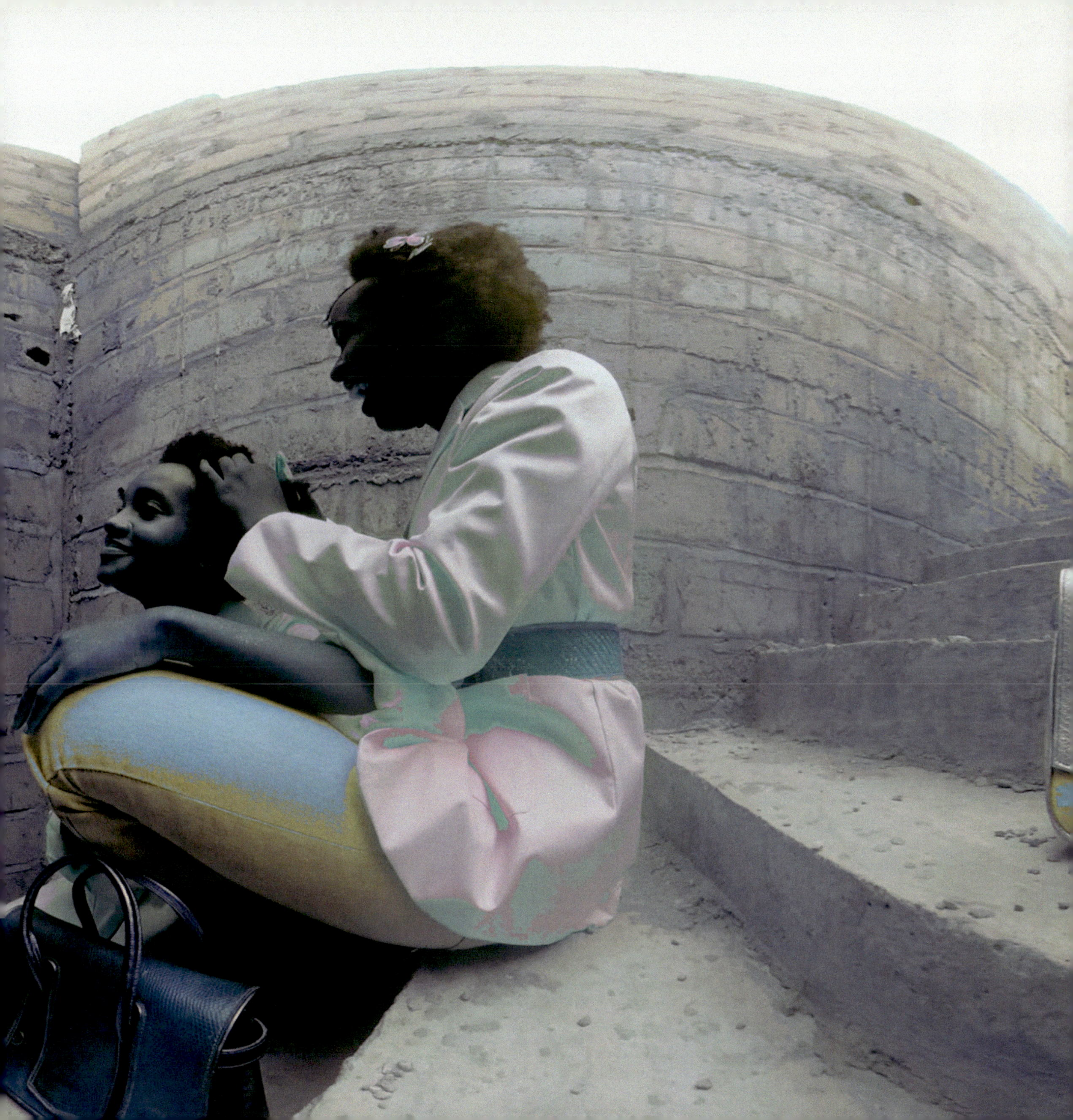

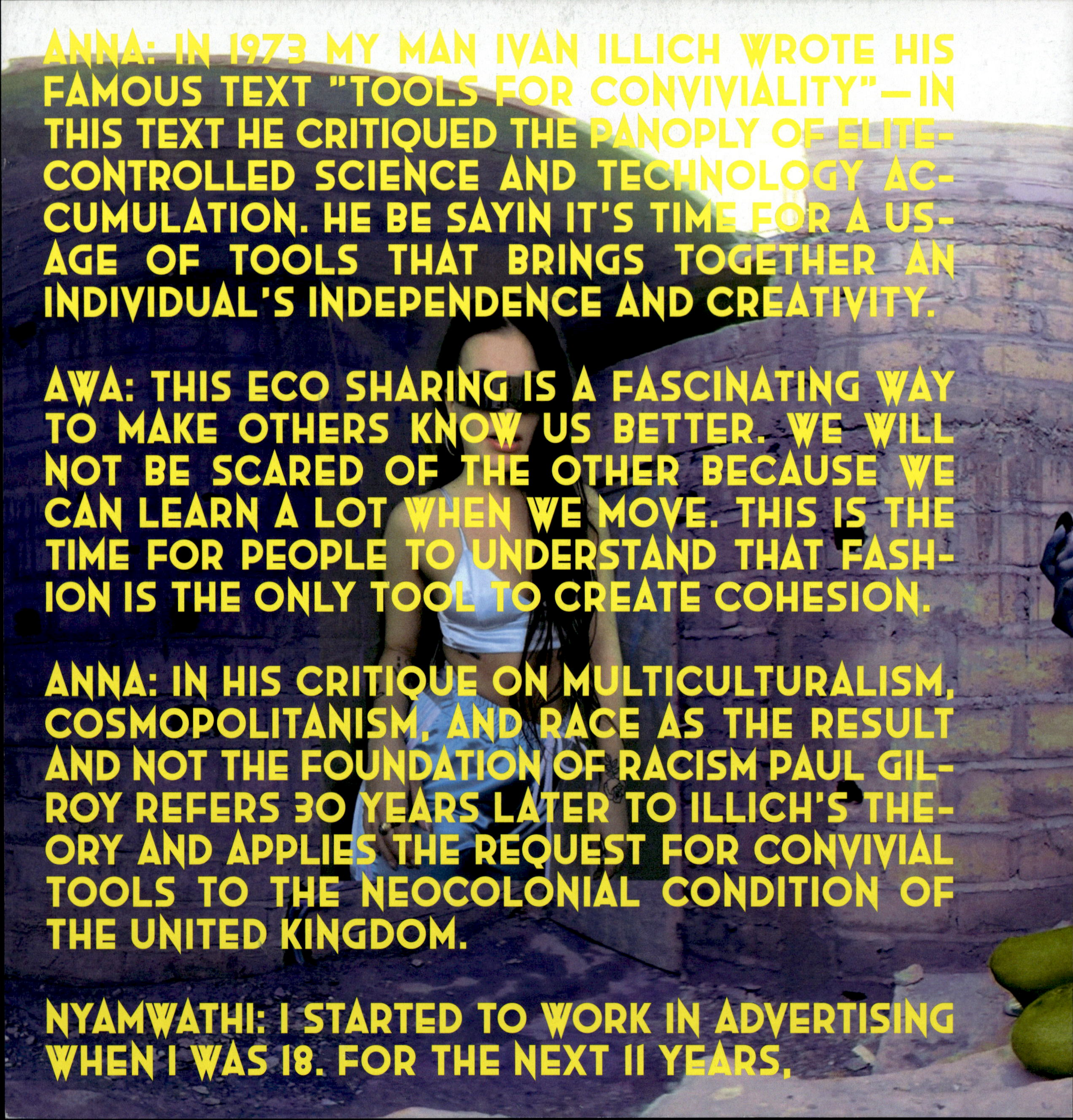

ANNA: IN 1973 MY MAN IVAN ILLICH WROTE HIS FAMOUS TEXT "TOOLS FOR CONVIVIALITY"—IN THIS TEXT HE CRITIQUED THE PANOPLY OF ELITE-CONTROLLED SCIENCE AND TECHNOLOGY AC-CUMULATION. HE BE SAYIN IT'S TIME FOR A US-AGE OF TOOLS THAT BRINGS TOGETHER AN INDIVIDUAL'S INDEPENDENCE AND CREATIVITY.

AWA: THIS ECO SHARING IS A FASCINATING WAY TO MAKE OTHERS KNOW US BETTER. WE WILL NOT BE SCARED OF THE OTHER BECAUSE WE CAN LEARN A LOT WHEN WE MOVE. THIS IS THE TIME FOR PEOPLE TO UNDERSTAND THAT FASH-ION IS THE ONLY TOOL TO CREATE COHESION.

ANNA: IN HIS CRITIQUE ON MULTICULTURALISM, COSMOPOLITANISM, AND RACE AS THE RESULT AND NOT THE FOUNDATION OF RACISM PAUL GIL-ROY REFERS 30 YEARS LATER TO ILLICH'S THE-ORY AND APPLIES THE REQUEST FOR CONVIVIAL TOOLS TO THE NEOCOLONIAL CONDITION OF THE UNITED KINGDOM.

NYAMWATHI: I STARTED TO WORK IN ADVERTISING WHEN I WAS 18. FOR THE NEXT 11 YEARS,

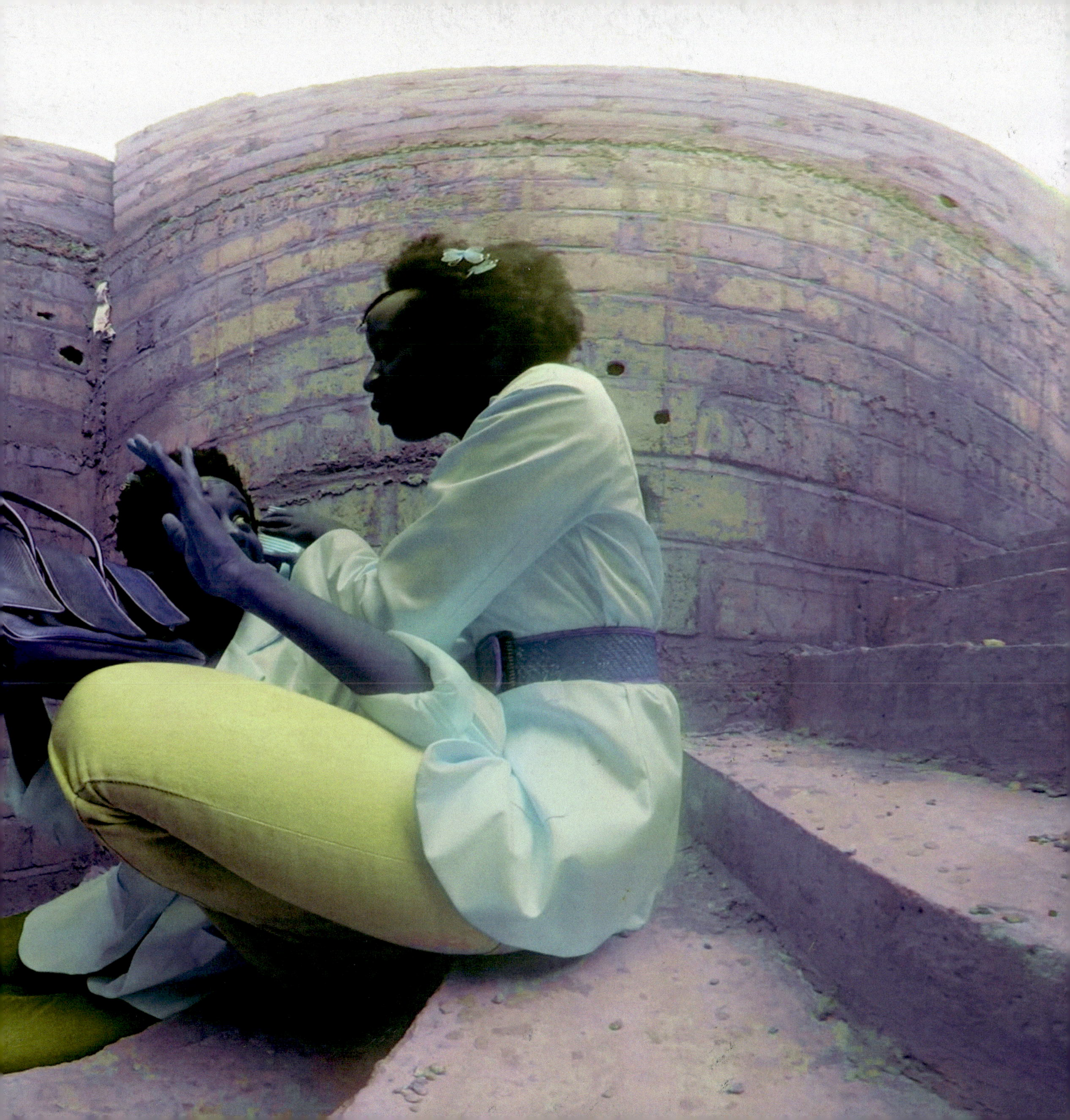

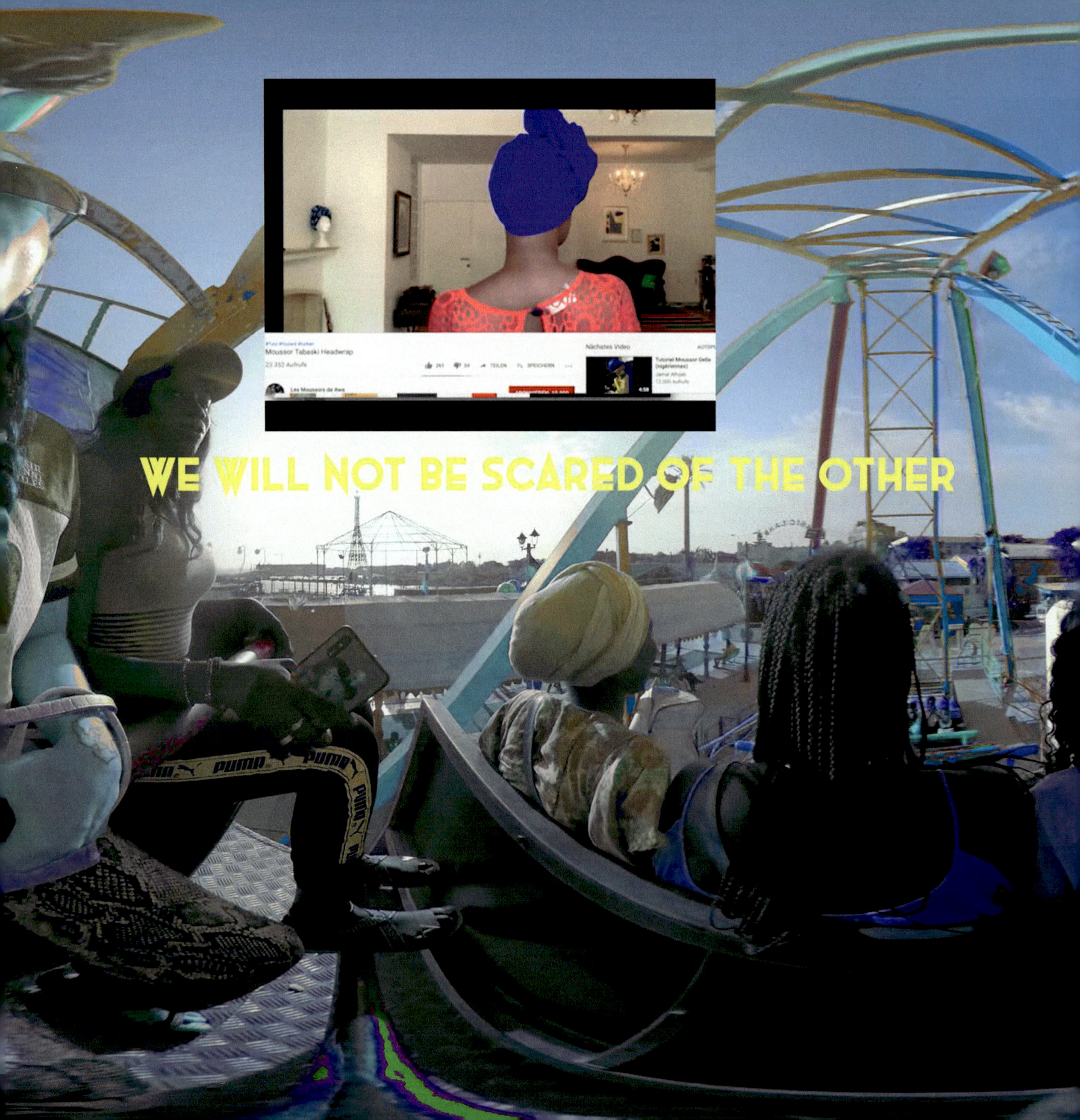

Moussor Tabaski Headwrap
23.352 Aufrufe
Les Moussoirs de Awa
Nächstes Video
Tutoriel Moussor Gele (nigériennes)
WE WILL NOT BE SCARED OF THE OTHER

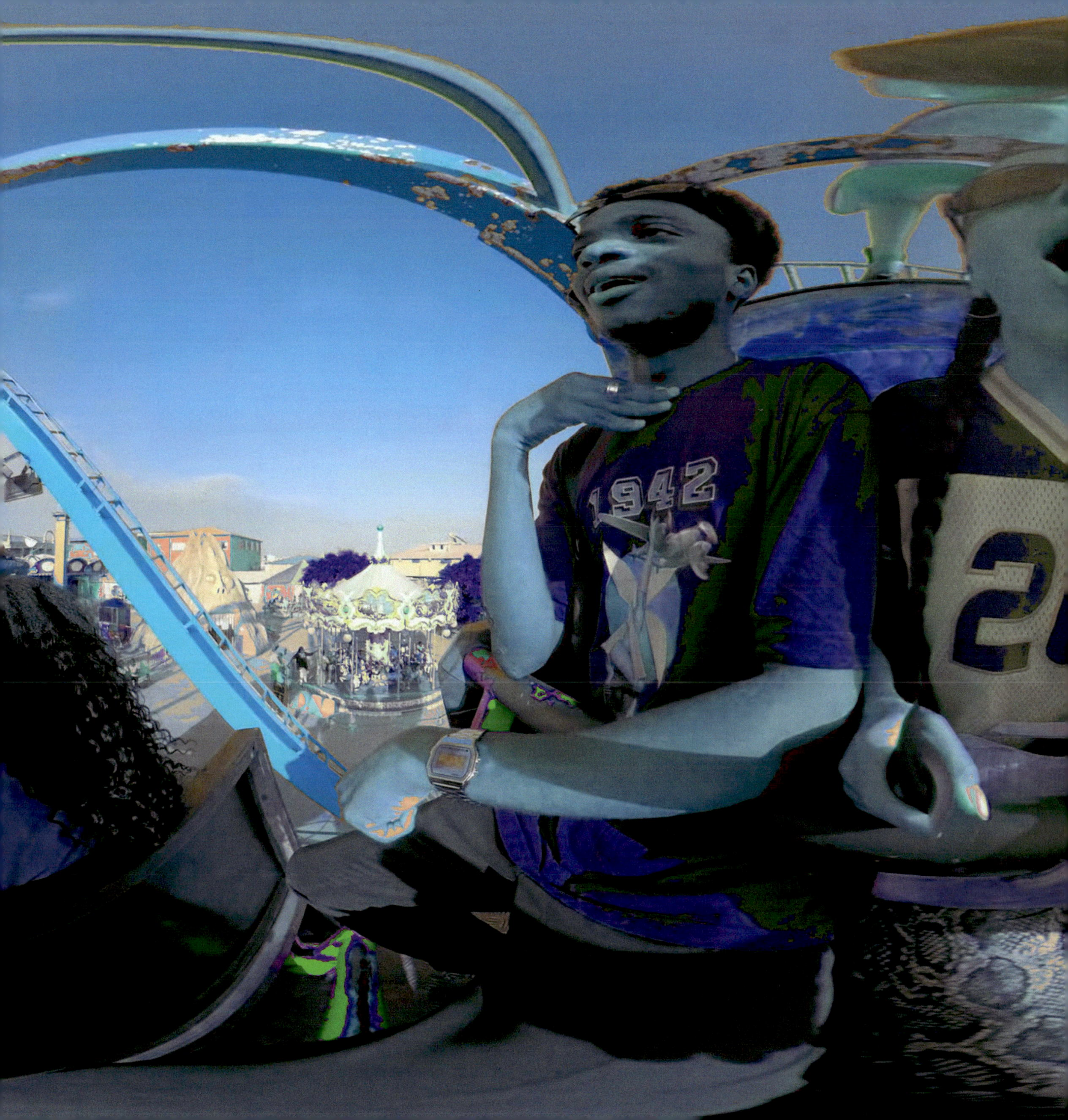

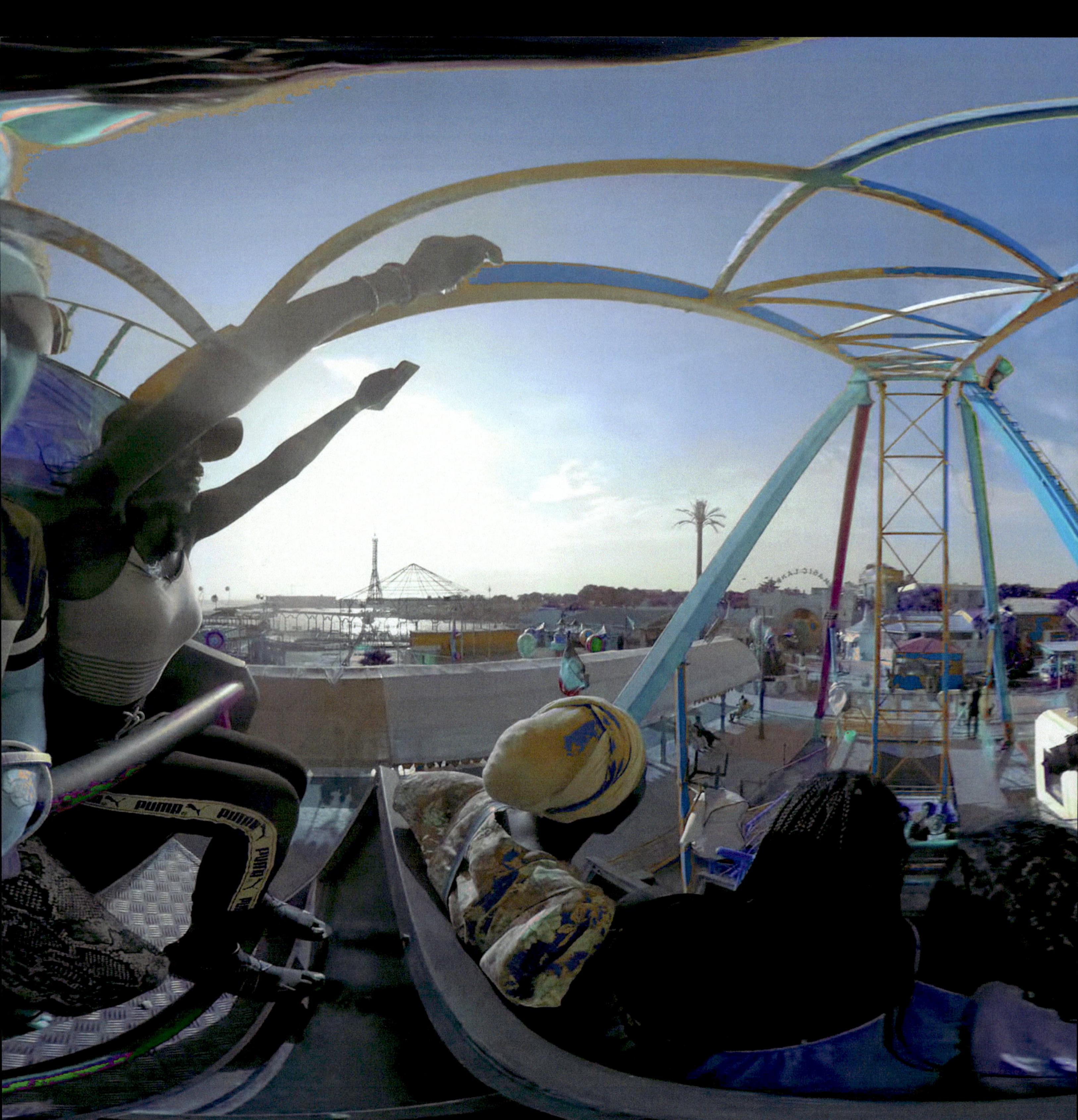

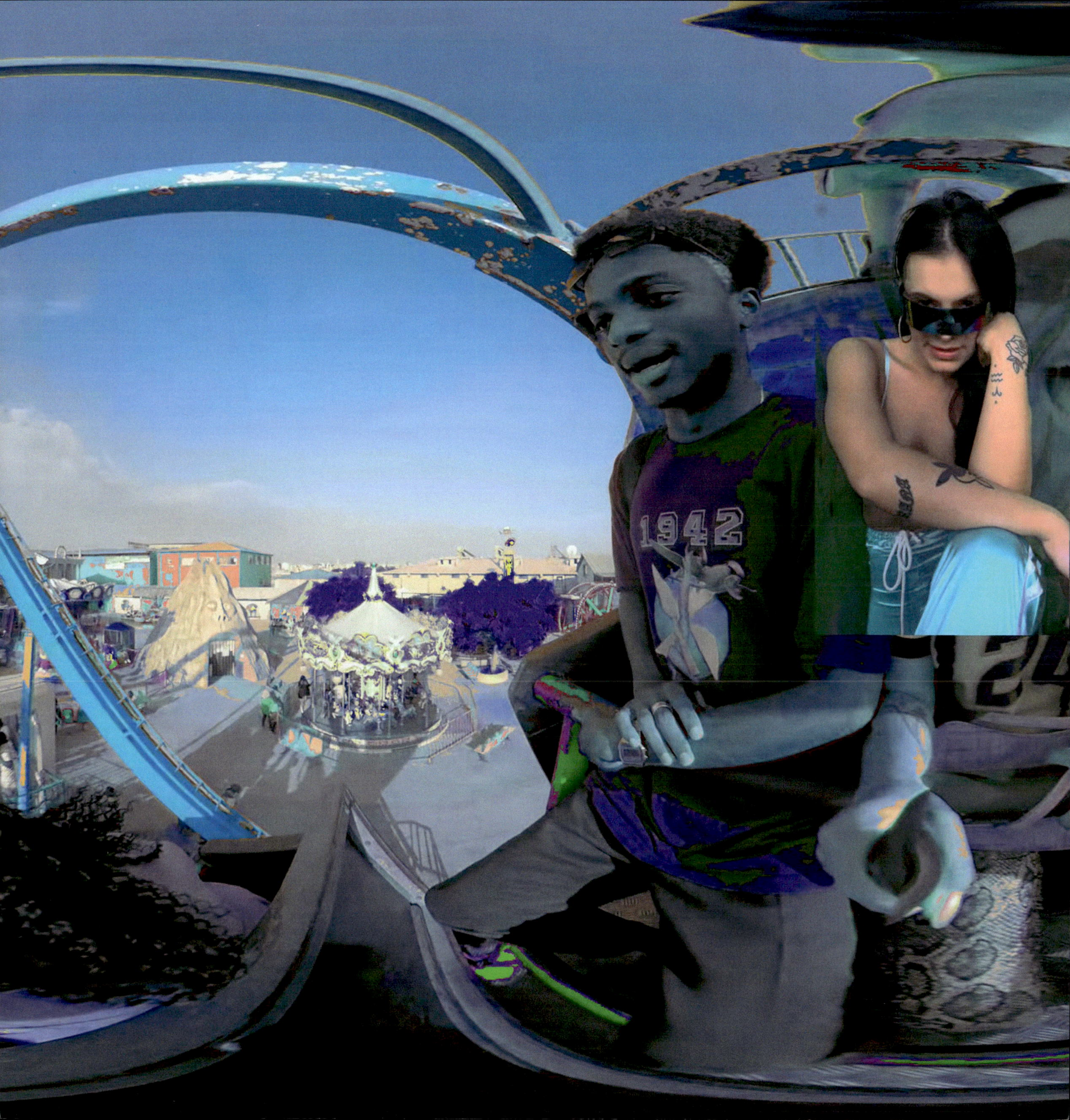

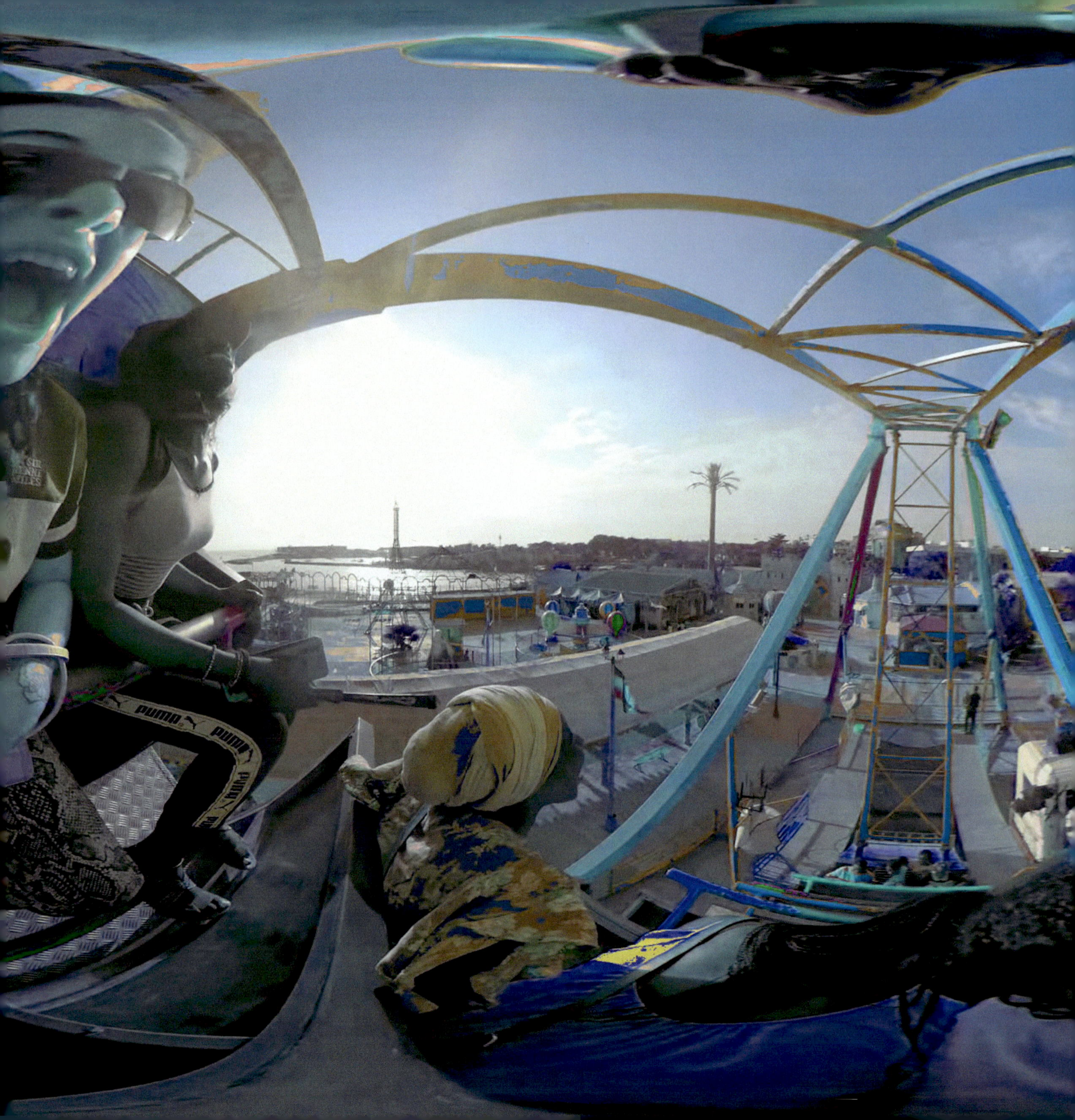

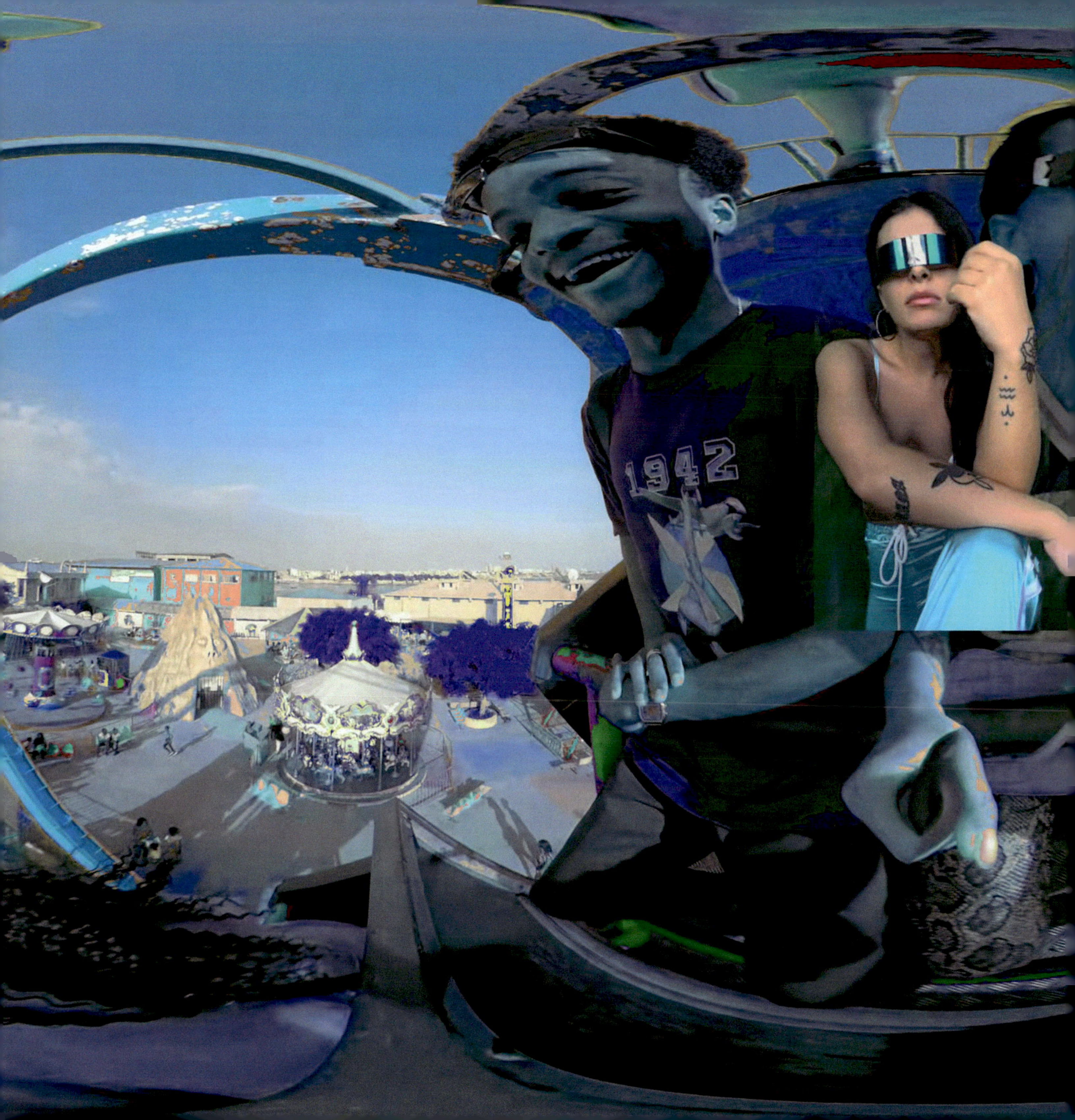
1942

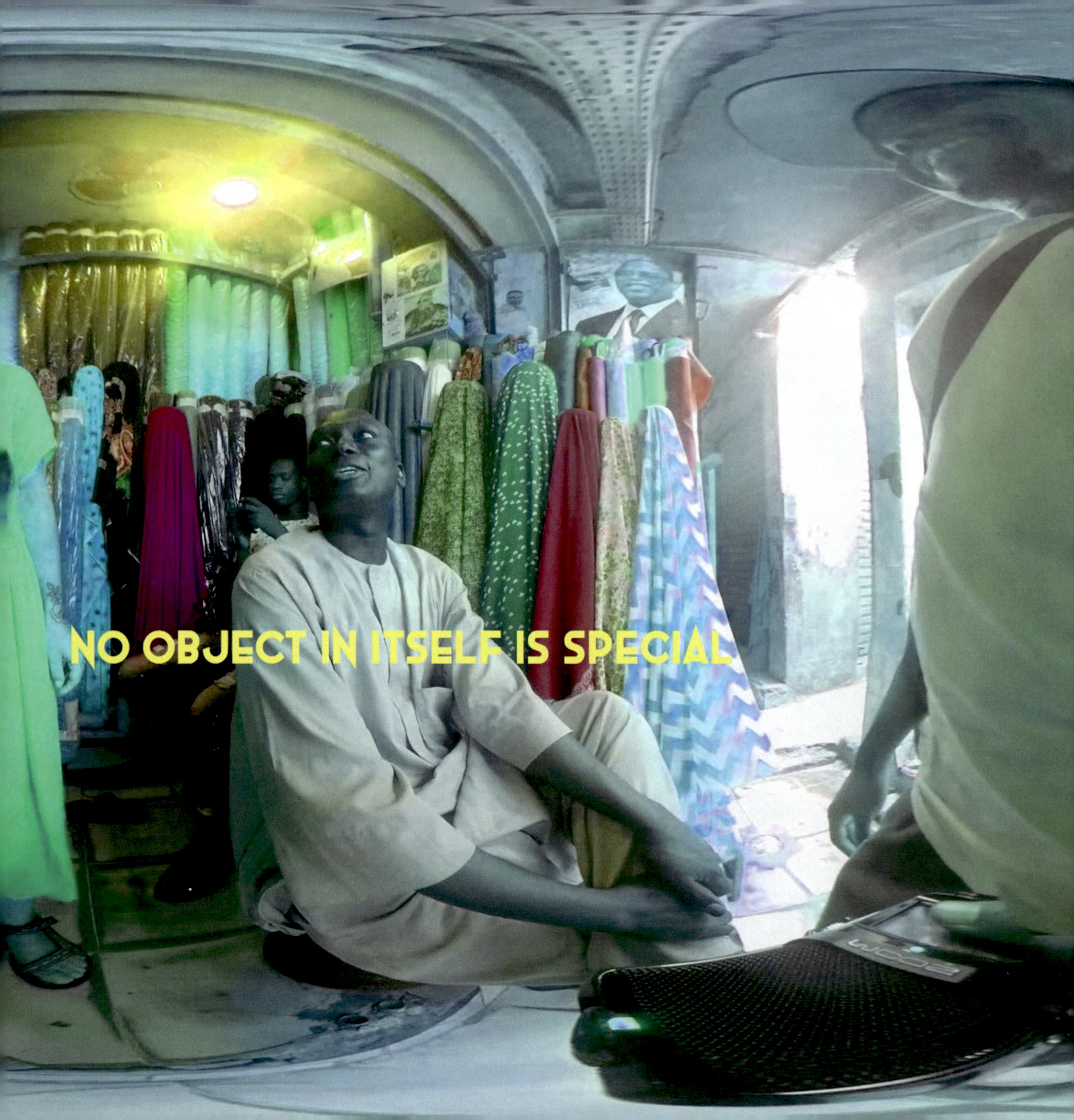
NO OBJECT IN ITSELF IS SPECIAL

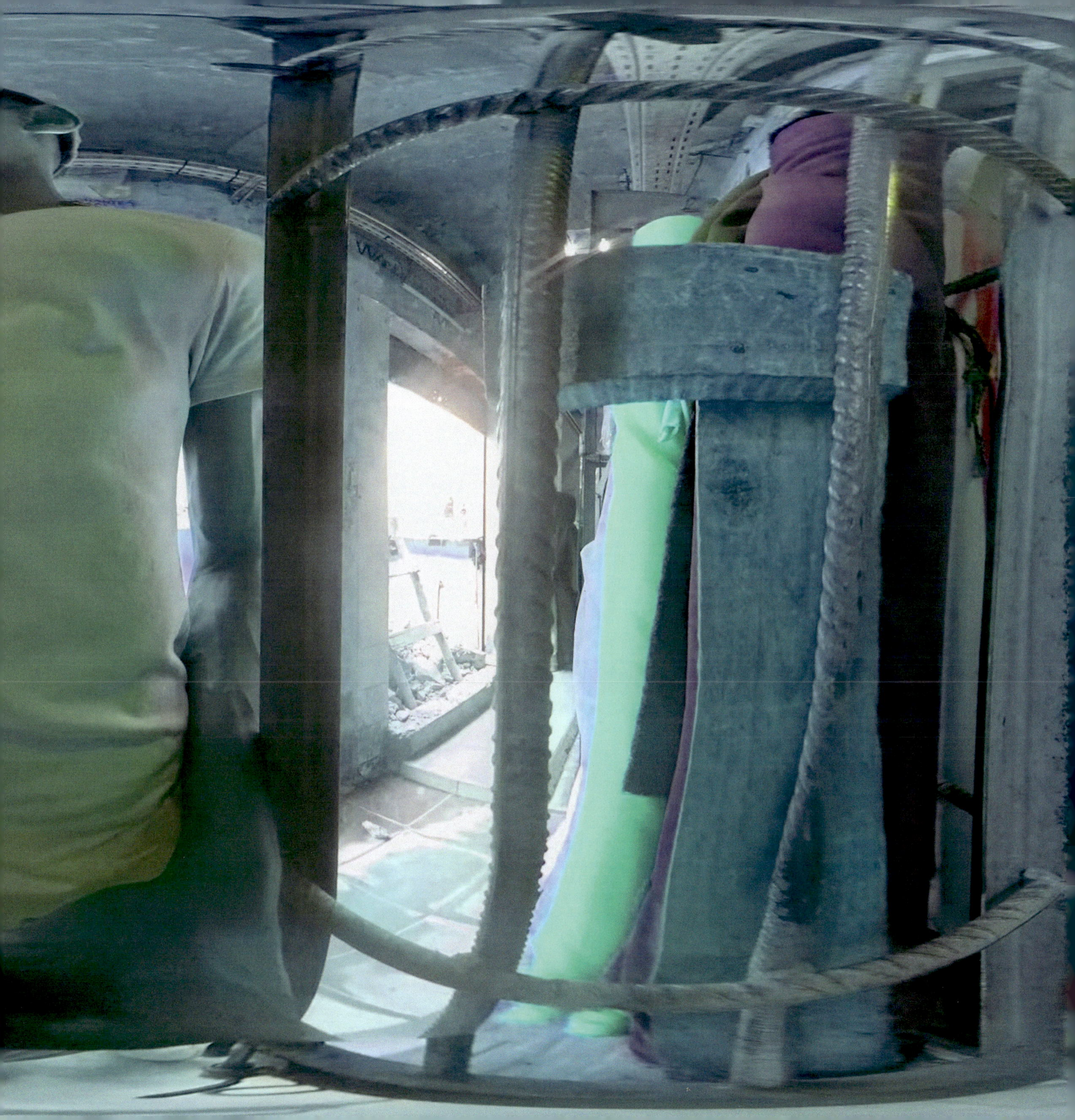

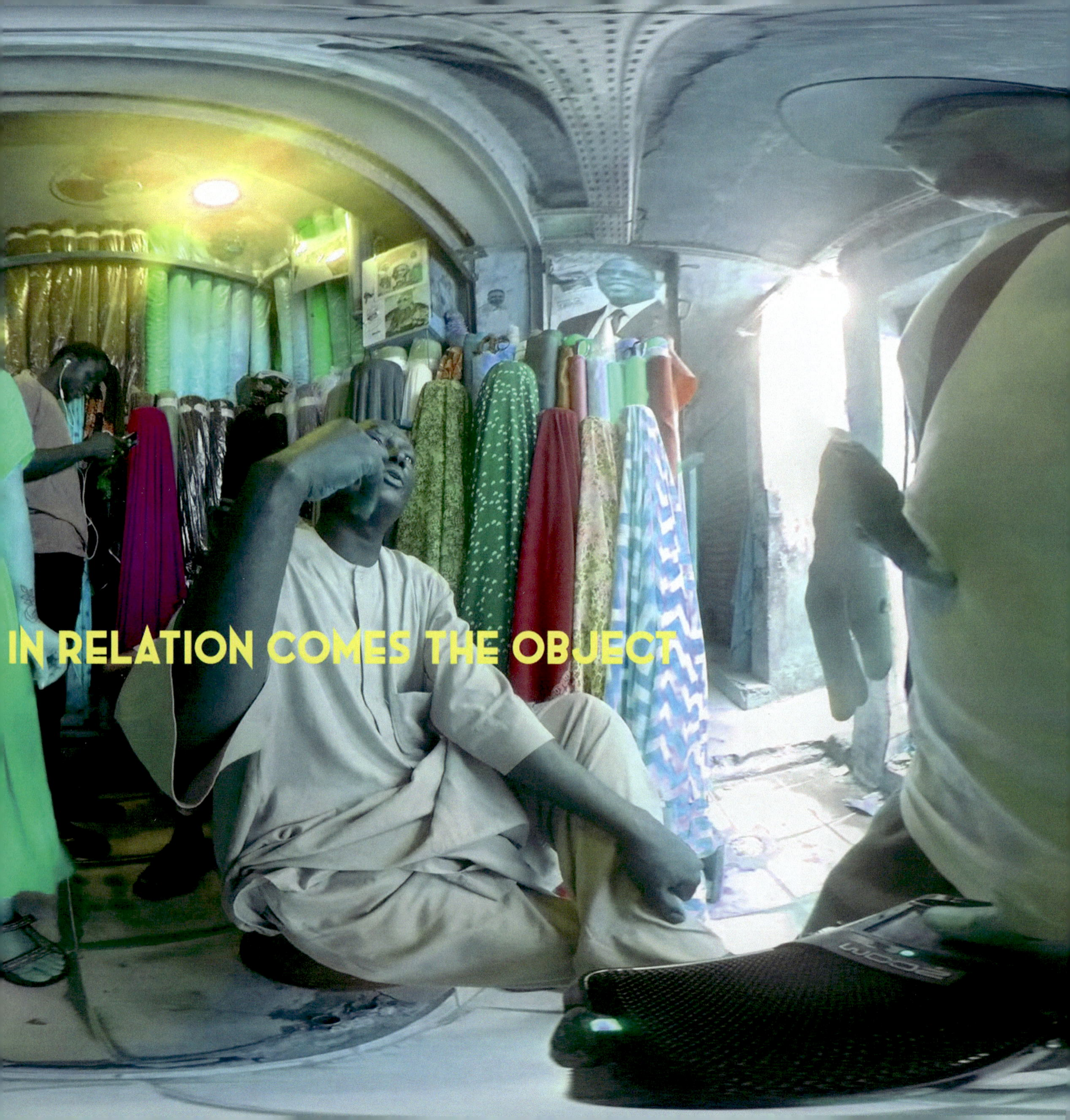

IN RELATION COMES THE OBJECT

I worked on strategic issues, first with corporations and then with NGOs and social activists. At one point, however, I had a meltdown and ended up being diagnosed with severe clinical depression. This was actually the same time when I removed myself from social media. I needed to take care of myself. If you are severely depressed and suicidal, you already believe that people do not care about you. Certain aspects of social media reinforce this idea. People pretend to care, but they are not showing up.

All the advertising agencies in Nairobi have been monopolized, the environment I was working in at that time was extremely toxic and continues to be emotionally abusive. In a single year, I lost three colleagues because they committed suicide.

As a person who respects herself, I did not want to work in an environment of constant abuse, so I resigned. For me, it

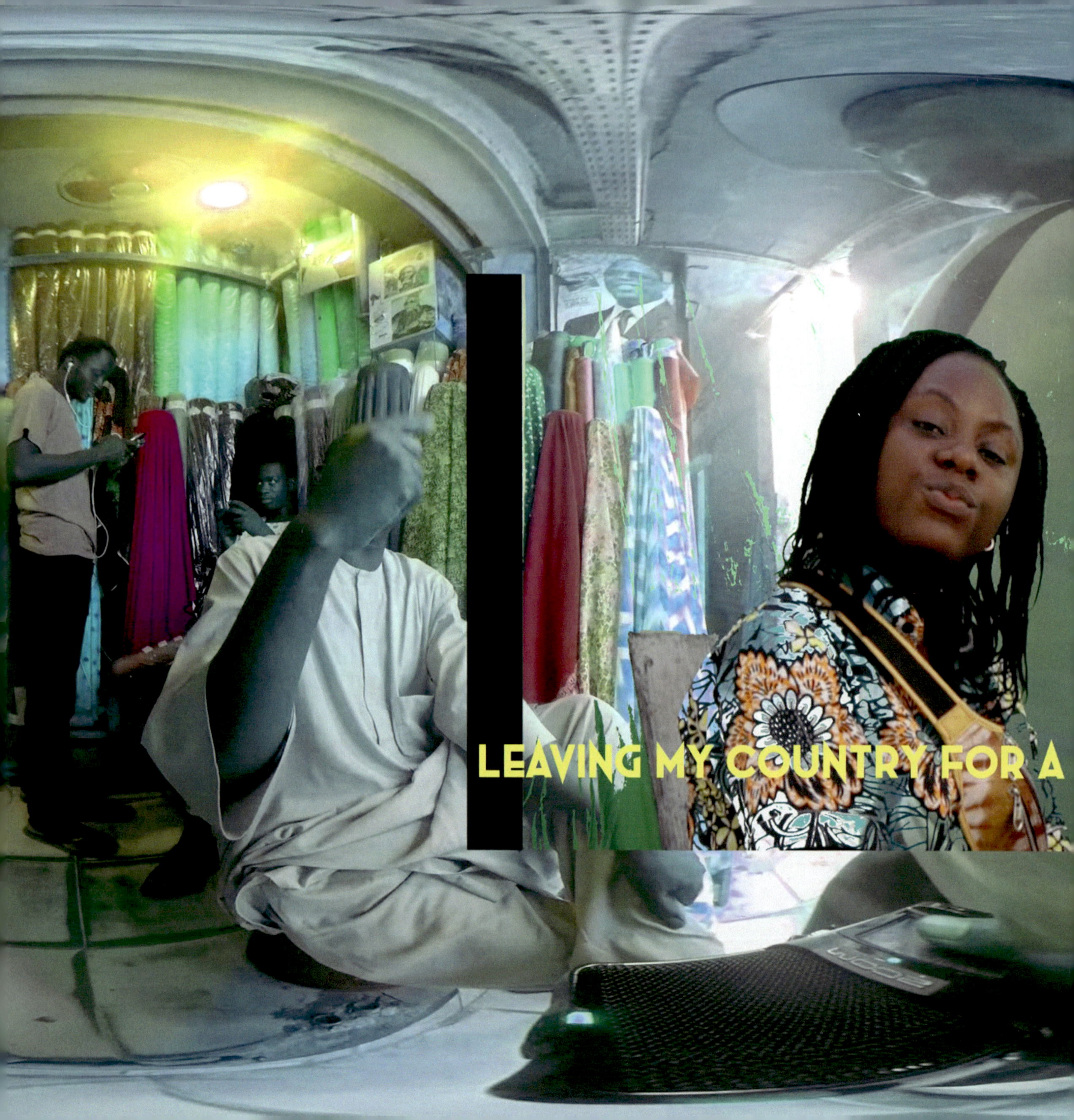

LEAVING MY COUNTRY FOR A

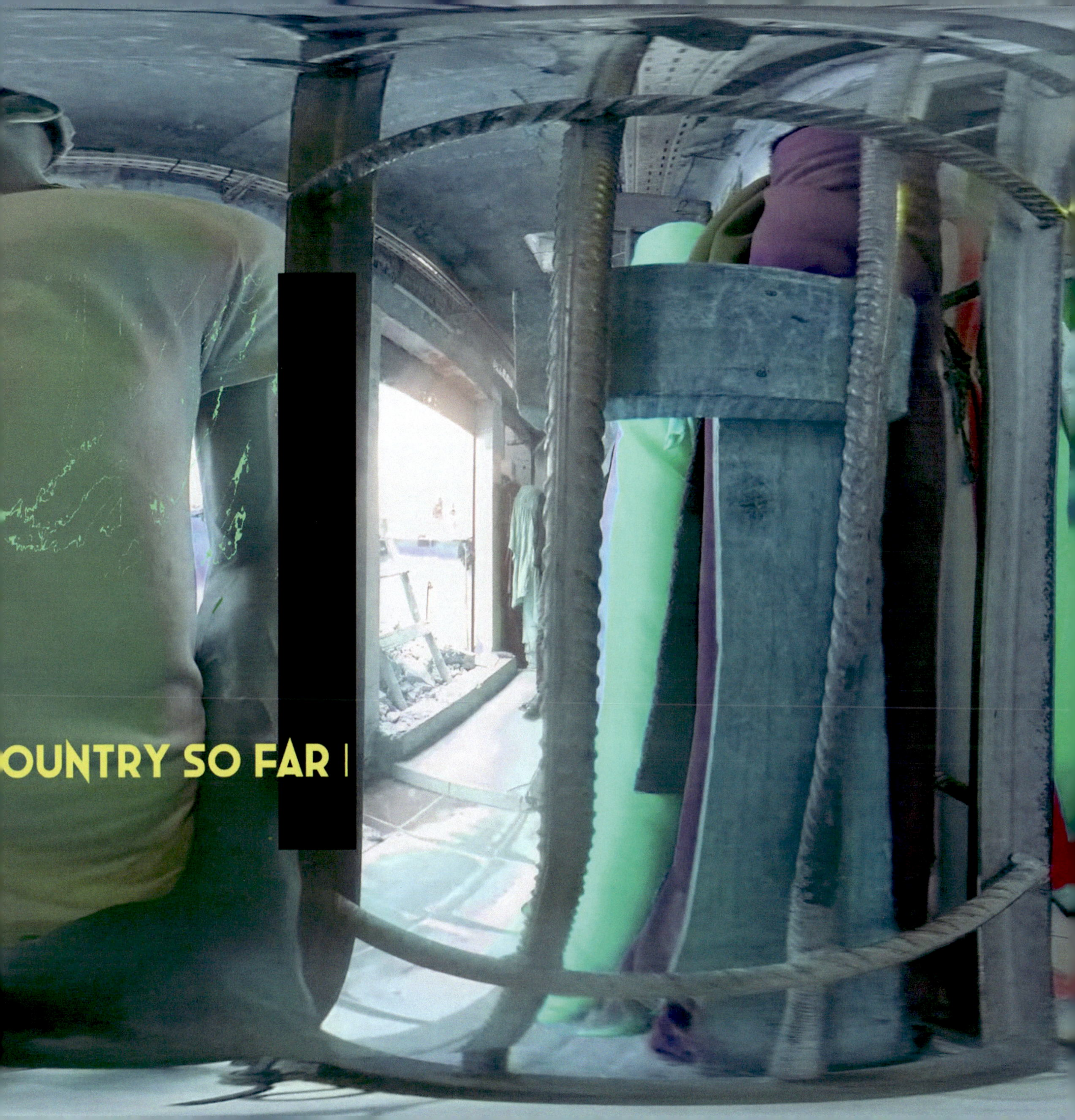
OUNTRY SO FAR I

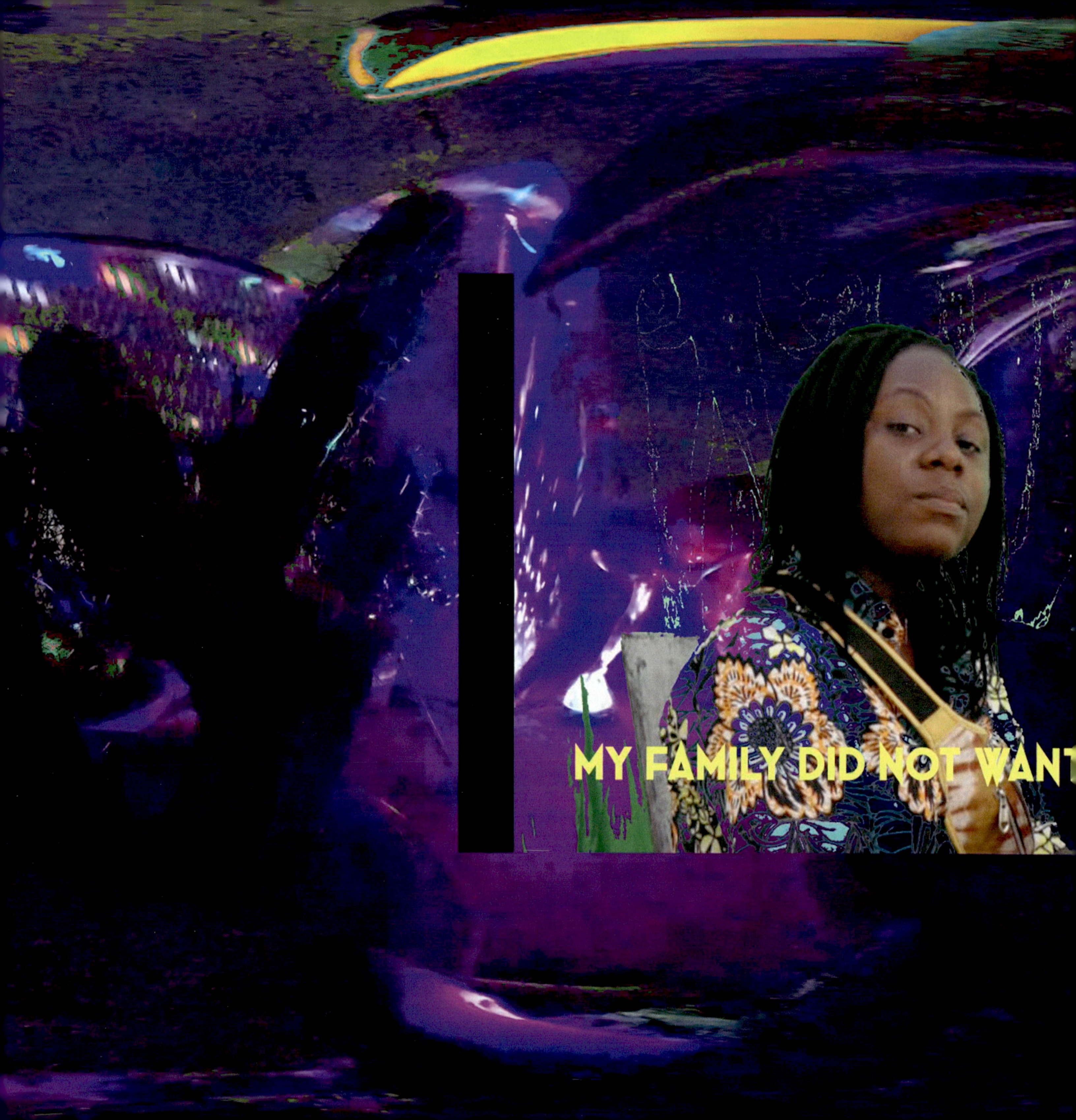
MY FAMILY DID NOT WANT

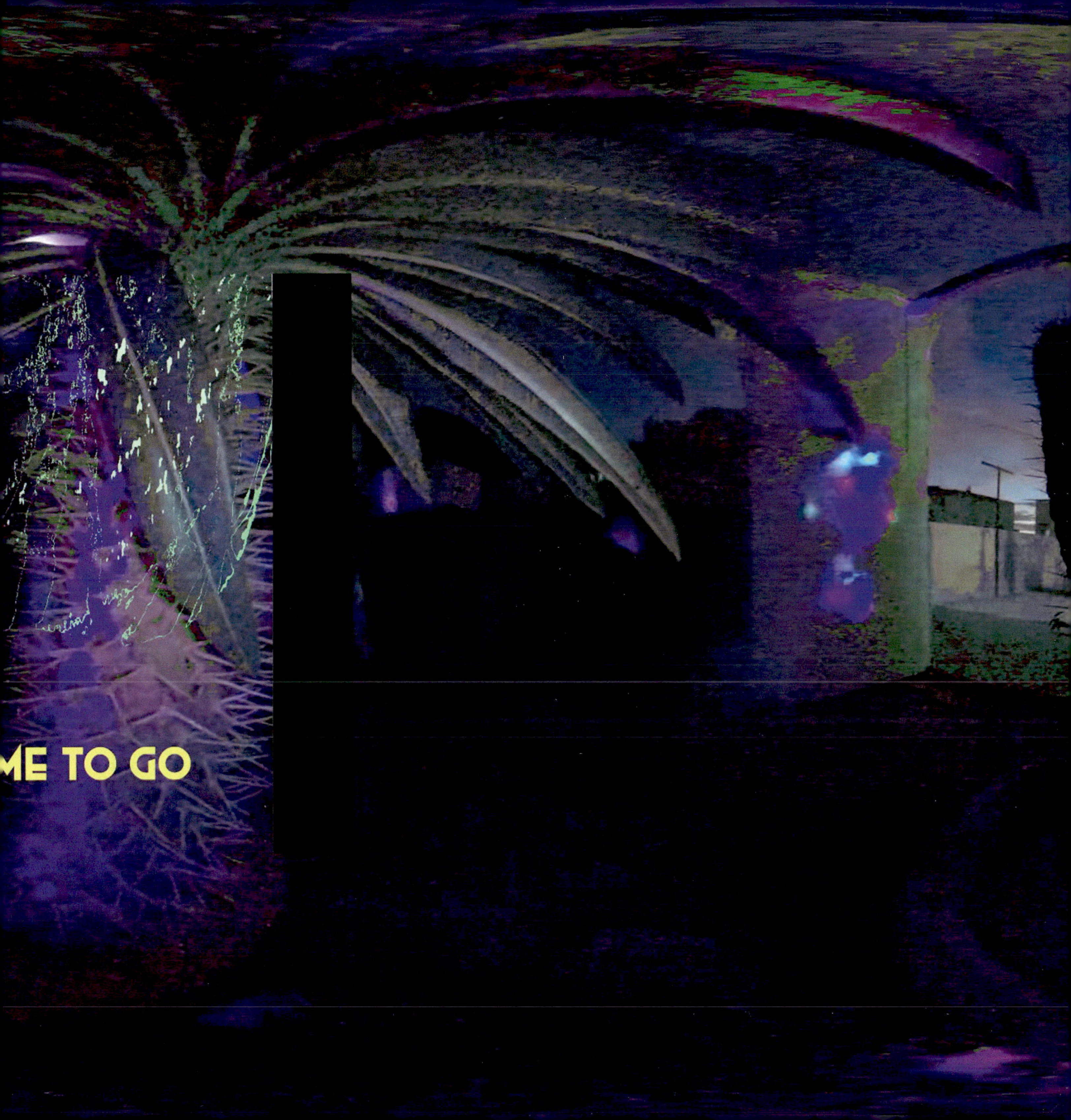
ME TO GO

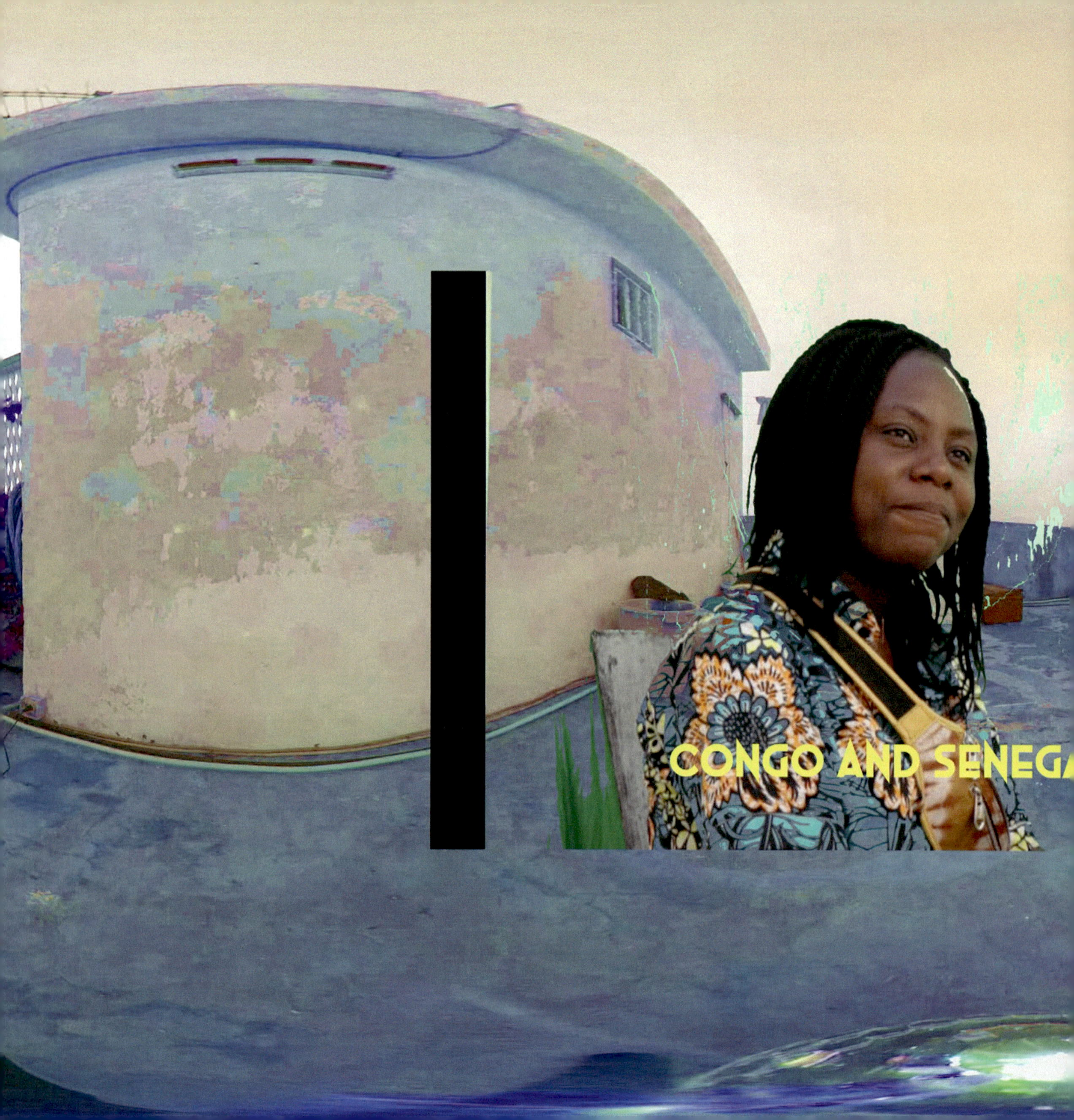
CONGO AND SENEGA

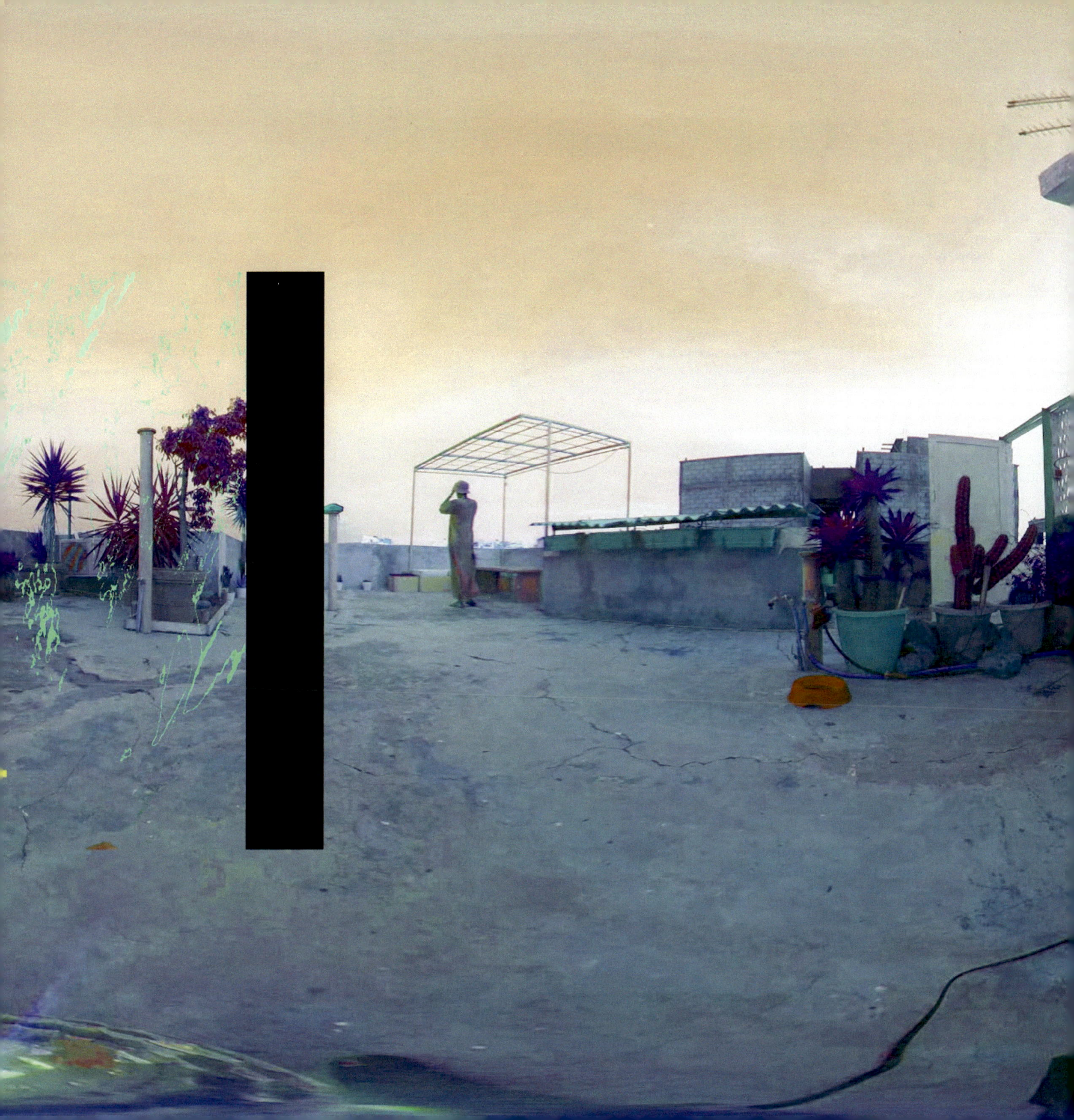

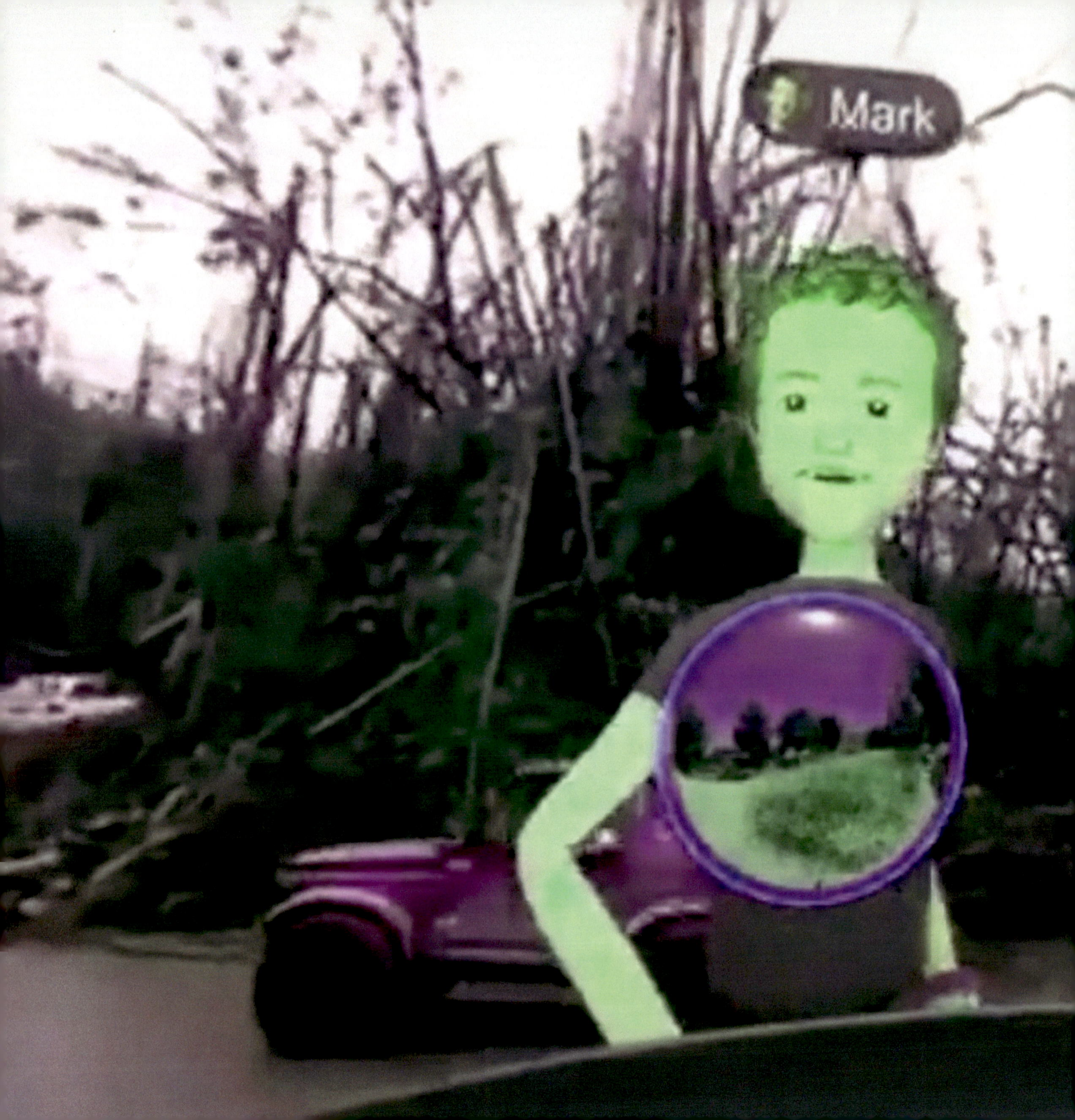
Mark

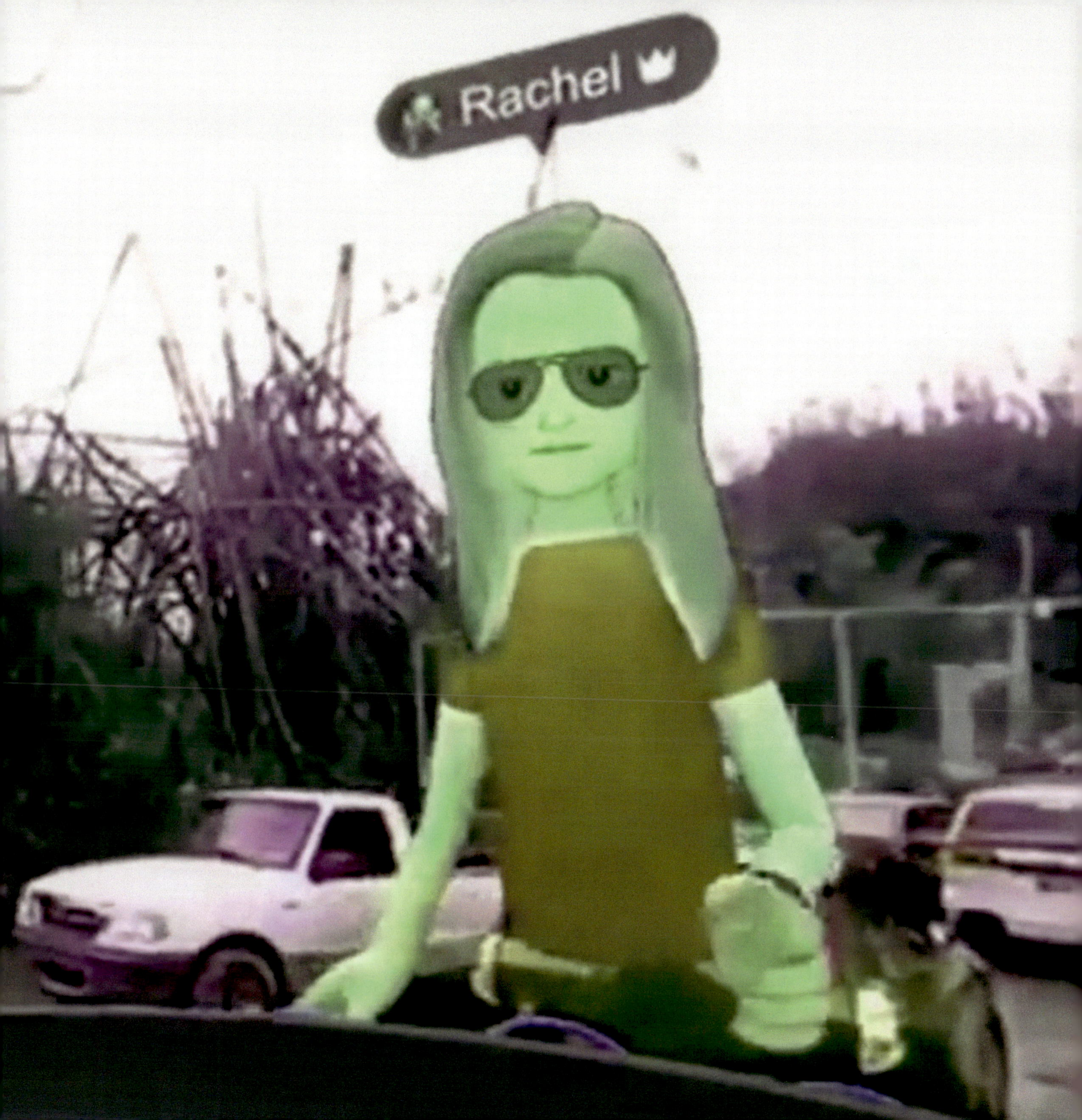
Rachel

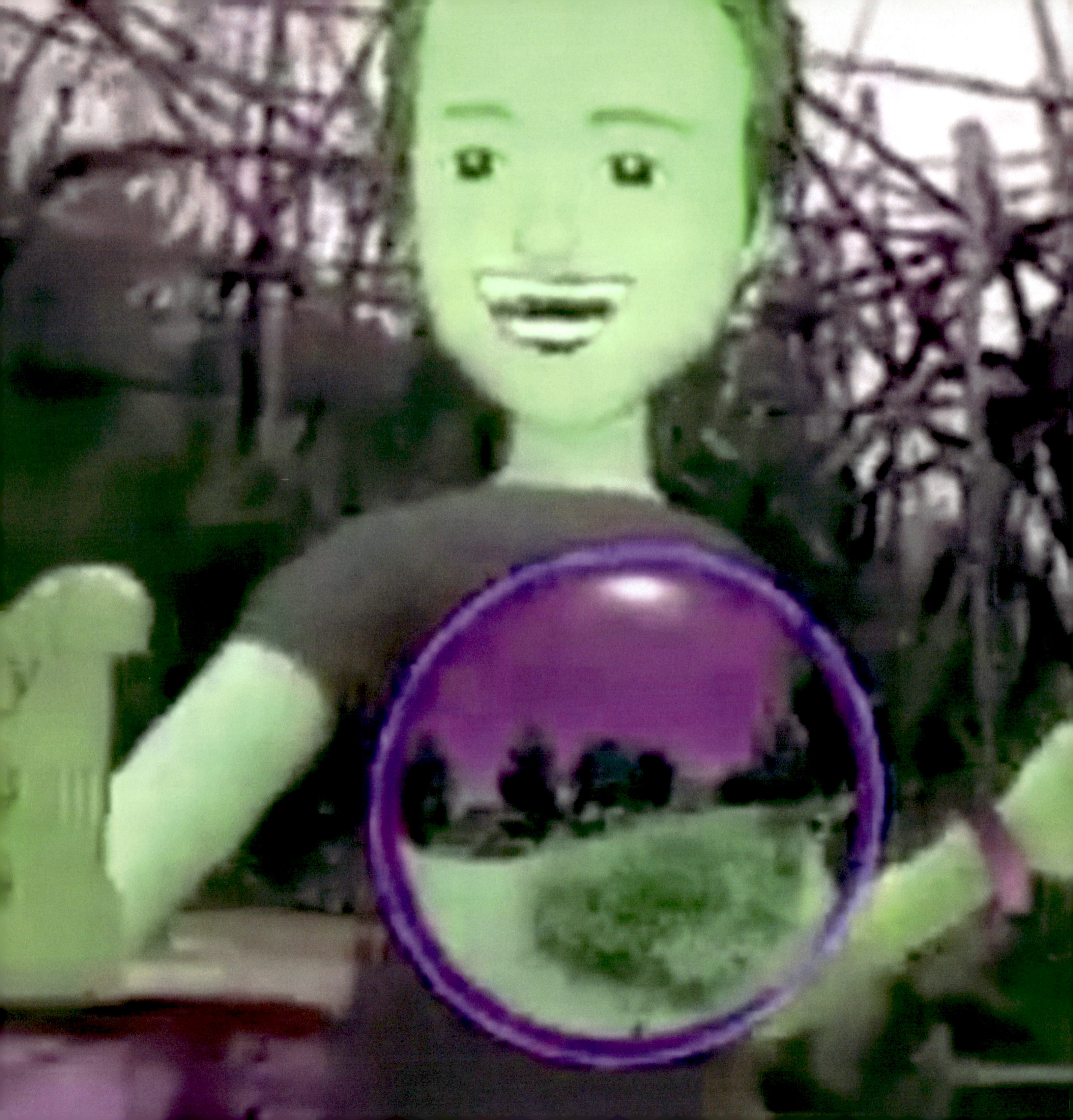

WAS A GOOD TURNING POINT. I HIT ROCK BOT-TOM AND HAD LOST ALL PURPOSE. IT PUSHED ME TO TRAIN AS A YOGA TEACHER AFTER HAVING PRACTICED YOGA MYSELF FOR 18 YEARS. IT WAS NOT A CONSCIOUS PLAN, BUT I WENT ROCK WITH MY INTUITION AND STARTED TEACHING STRAIGHT AFTER COMPLETING MY TRAINING.

THE THERAPIST I WAS SEEING AT THAT TIME PRE-SCRIBED ME A DRUG CALLED ZOLOFT, BECAUSE I WAS SO COMPLETELY OFF AND SUICIDAL. A WAKE-UP CALL! I TOLD HIM, WITH ALL RESPECT, I WILL NOT USE THE DRUG. I WILL USE THE HEALING MODALITIES I HAD BEEN USING ON OTHER PEO-PLE. AS A RESULT I STARTED USING THE TOOLS INTERNALLY.

ANNA: ABOUT ANOTHER DECADE LATER INTO THE AGE OF THE SURVEILLANCE ALGORITHM TECH-NOCRATIC NECROPOLITICS IS THREATENING TO TURN US ALL INTO FOSSILS. WHILE WESTERN MAINSTREAM ADRESSES MIGRATION AND MULTI-CULTURAL INTIMACY AS A PHENOMENON OF SOLELY THEIR OWN CONCERN AND MENACE

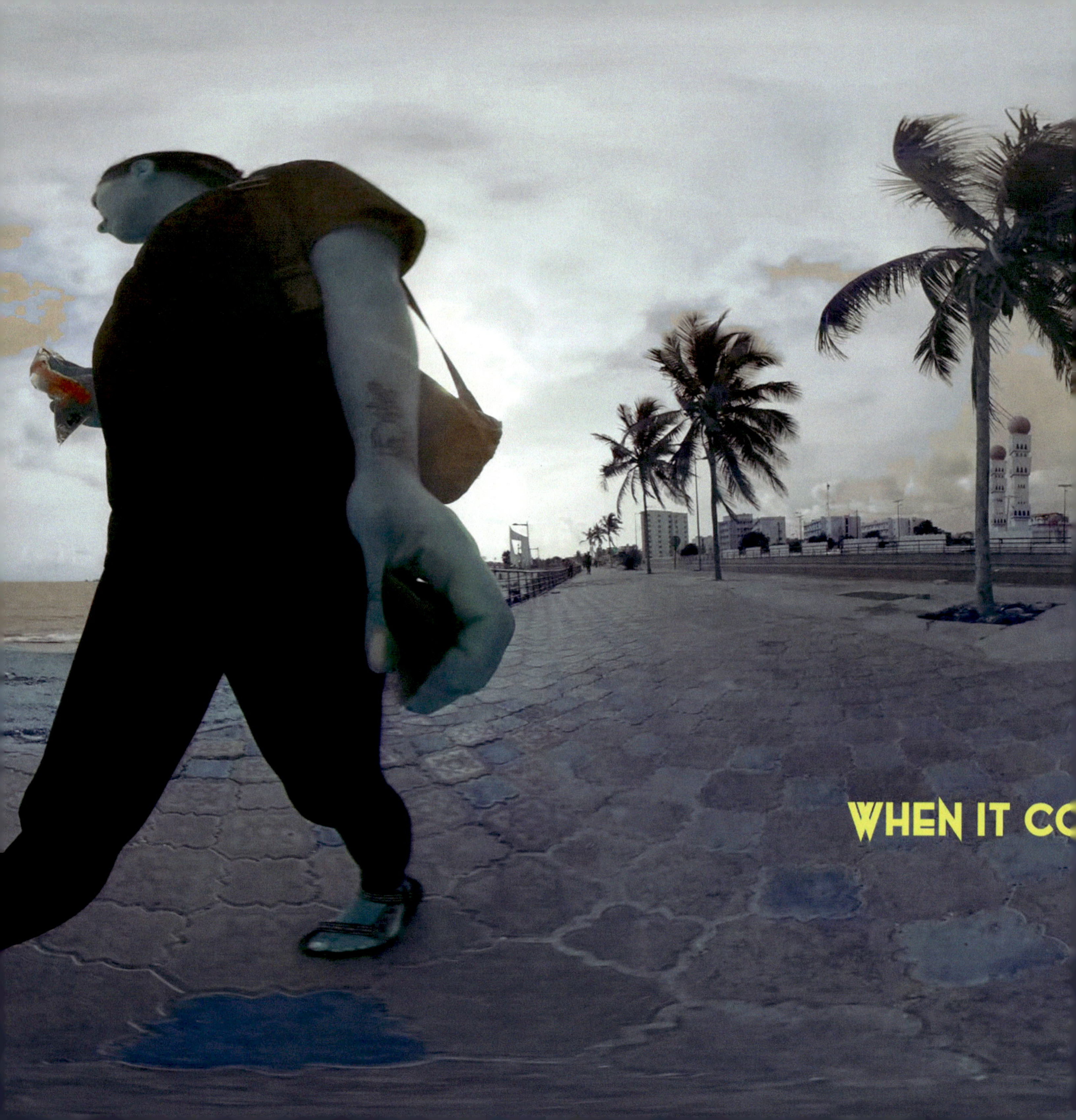

WHEN IT CO

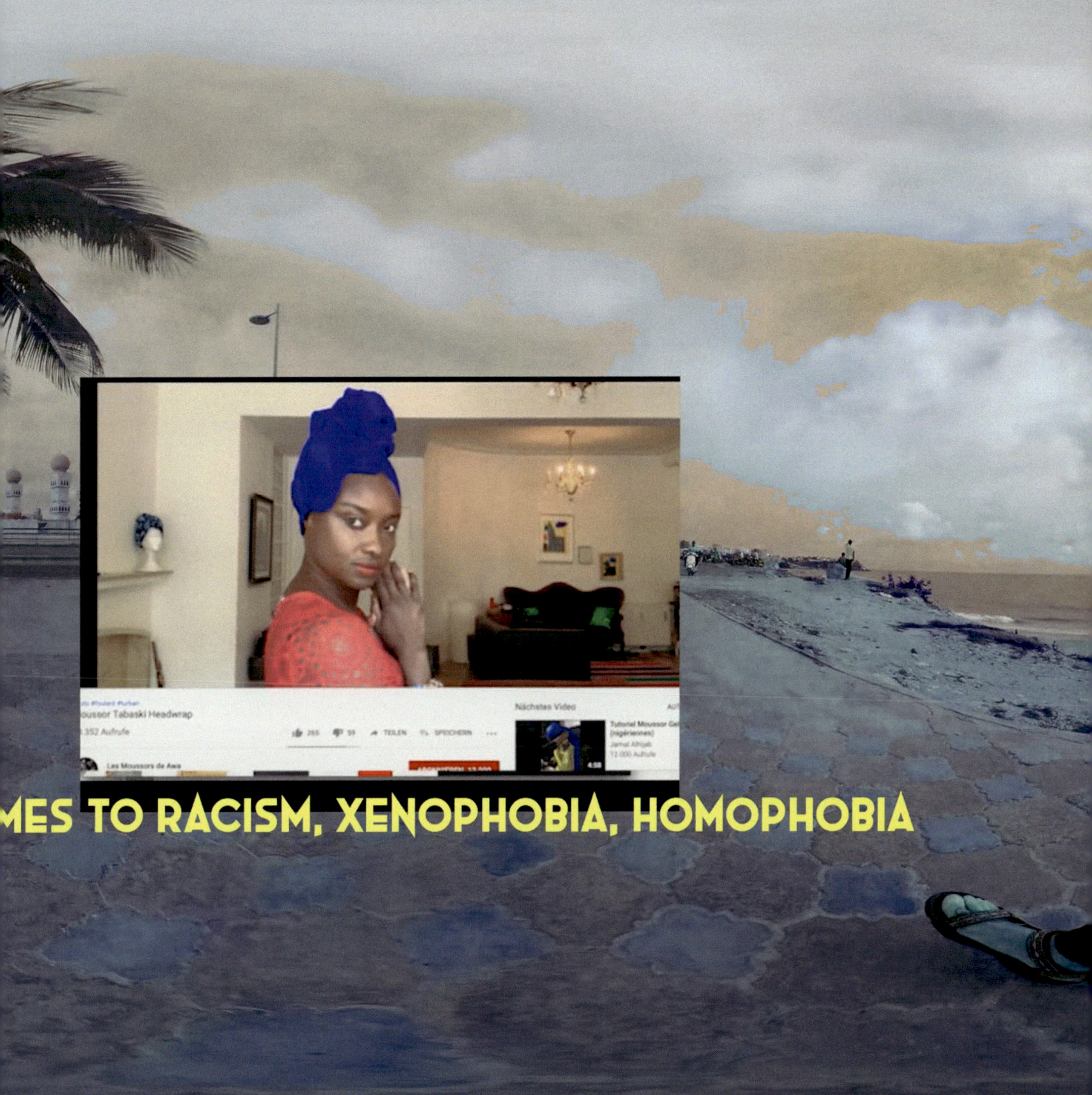
Moussor Tabaski Headwrap
.352 Aufrufe
265
59
TEILEN
SPEICHERN
Les Moussors de Awa
Nächstes Video
Tutorial Moussor Ge
(nigériennes)
Jamal Alhijab
12.000 Aufrufe
4:58
MES TO RACISM, XENOPHOBIA, HOMOPHOBIA

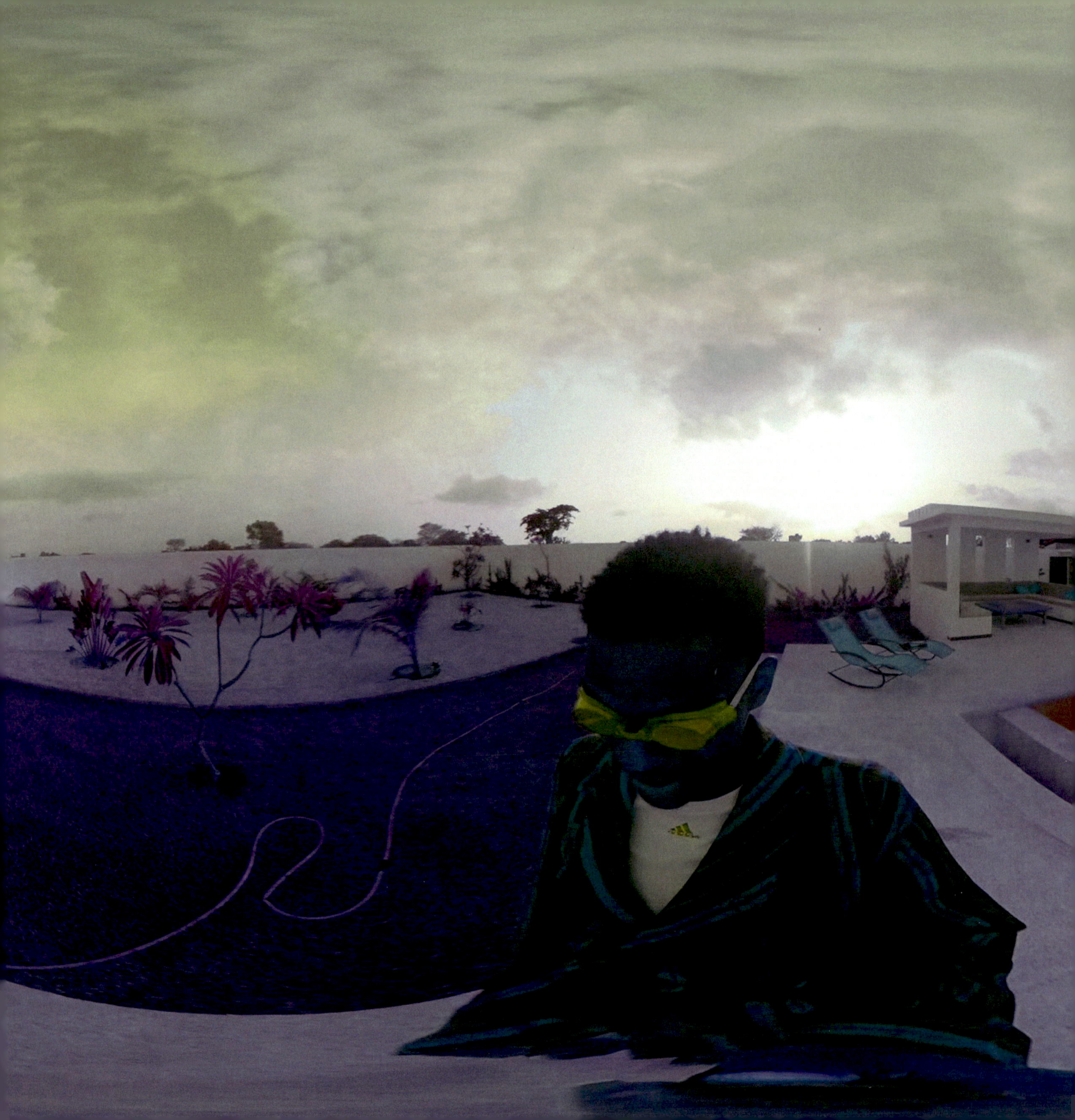

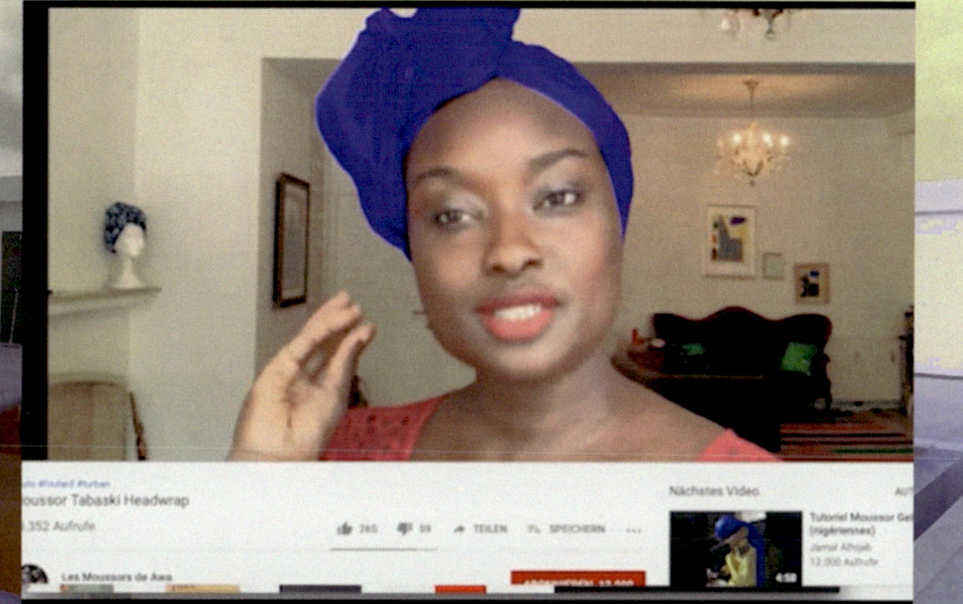

THERE IS ABUSE IN EVERYTHING

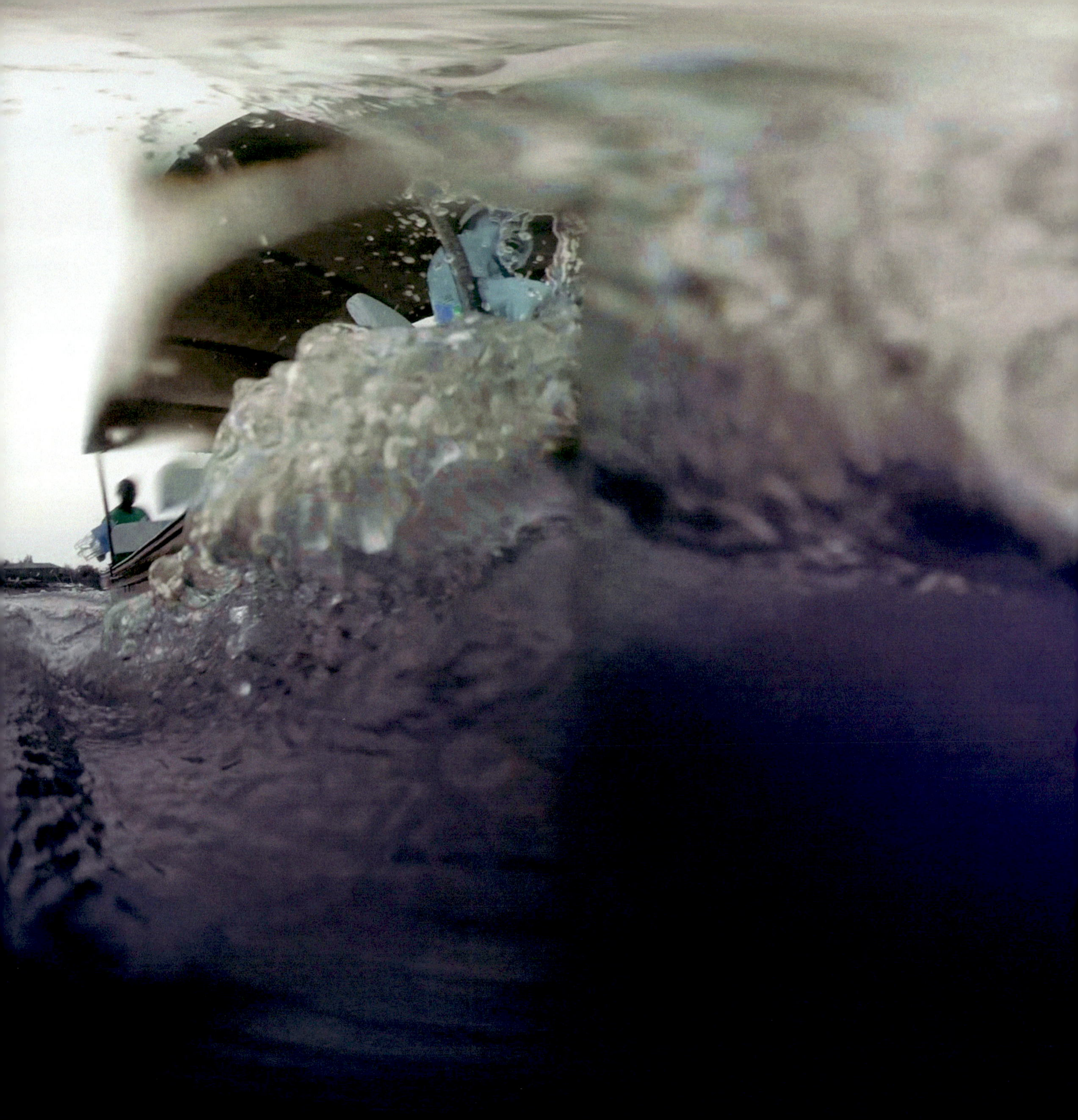

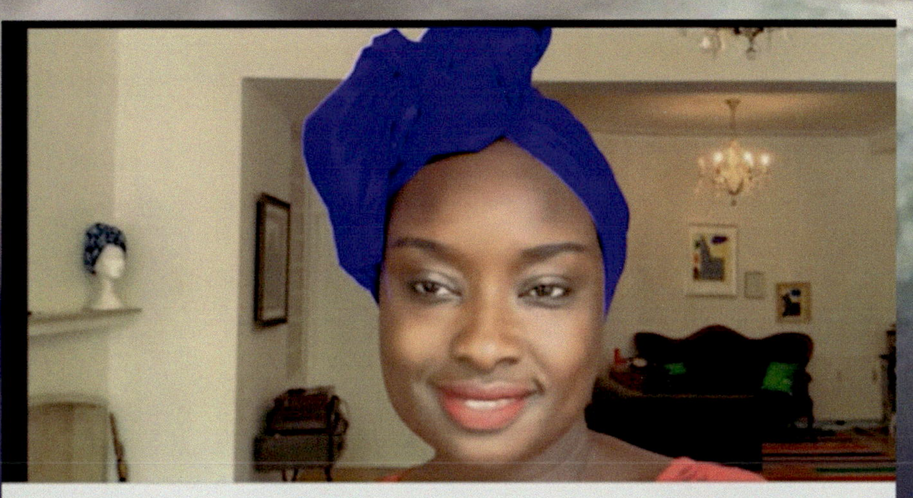

END UP RUINING US.

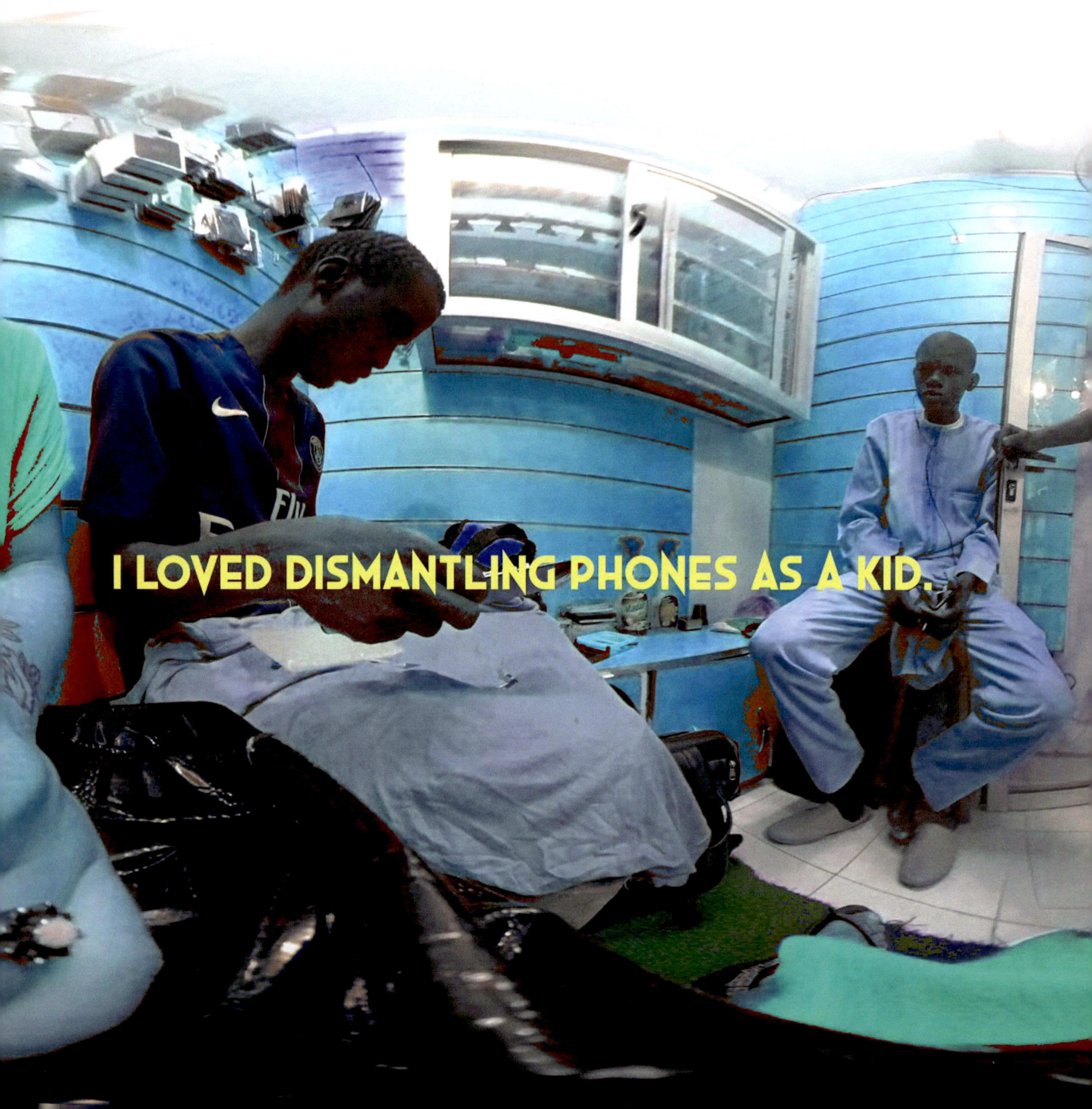
I LOVED DISMANTLING PHONES AS A KID.

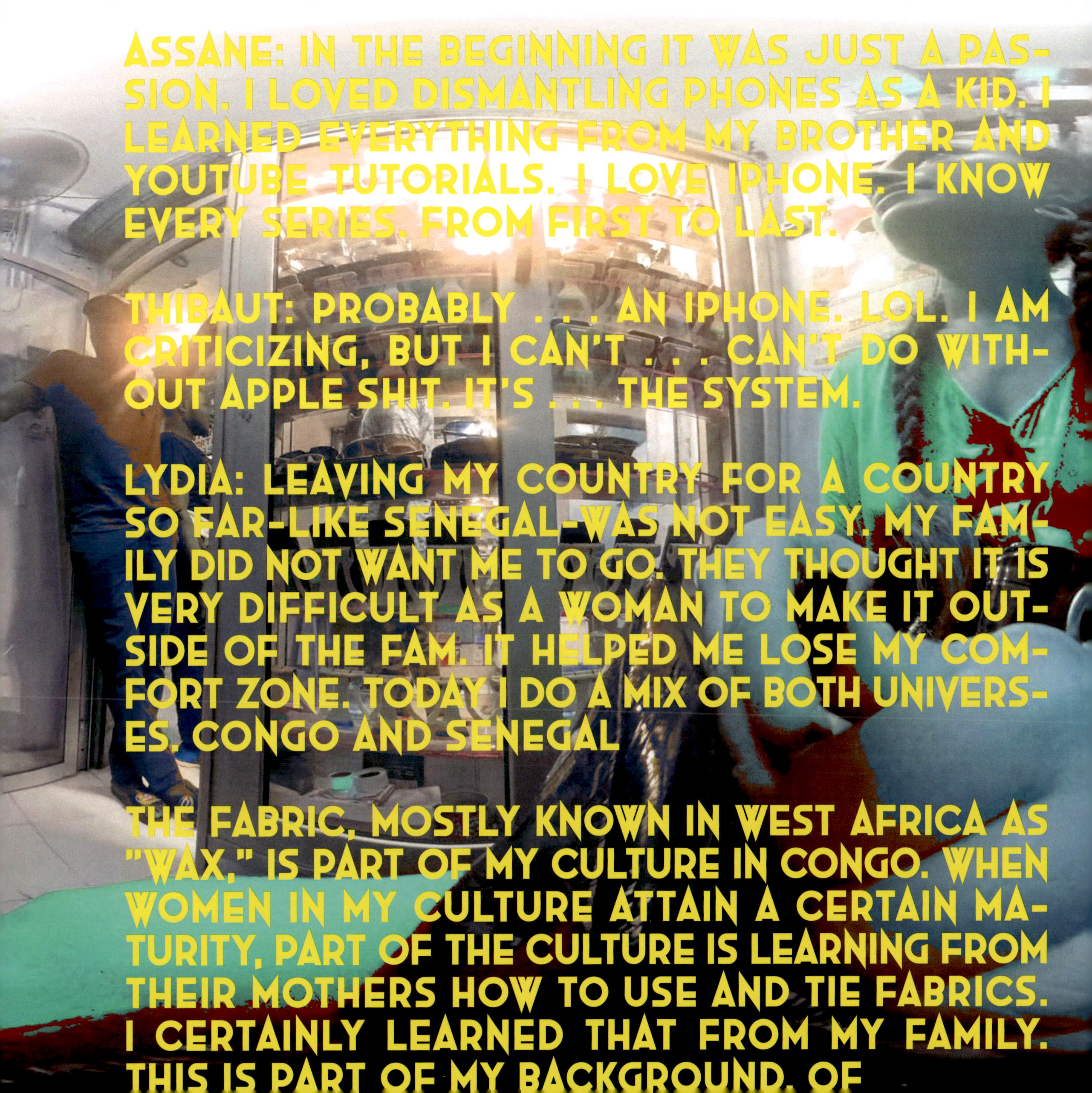

ASSANE: IN THE BEGINNING IT WAS JUST A PASSION. I LOVED DISMANTLING PHONES AS A KID. I LEARNED EVERYTHING FROM MY BROTHER AND YOUTUBE TUTORIALS. I LOVE IPHONE. I KNOW EVERY SERIES. FROM FIRST TO LAST.

THIBAUT: PROBABLY . . . AN IPHONE. LOL. I AM CRITICIZING, BUT I CAN'T . . . CAN'T DO WITHOUT APPLE SHIT. IT'S . . . THE SYSTEM.

LYDIA: LEAVING MY COUNTRY FOR A COUNTRY SO FAR—LIKE SENEGAL—WAS NOT EASY. MY FAMILY DID NOT WANT ME TO GO. THEY THOUGHT IT IS VERY DIFFICULT AS A WOMAN TO MAKE IT OUTSIDE OF THE FAM. IT HELPED ME LOSE MY COMFORT ZONE. TODAY I DO A MIX OF BOTH UNIVERSES. CONGO AND SENEGAL

THE FABRIC, MOSTLY KNOWN IN WEST AFRICA AS "WAX," IS PART OF MY CULTURE IN CONGO. WHEN WOMEN IN MY CULTURE ATTAIN A CERTAIN MATURITY, PART OF THE CULTURE IS LEARNING FROM THEIR MOTHERS HOW TO USE AND TIE FABRICS. I CERTAINLY LEARNED THAT FROM MY FAMILY. THIS IS PART OF MY BACKGROUND. OF

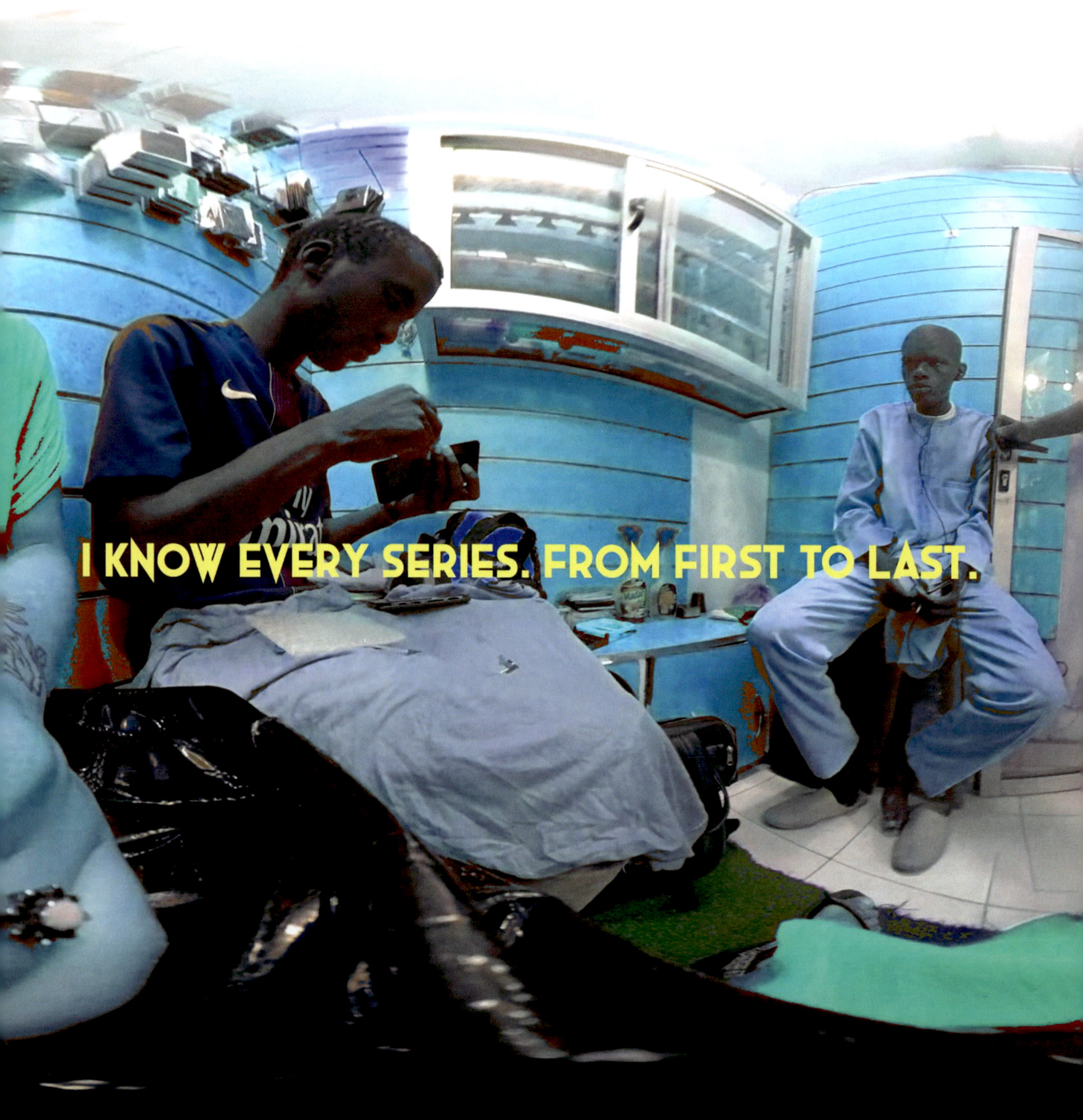
I KNOW EVERY SERIES. FROM FIRST TO LAST.

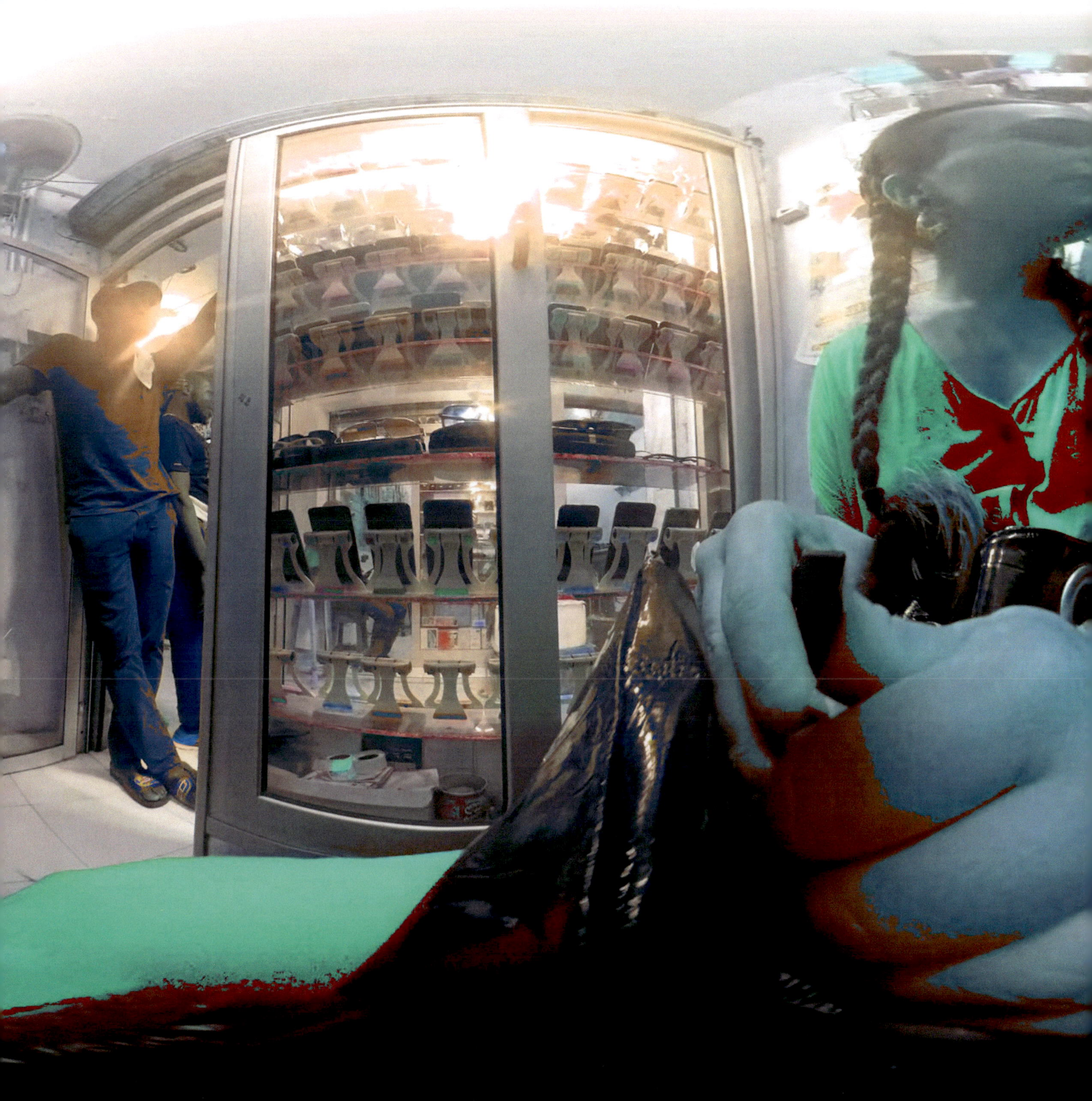

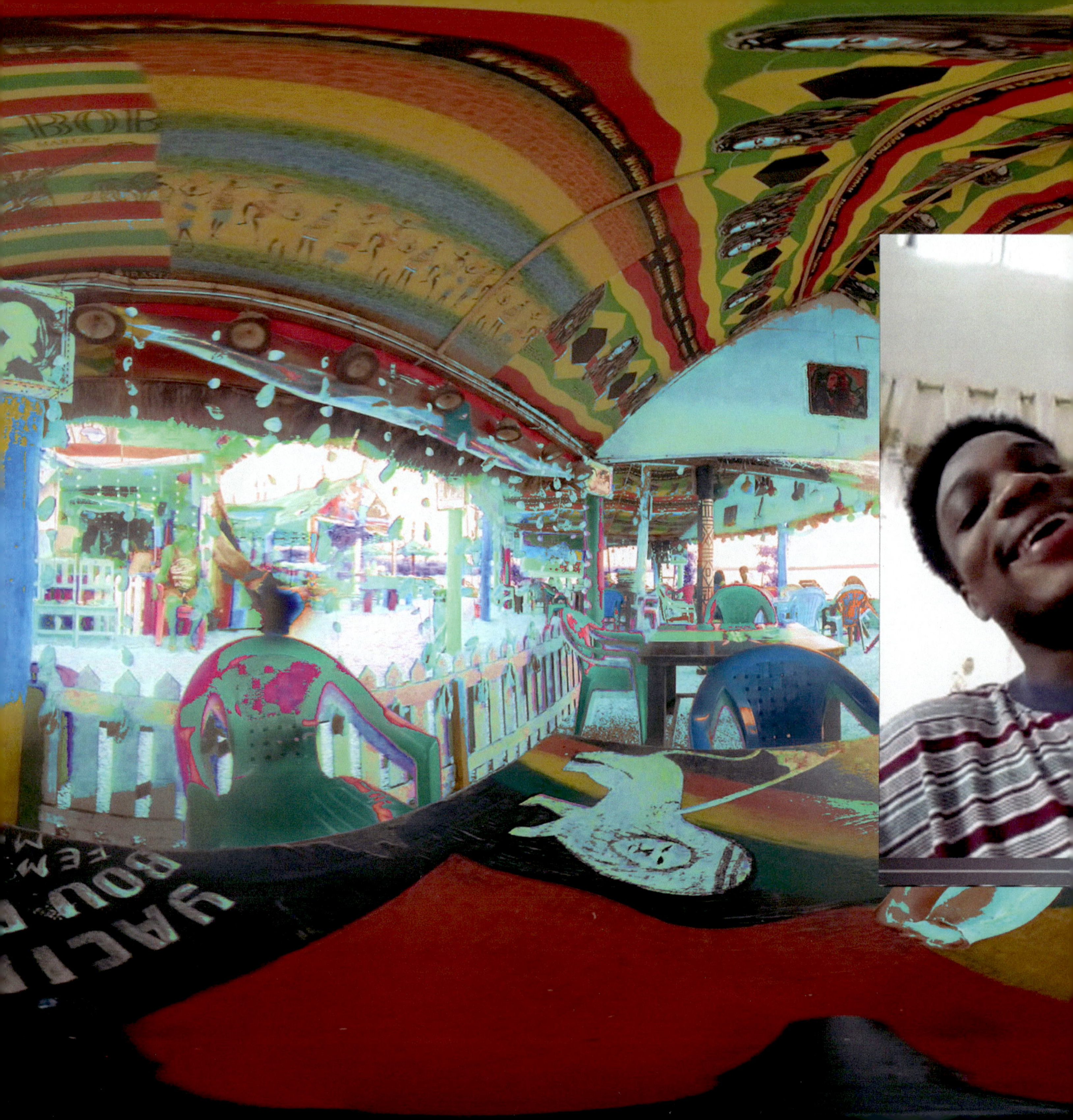

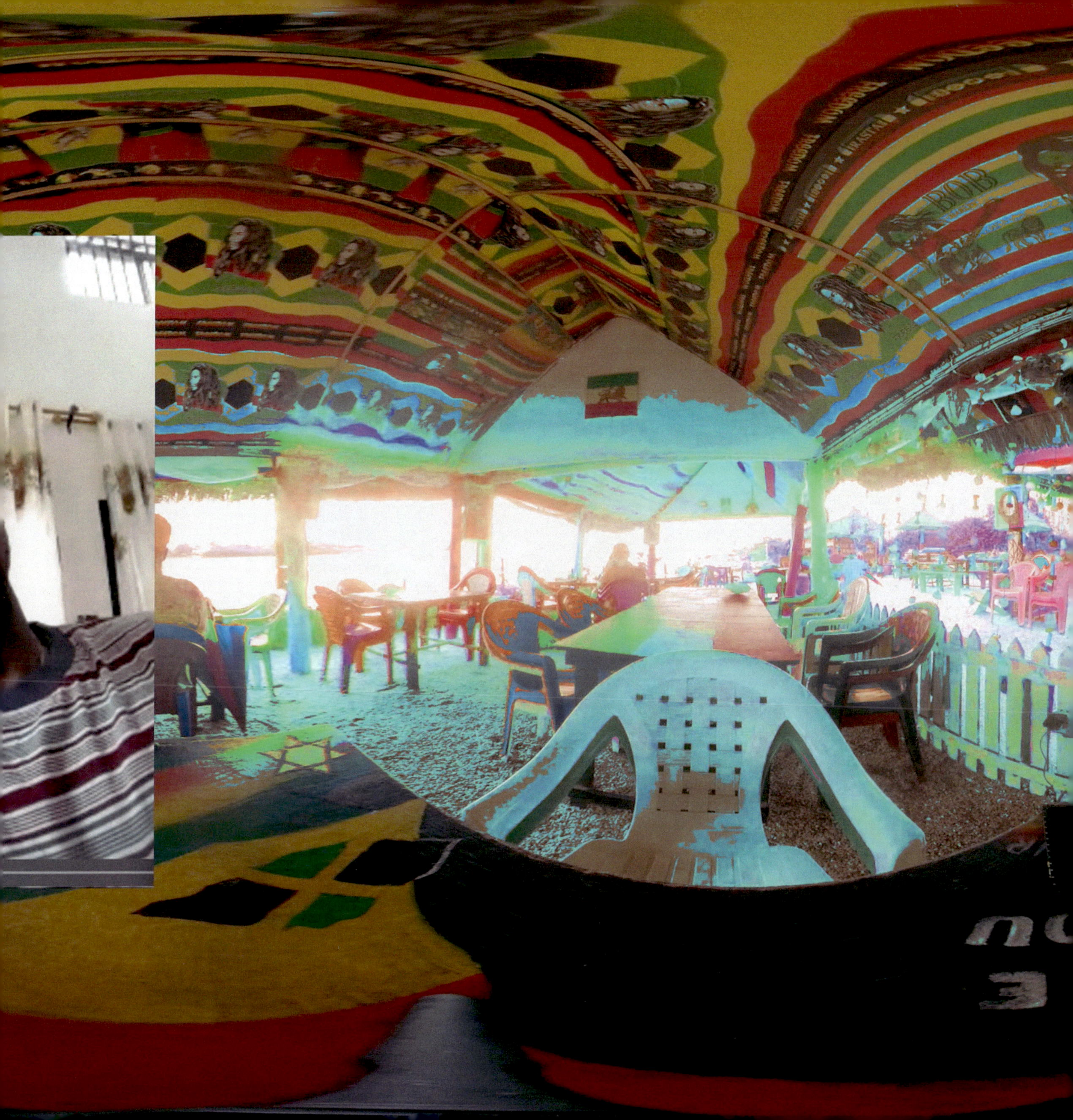

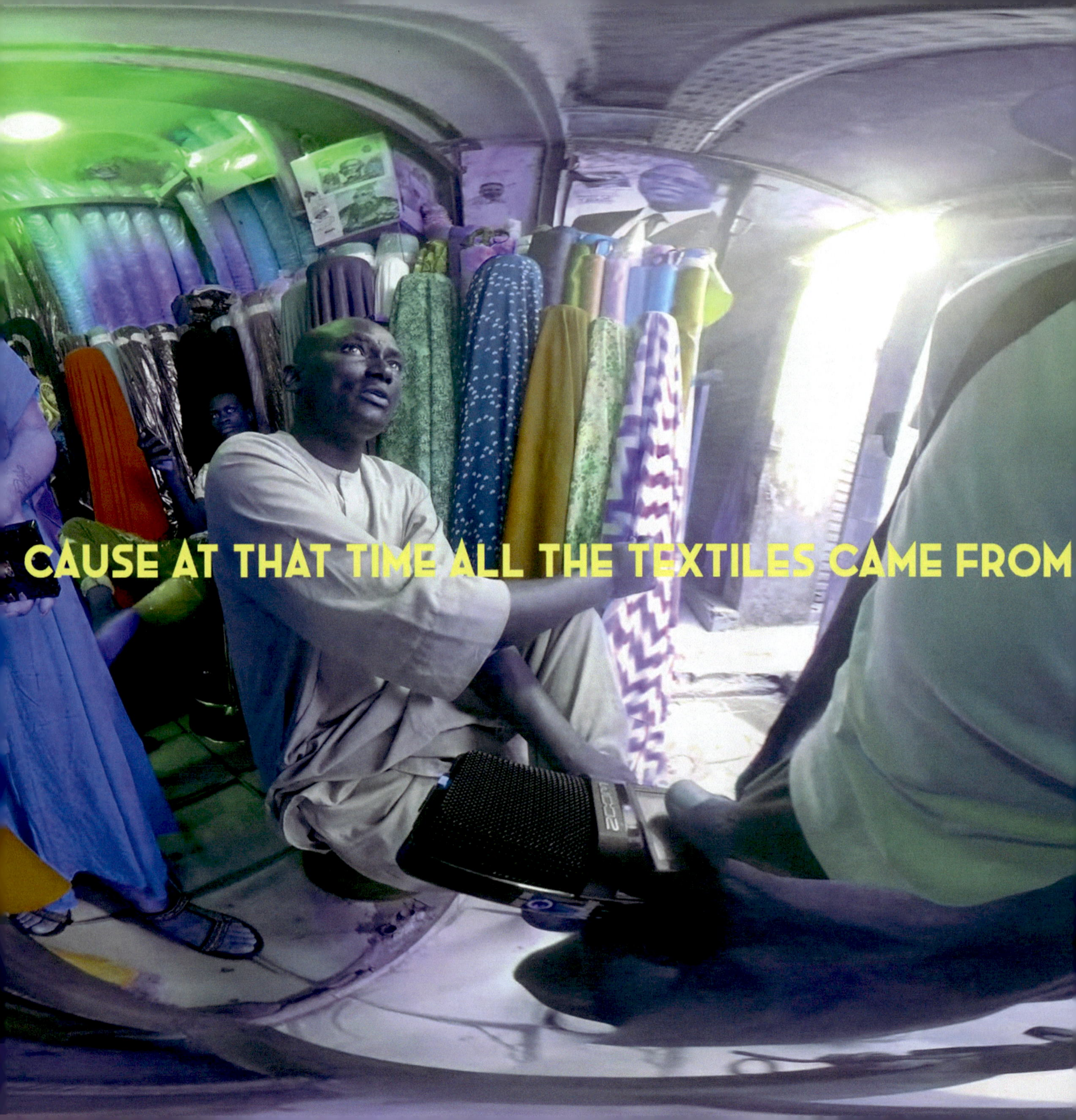
CAUSE AT THAT TIME ALL THE TEXTILES CAME FROM

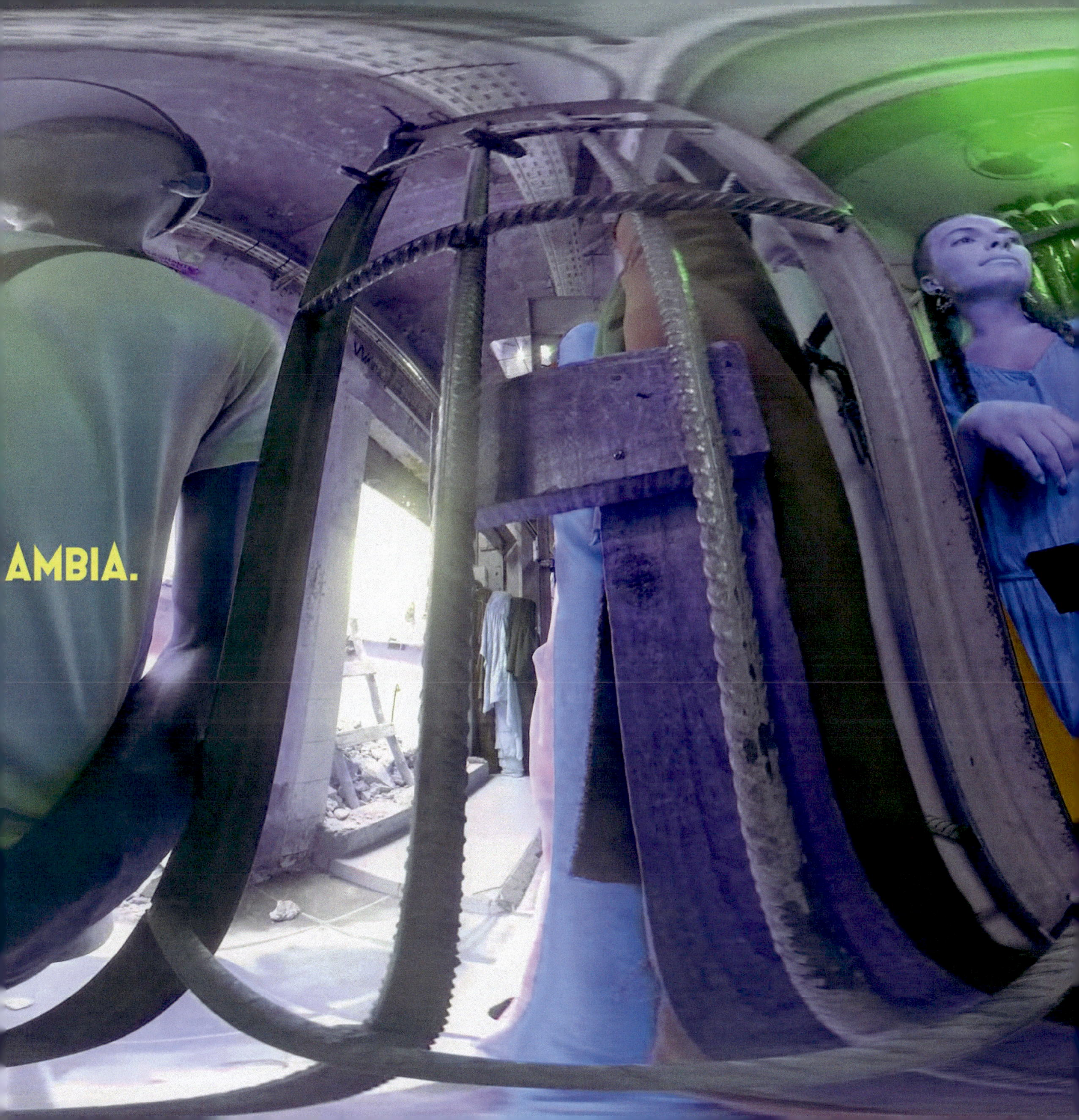
AMBIA.

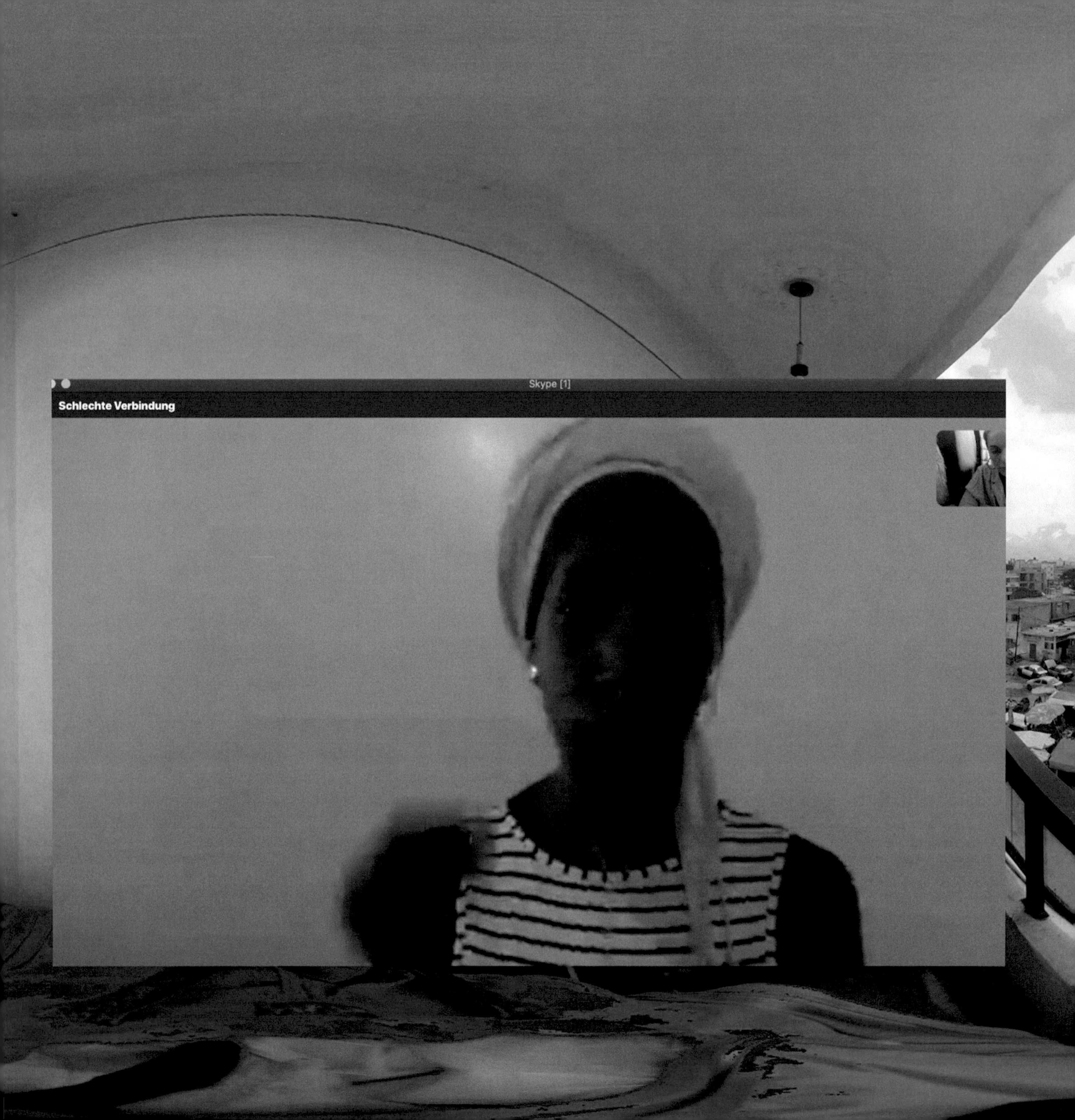

Skype [1]
Schlechte Verbindung

MY CULTURE. IT INFLUENCES MY DECISION IN CHOOSING WHICH TYPE OF TEXTILES TO USE, THE DESIGNS AND MORE. LIVING IN SENEGAL AND WORKING HERE, I TAKE ADVANTAGE OF AND AM INFLUENCED BY WHAT IS GOING ON AROUND ME. THIS VIBRATING ECOSYSTEM, ALL THESE COLORS AND ENERGIES.

AWA: WHEN IT COMES TO RACISM, XENOPHOBIA, HOMOPHOBIA, OR ISLAMOPHOBIA, PEOPLE USE ONLINE COMMUNICATION CARELESSLY-WRITING HATE SPEECH OUT OF THE SAFE SURROUNDING OF THEIR HOME. BUT PEOPLE LIKE YOU AND ME HAVE THE RESPONSIBILITY TO SAY NO. WE HAVE TO SET LIMITS AND BE VERY DEMANDING ABOUT HOW TO USE THESE NETWORKS. THERE IS ABUSE IN EVERYTHING- EVEN IN EATING OR DRINKING. MANY THINGS THAT ARE GOOD FOR US END UP RUINING US. WE NEED TO TAKE ACTIONS, MAKE THIS CHANGE A POSITIVE THING. MY ESSENTIAL JOB IS SPEAKING TO WOMEN. MAKING HEADWRAPS FOR THEM, SO THAT THEY ARE SEEN EVERYWHERE AROUND THE GLOBE. WE LIVE IN A SOCIETY RULED BY MEN, MADE BY MEN. NO MATTER WHERE WE COME FROM OR

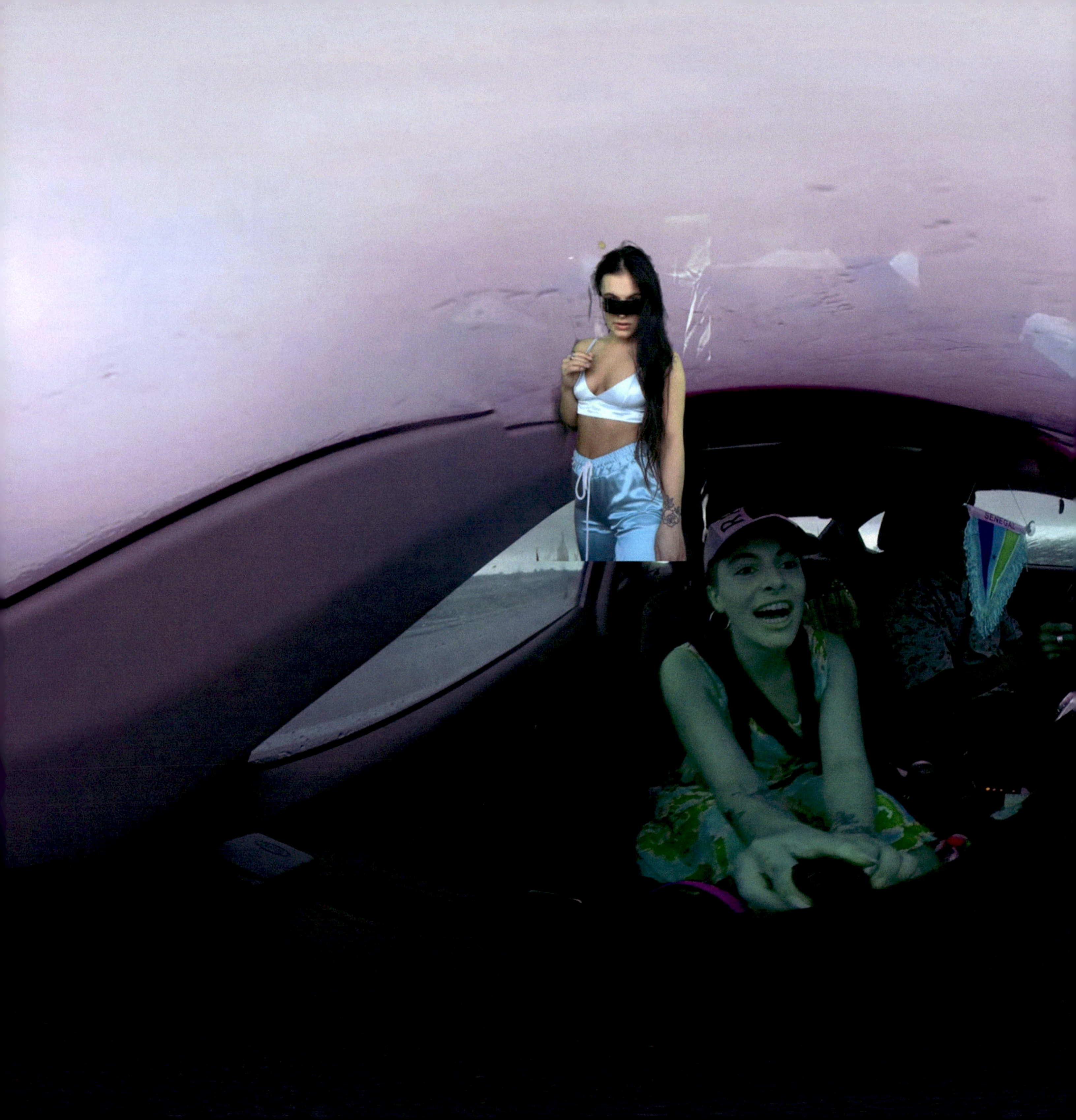

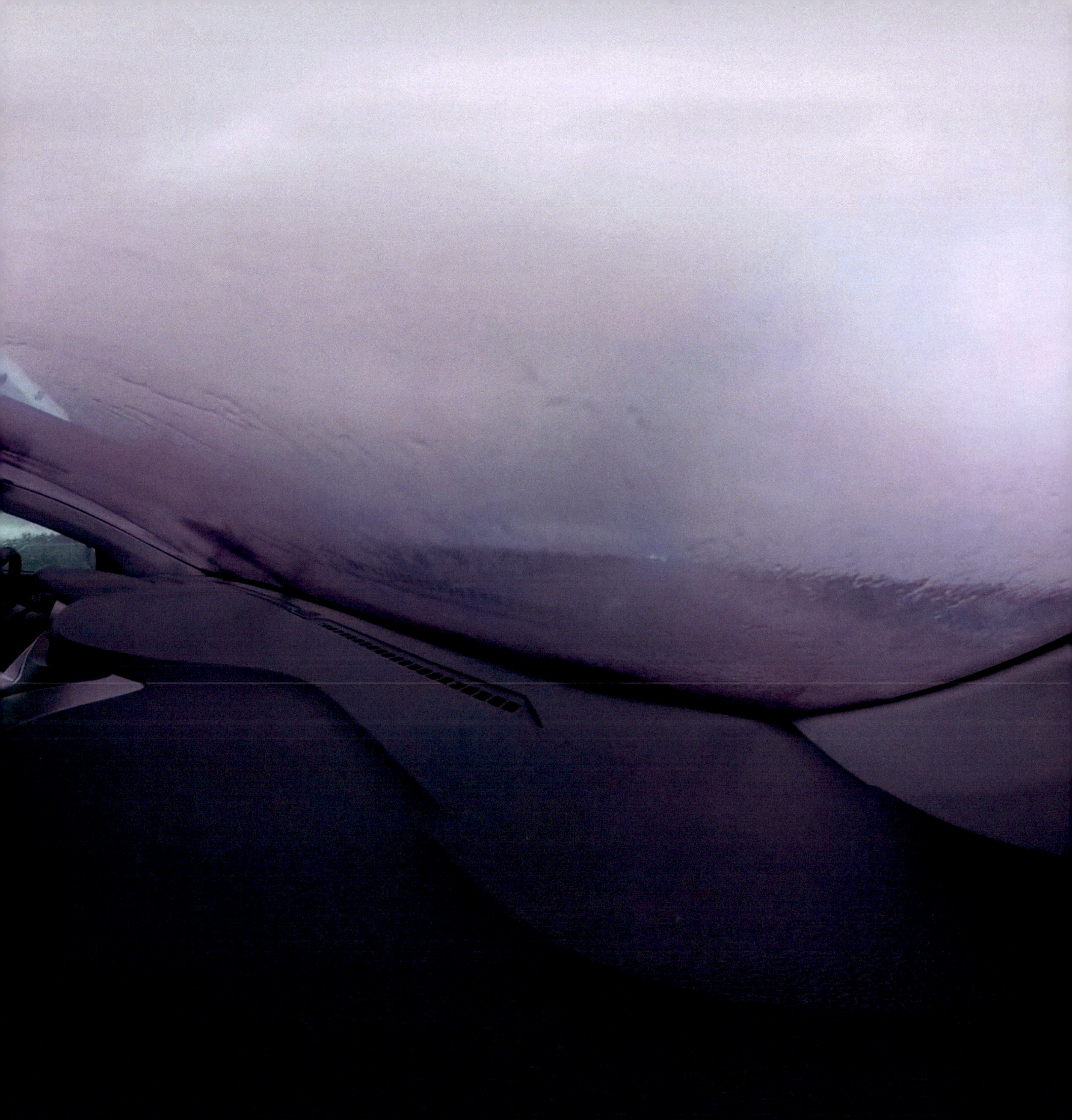

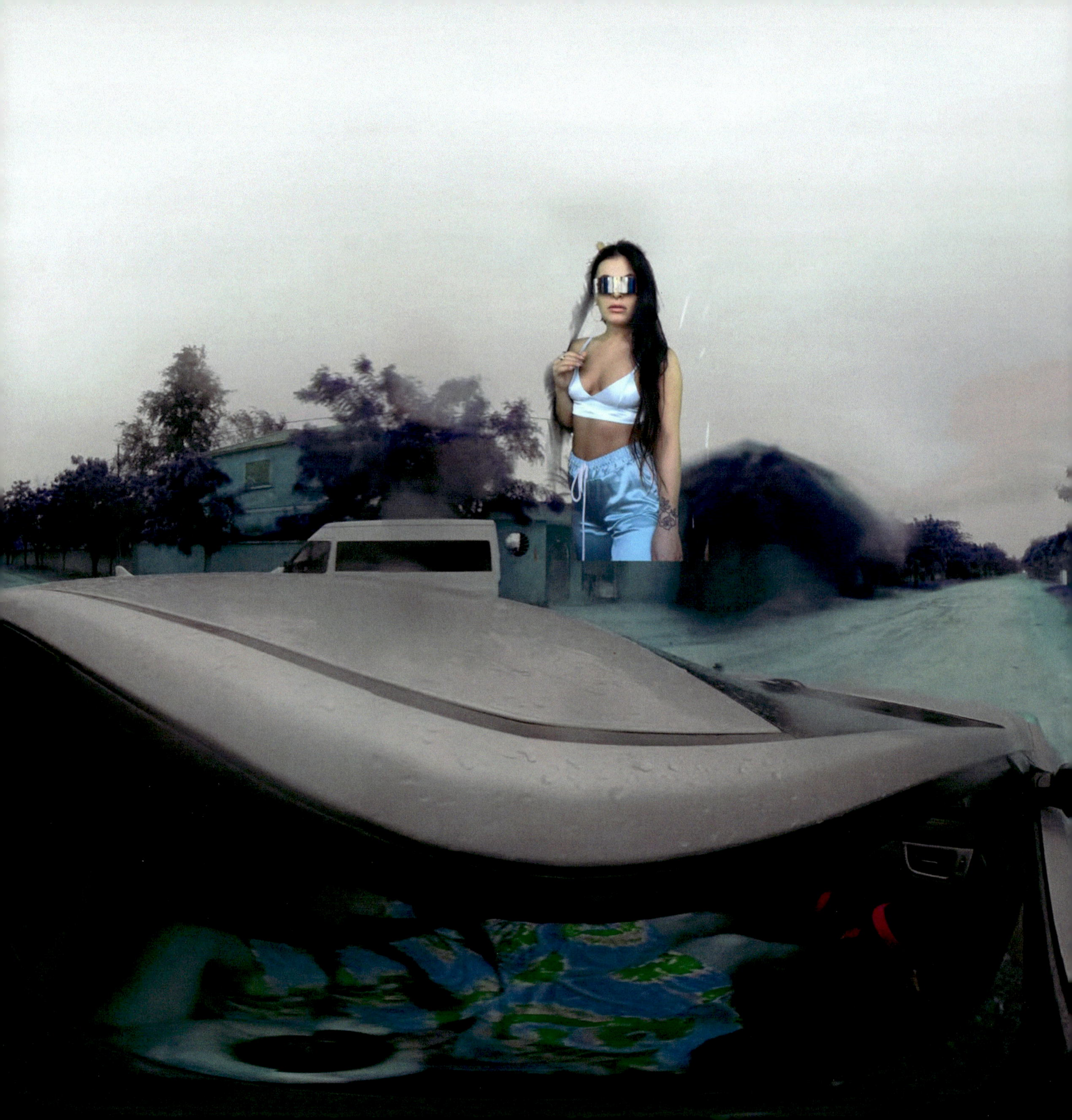

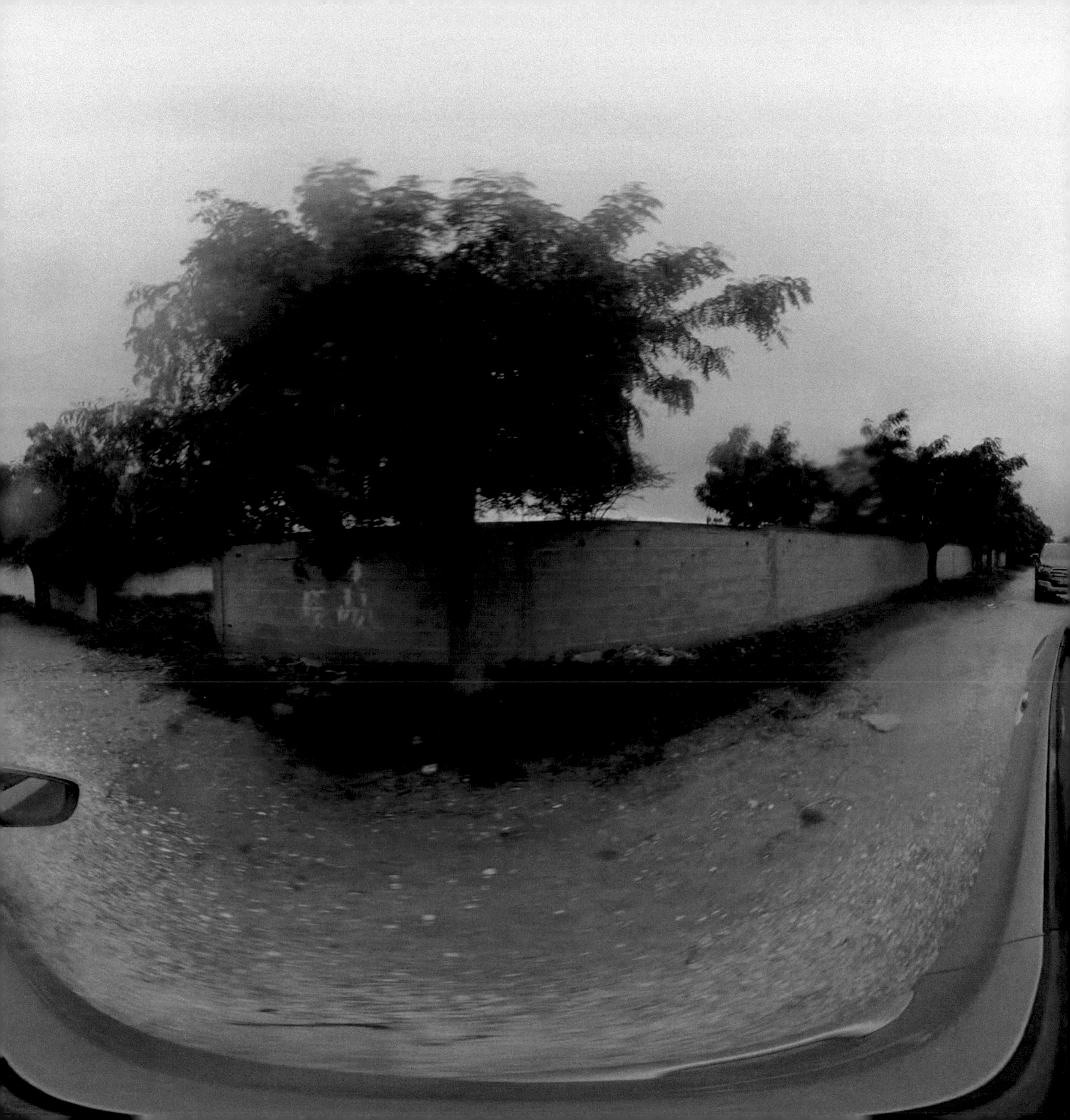

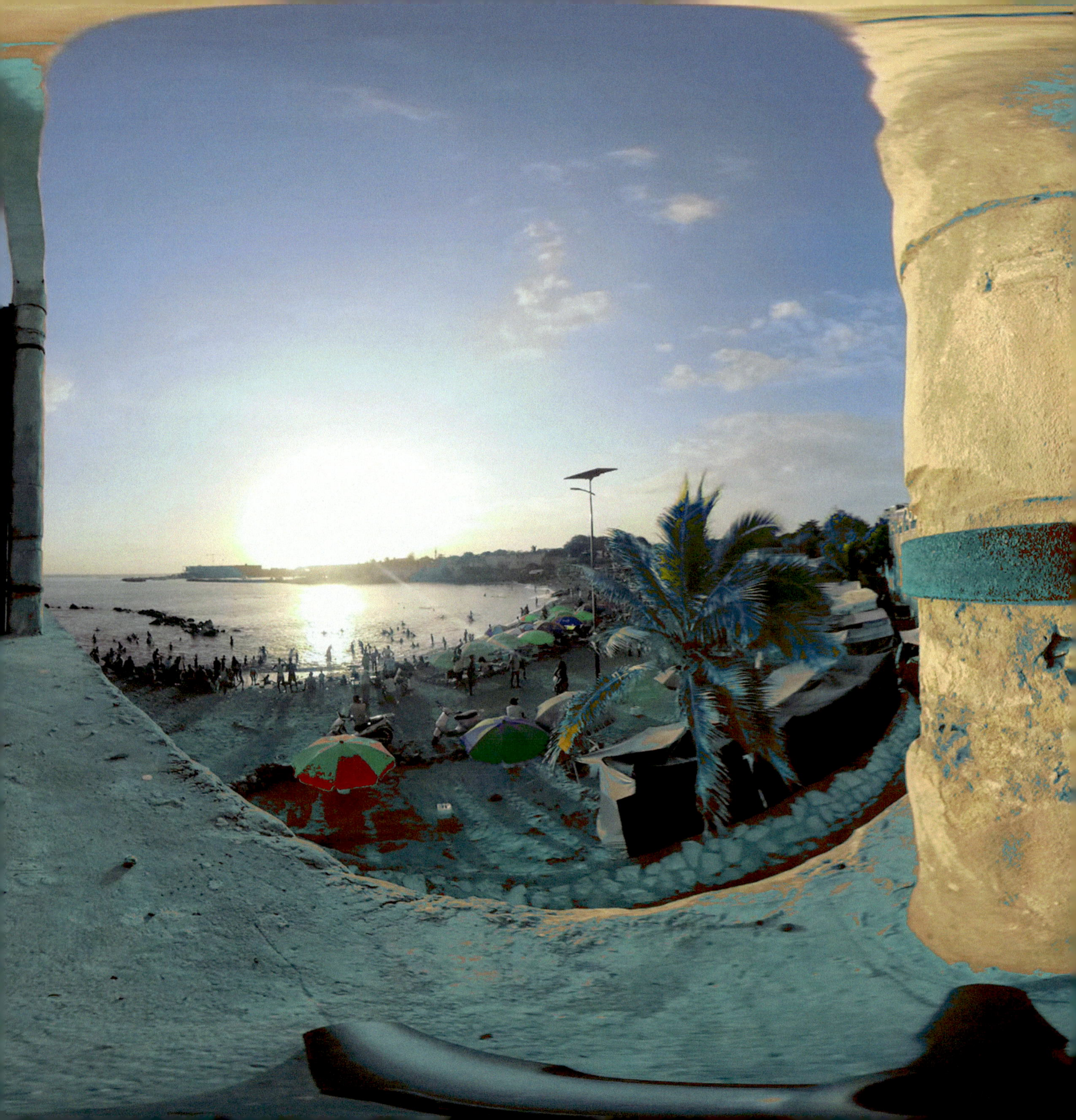

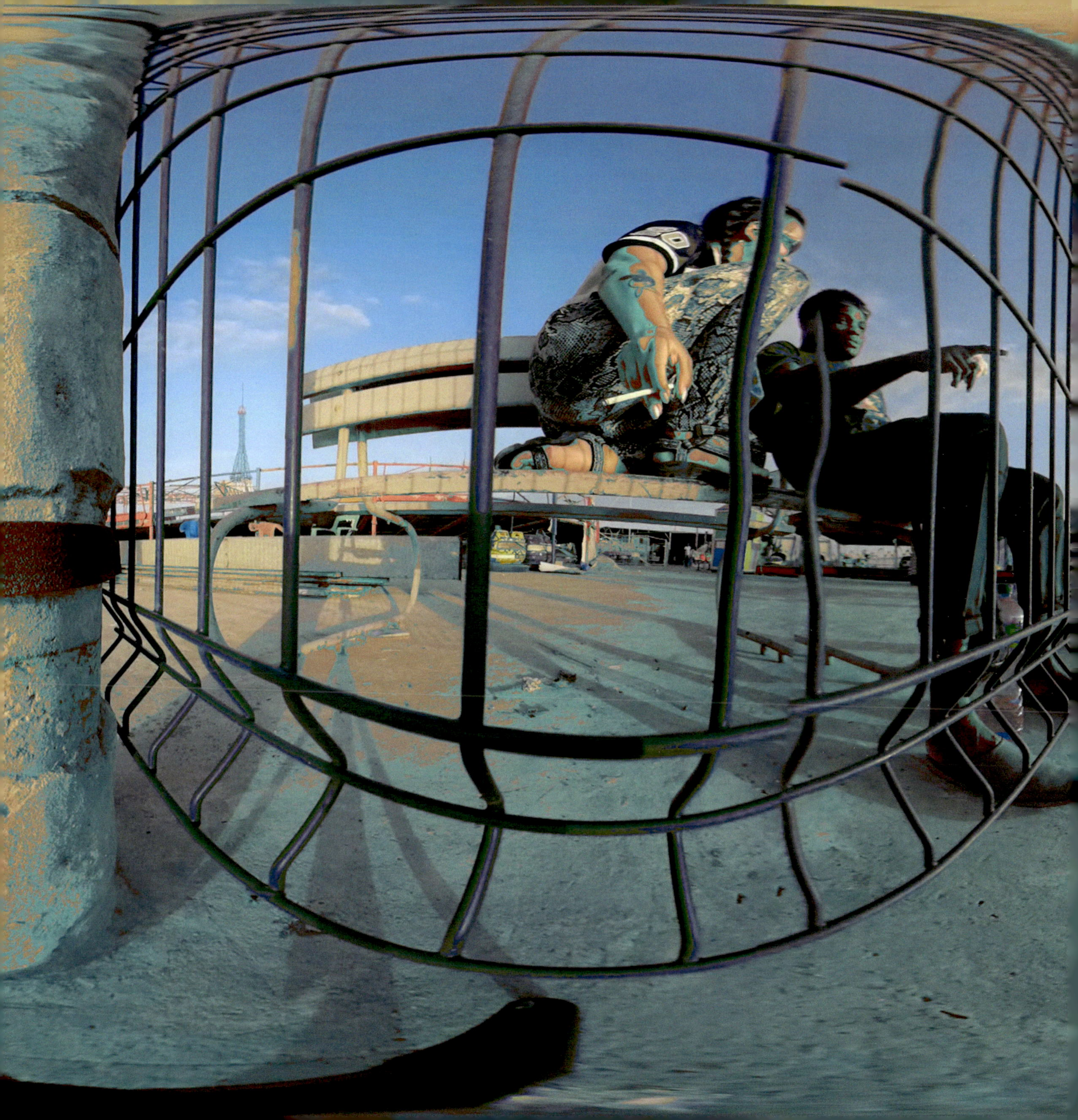

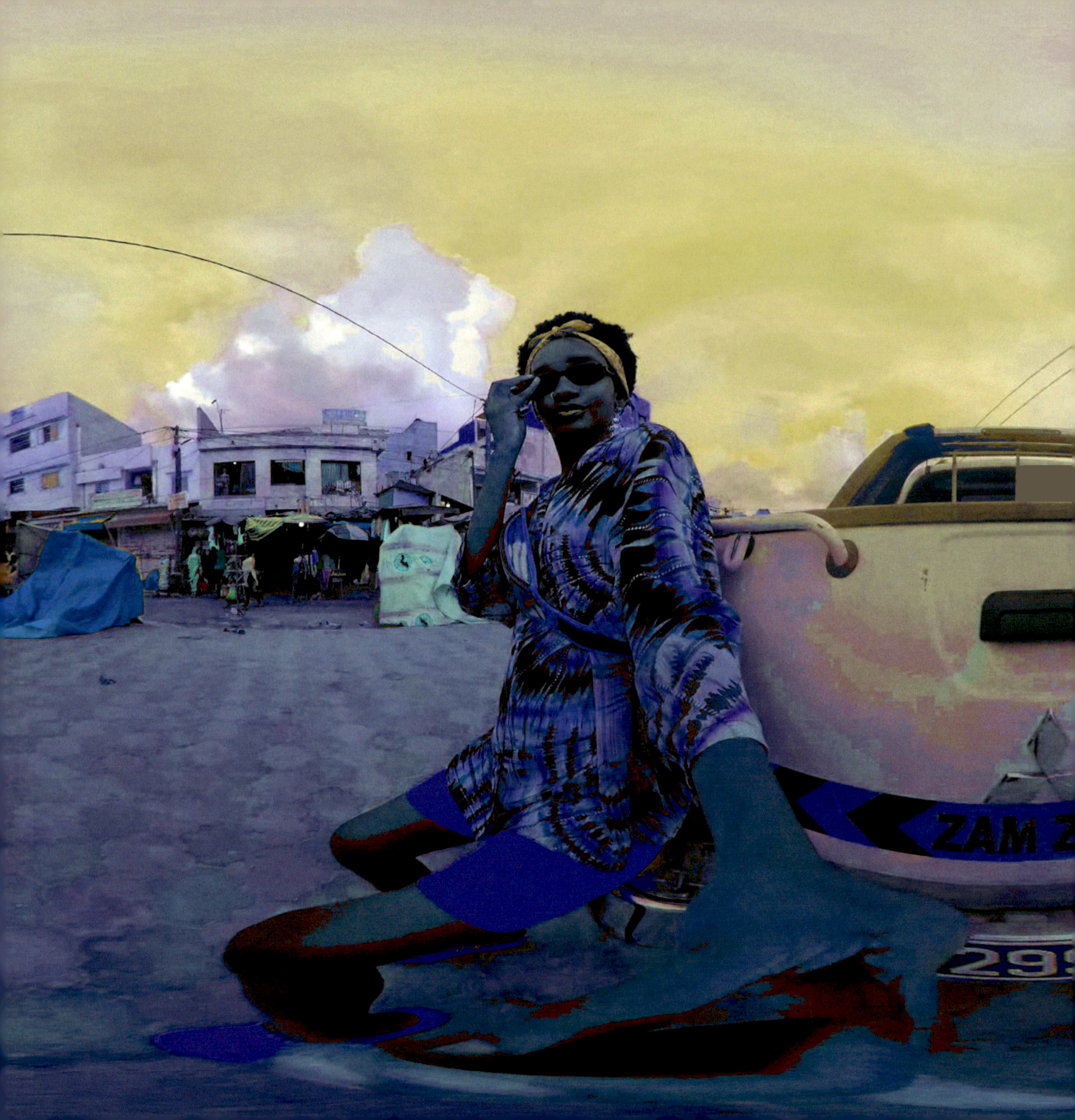

ZAM Z
295

OUR RELIGIOUS BACKGROUNDS, WE HAVE AL-WAYS BEEN TOLD HOW WE SHOULD DRESS.

MARK ZUCKERBERG: THE FIRST PLACE WE WANT TO GO TODAY IS PUERTO RICO. WE WILL QUICK-LY TELEPORT THERE . . . OKAY . . . NOW WE'RE IN PUERTO RICO . . . YOU CAN KIND OF GET A SENSE OF WHAT IS. WE'RE ON A BRIDGE. IT'S FLOODED. YOU CAN KIND OF GET A SENSE OF THE DAMAGE THAT THE HURRICANES HAVE DONE. AND THIS IS ONE OF THE THINGS THAT IS REALLY MAGICAL ABOUT VIRTUAL REALITY. YOU CAN GET THE FEELING THAT YOU ARE REALLY IN A PLACE. RIGHT?

THIBAUT: SORRY, AIN'T NOBODY GOT TIME FOR YOUR DISASTER PORN FETISH. WE RULE OUR TOOLS FOR PLANETARY REDISTRIBUTION OF AC-CESS TO RECOURSES.

TO THE BRIGHT AND GLITTERING DAYBREAK OF FREEDOM AND JUSTICE.

ANNA: THE CONTINUOUSLY RENDERING OF BOD-IES SUPERFLUOUS TO CAPITAL IS PRODUCING

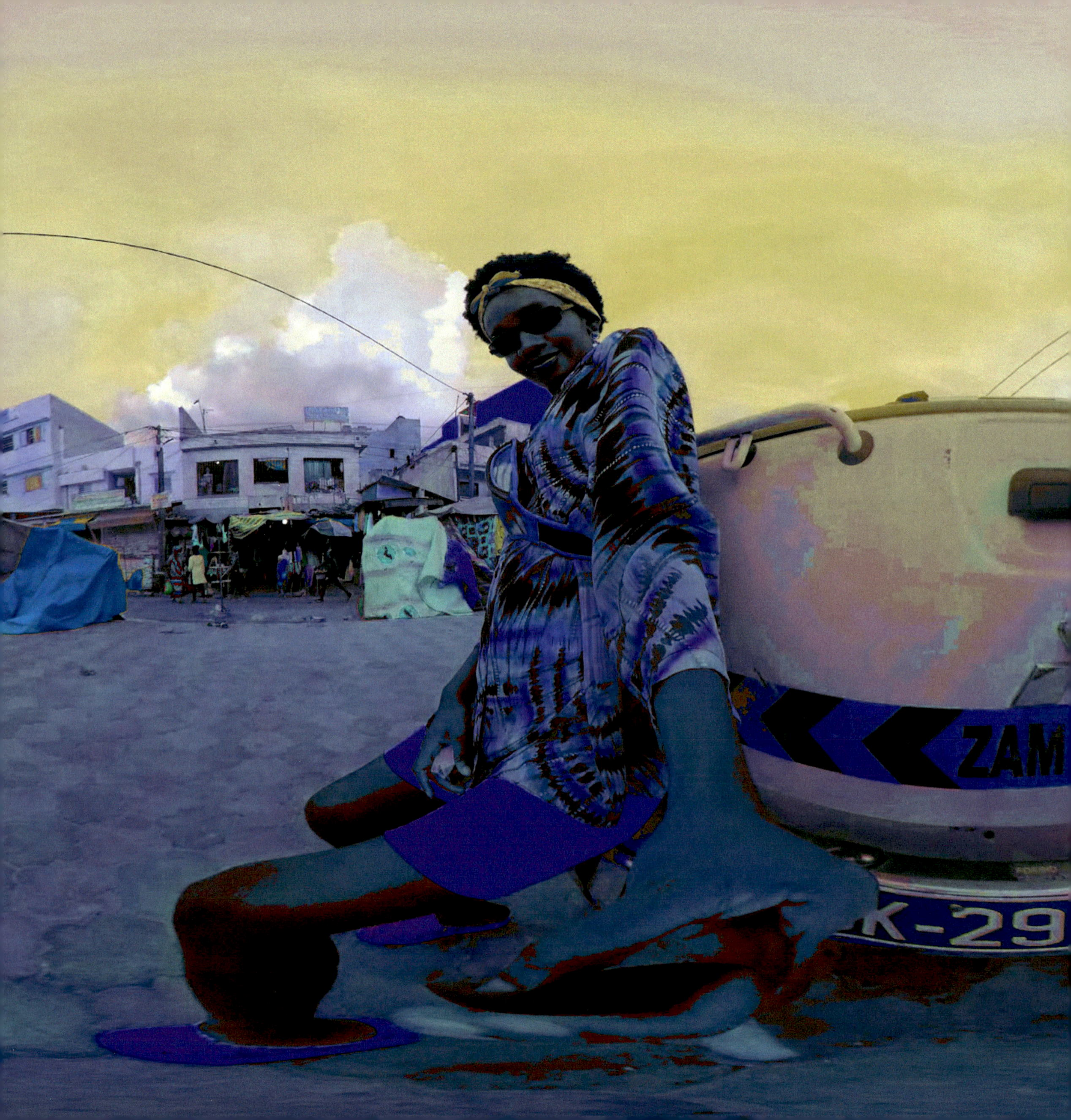
ZAM
K-29

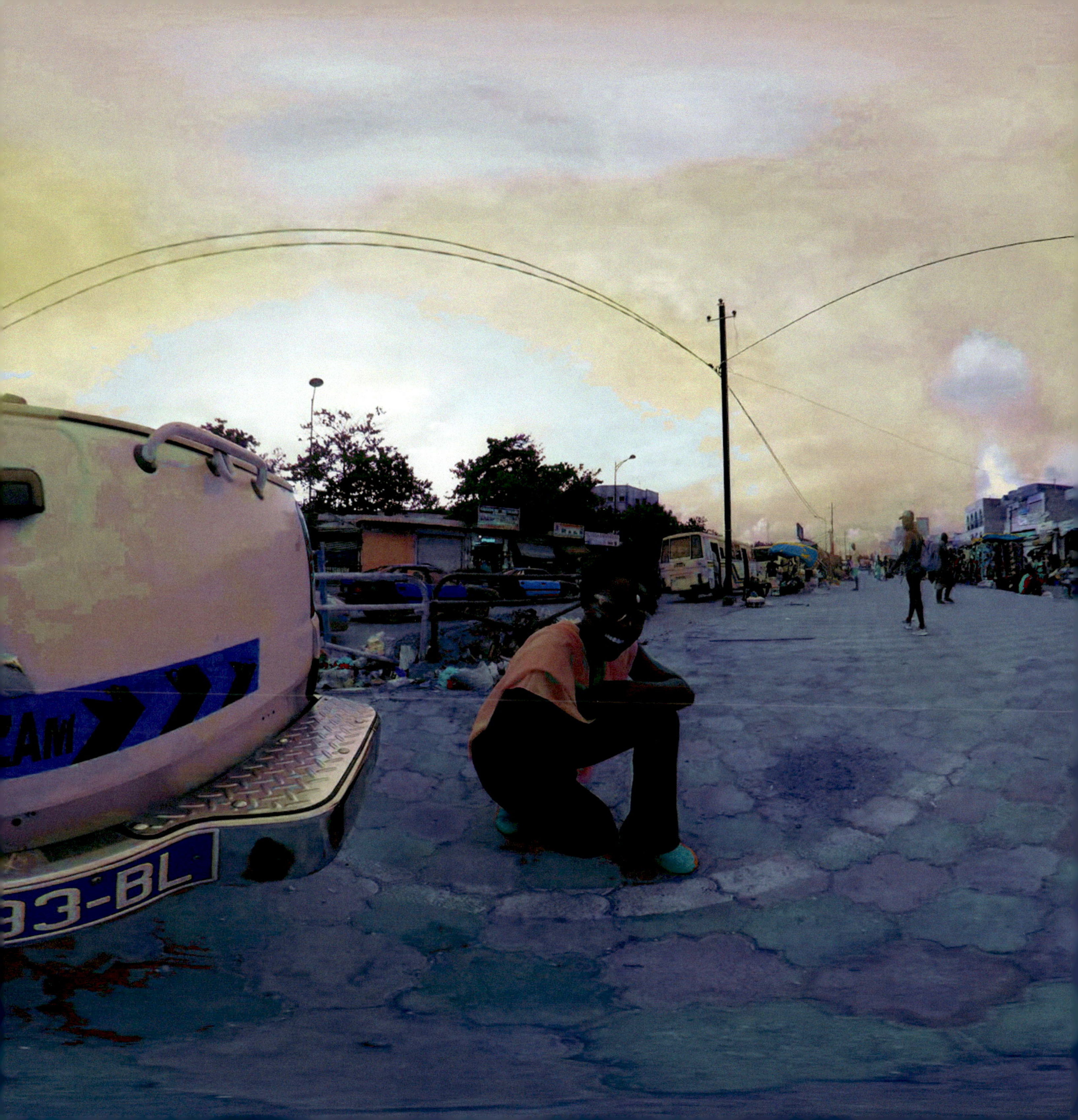

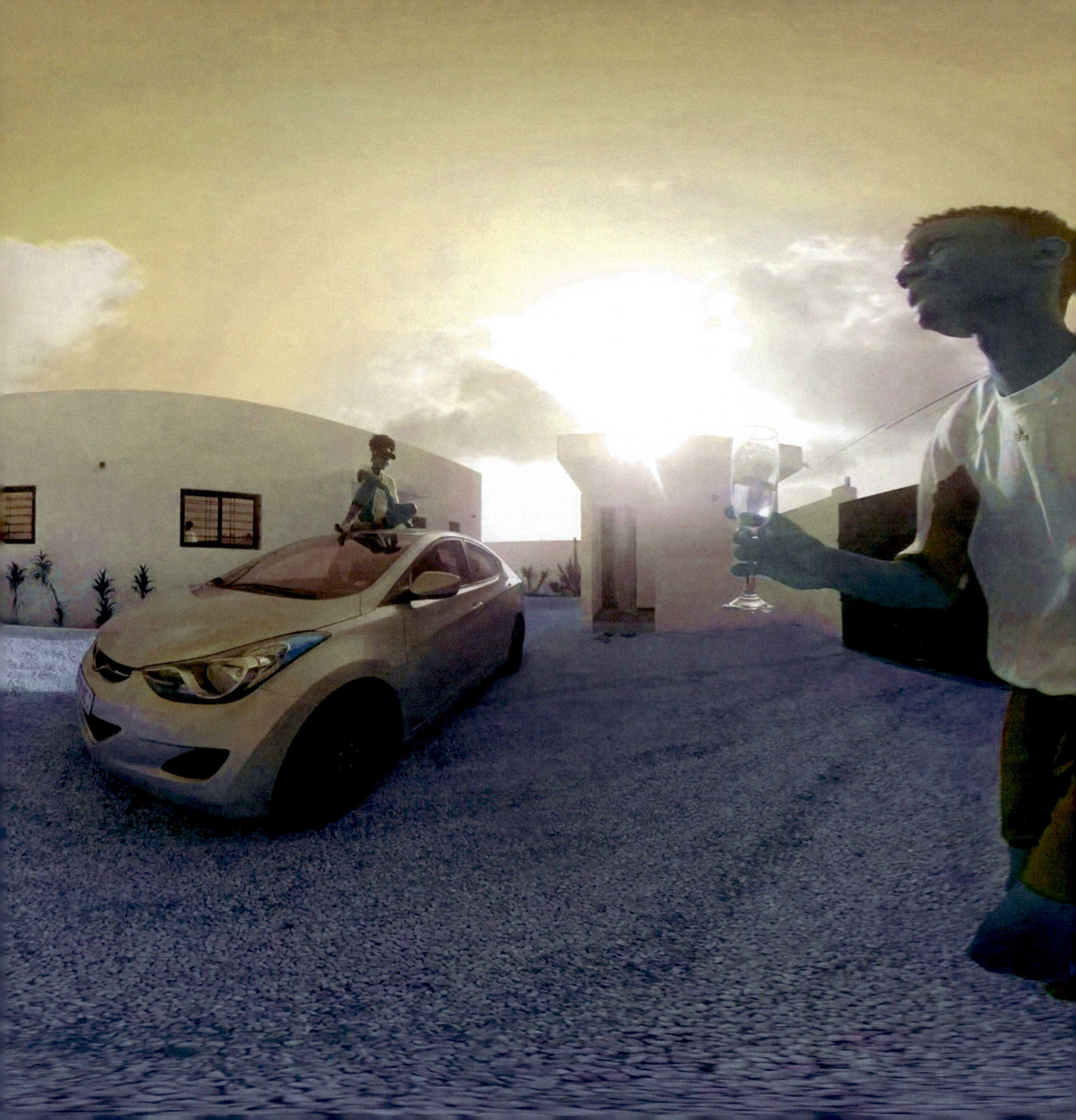

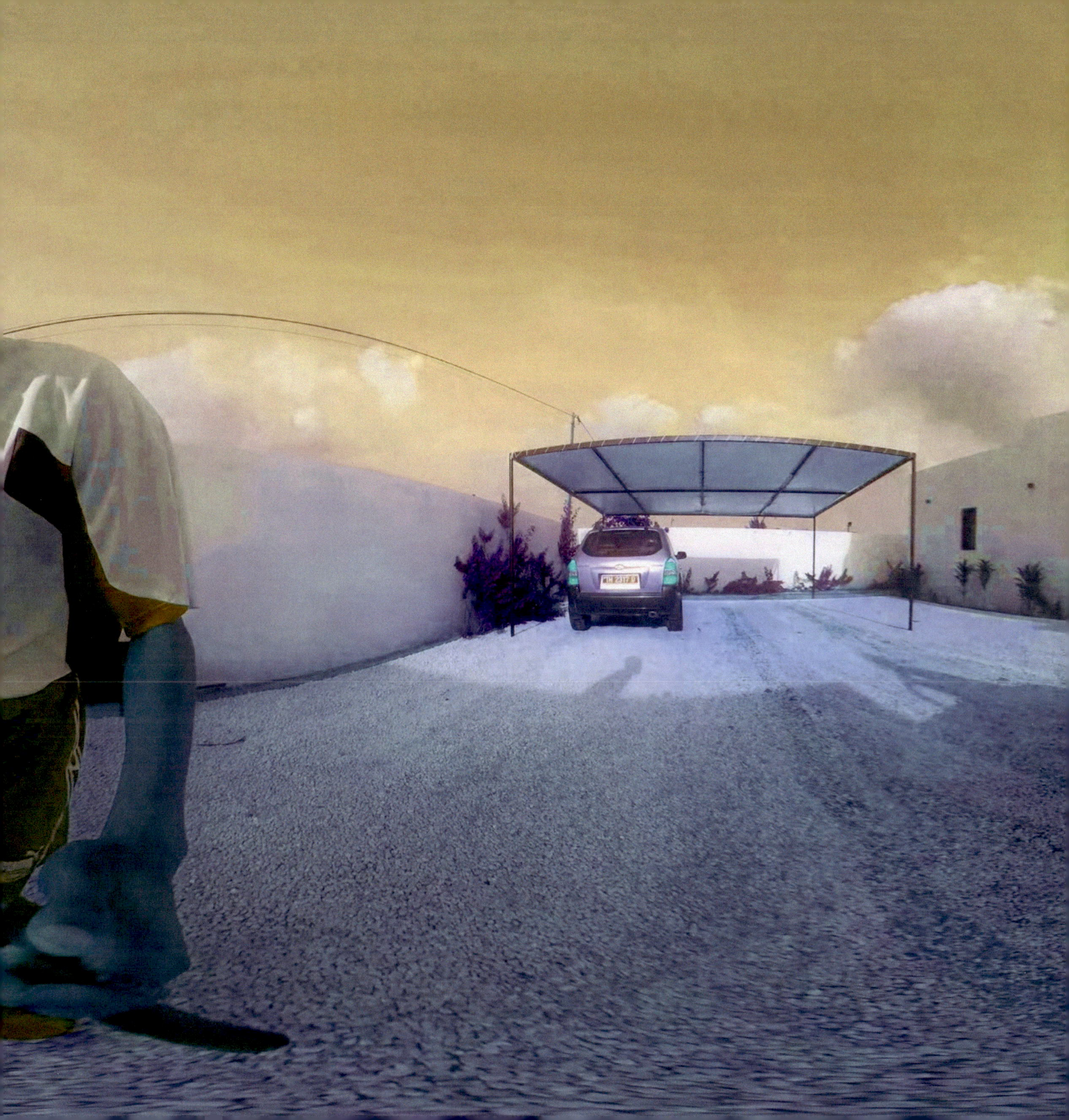

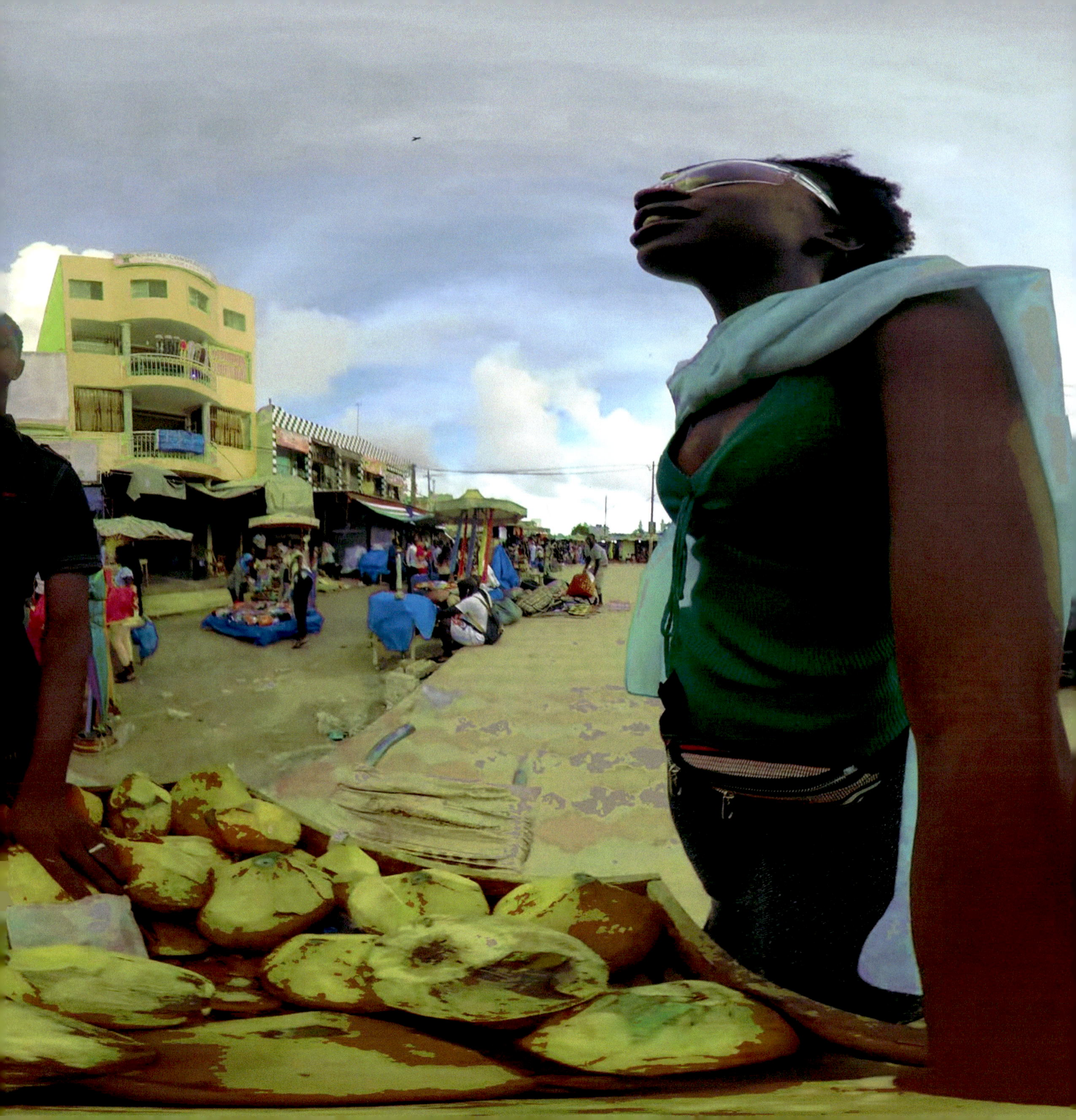

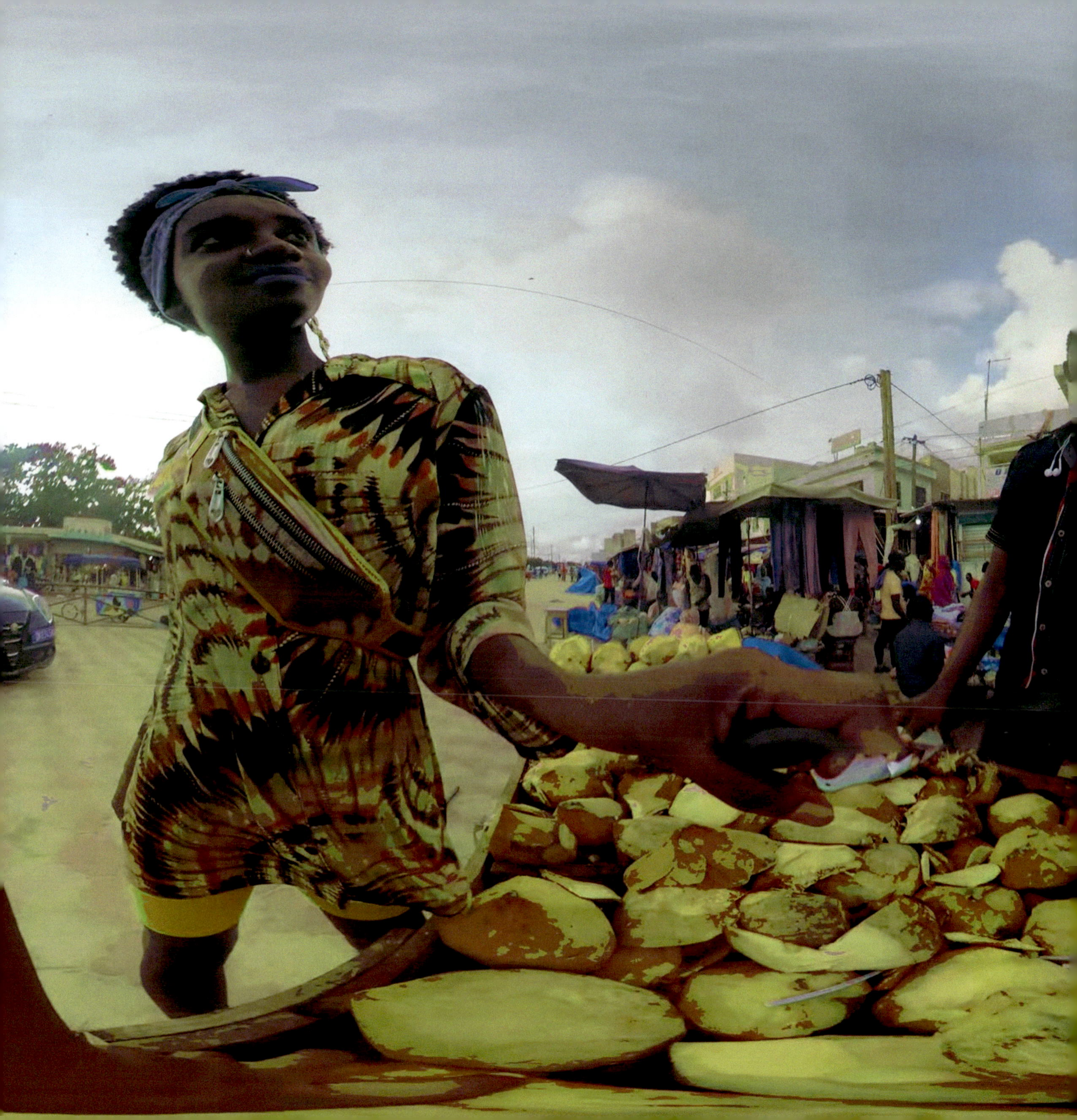

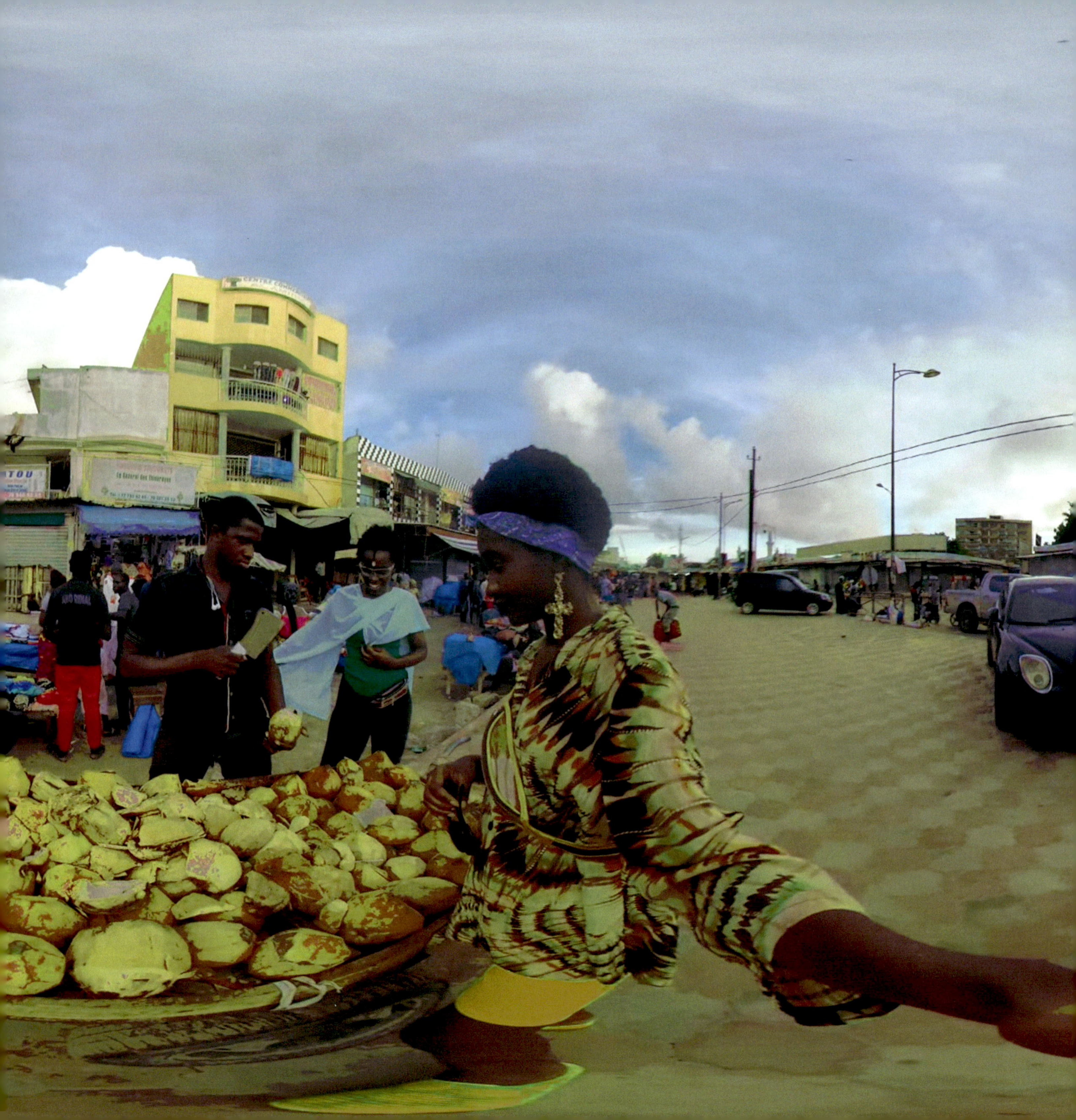

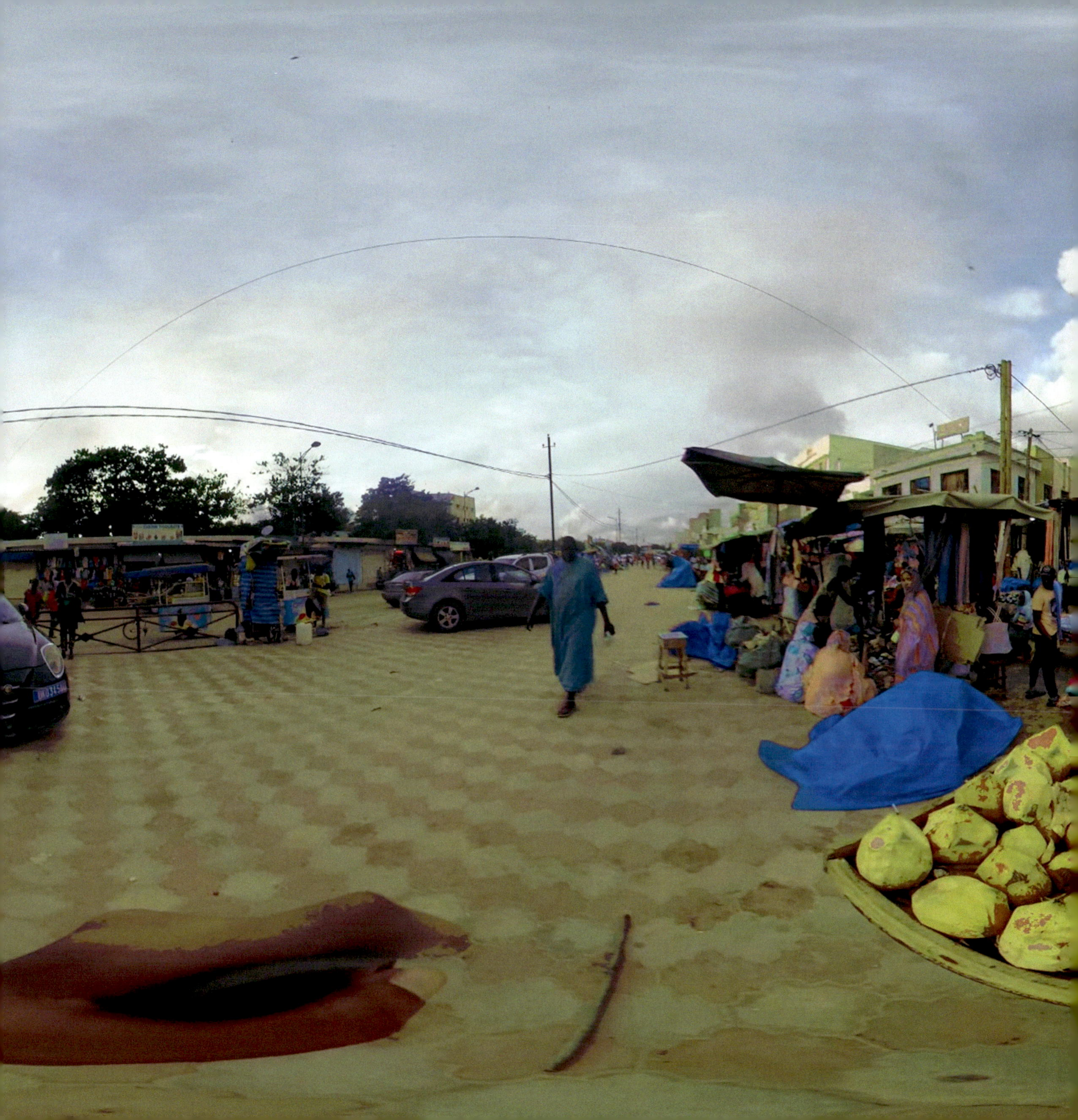

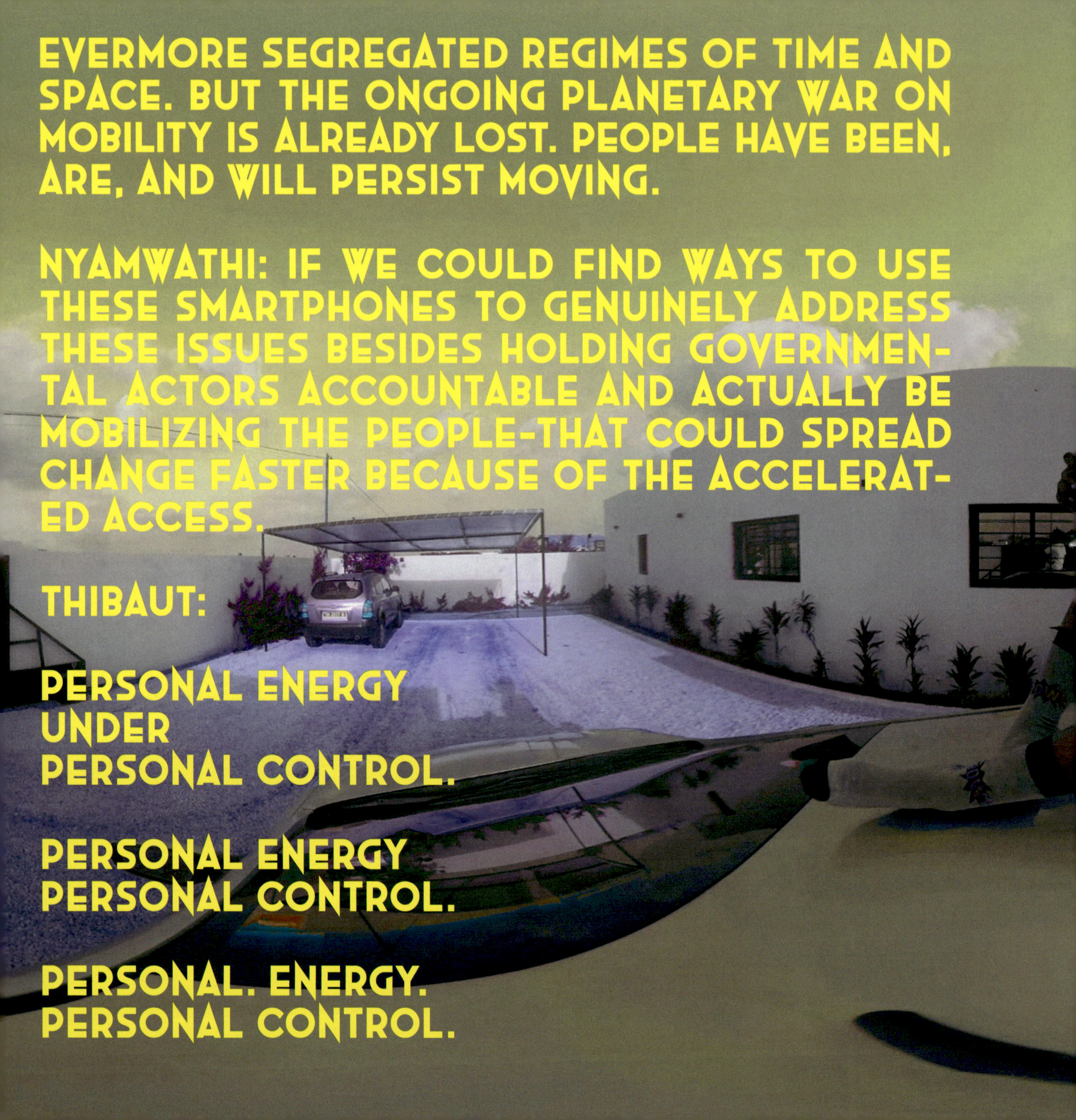

EVERMORE SEGREGATED REGIMES OF TIME AND SPACE. BUT THE ONGOING PLANETARY WAR ON MOBILITY IS ALREADY LOST. PEOPLE HAVE BEEN, ARE, AND WILL PERSIST MOVING.

NYAMWATHI: IF WE COULD FIND WAYS TO USE THESE SMARTPHONES TO GENUINELY ADDRESS THESE ISSUES BESIDES HOLDING GOVERNMEN-TAL ACTORS ACCOUNTABLE AND ACTUALLY BE MOBILIZING THE PEOPLE-THAT COULD SPREAD CHANGE FASTER BECAUSE OF THE ACCELERAT-ED ACCESS.

THIBAUT:

PERSONAL ENERGY
UNDER
PERSONAL CONTROL.

PERSONAL ENERGY
PERSONAL CONTROL.

PERSONAL. ENERGY.
PERSONAL CONTROL.

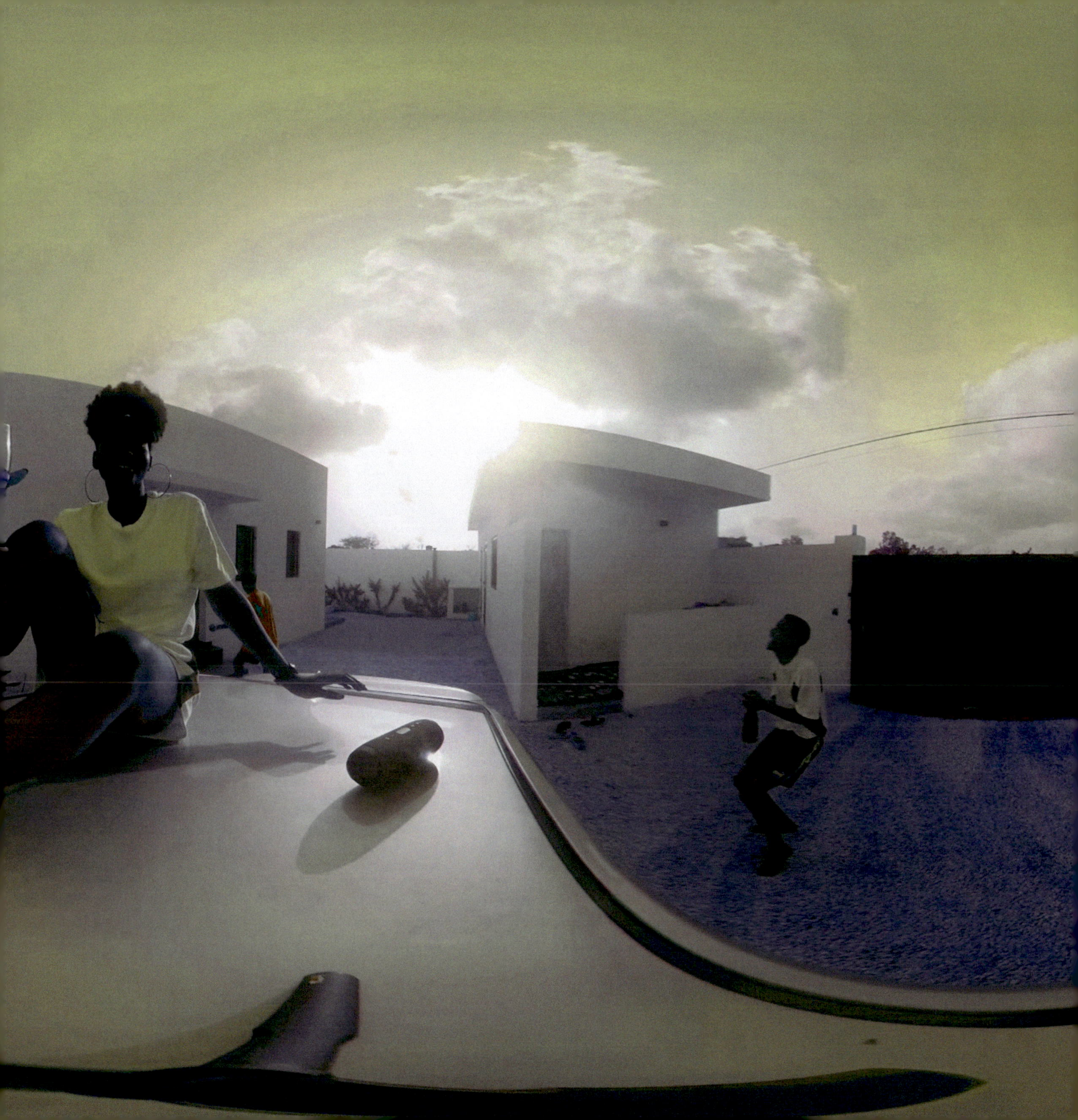

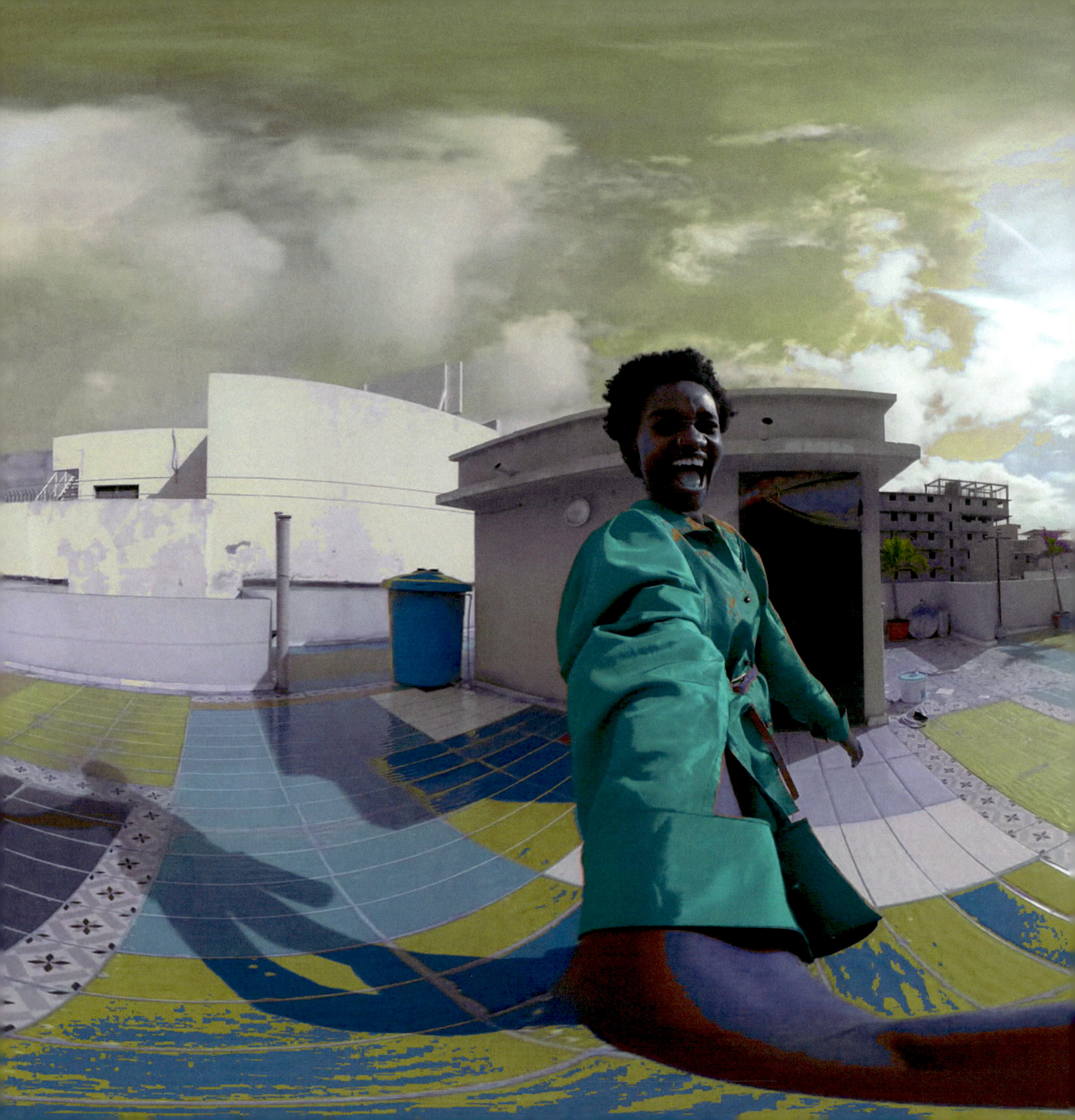

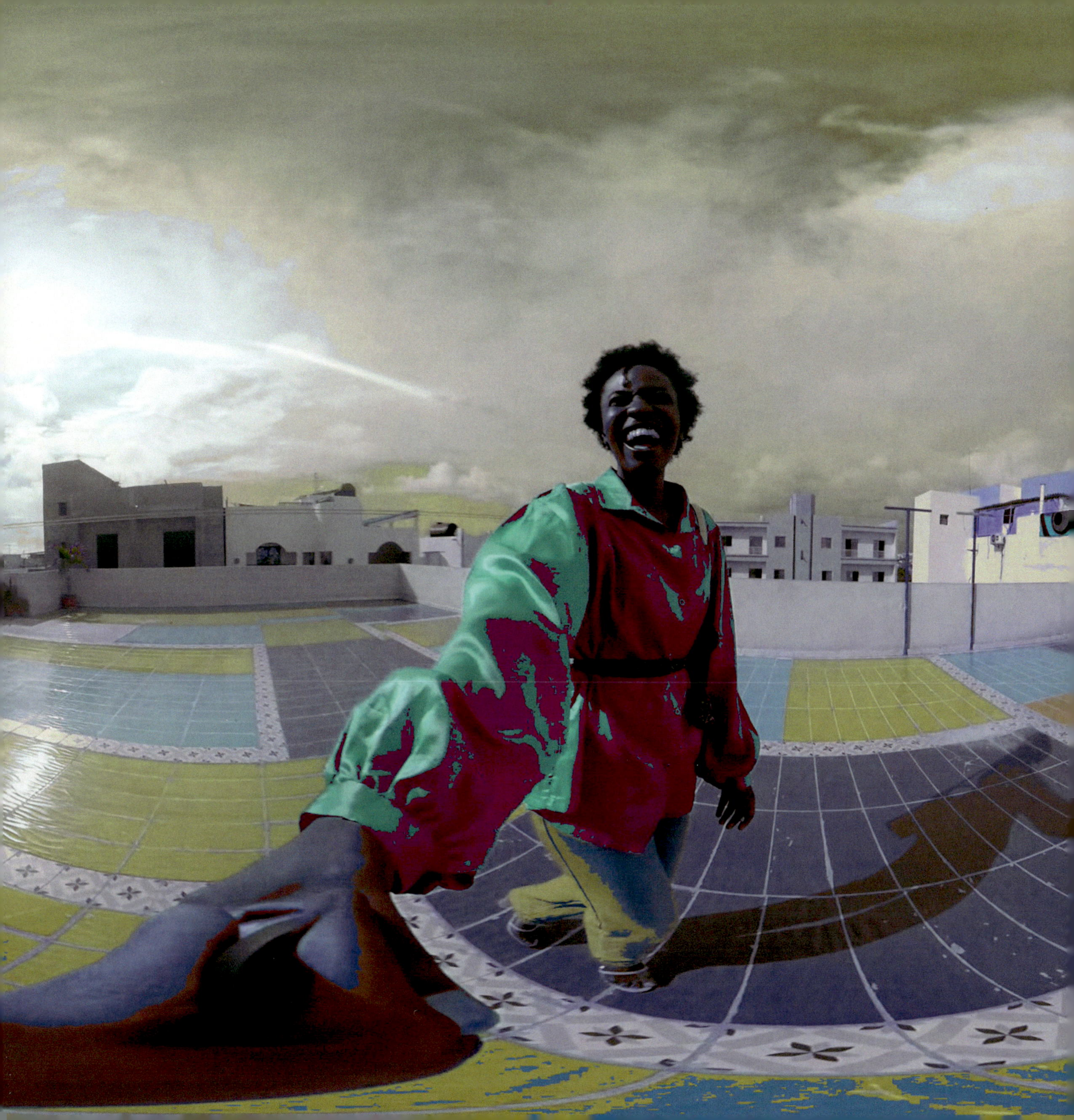

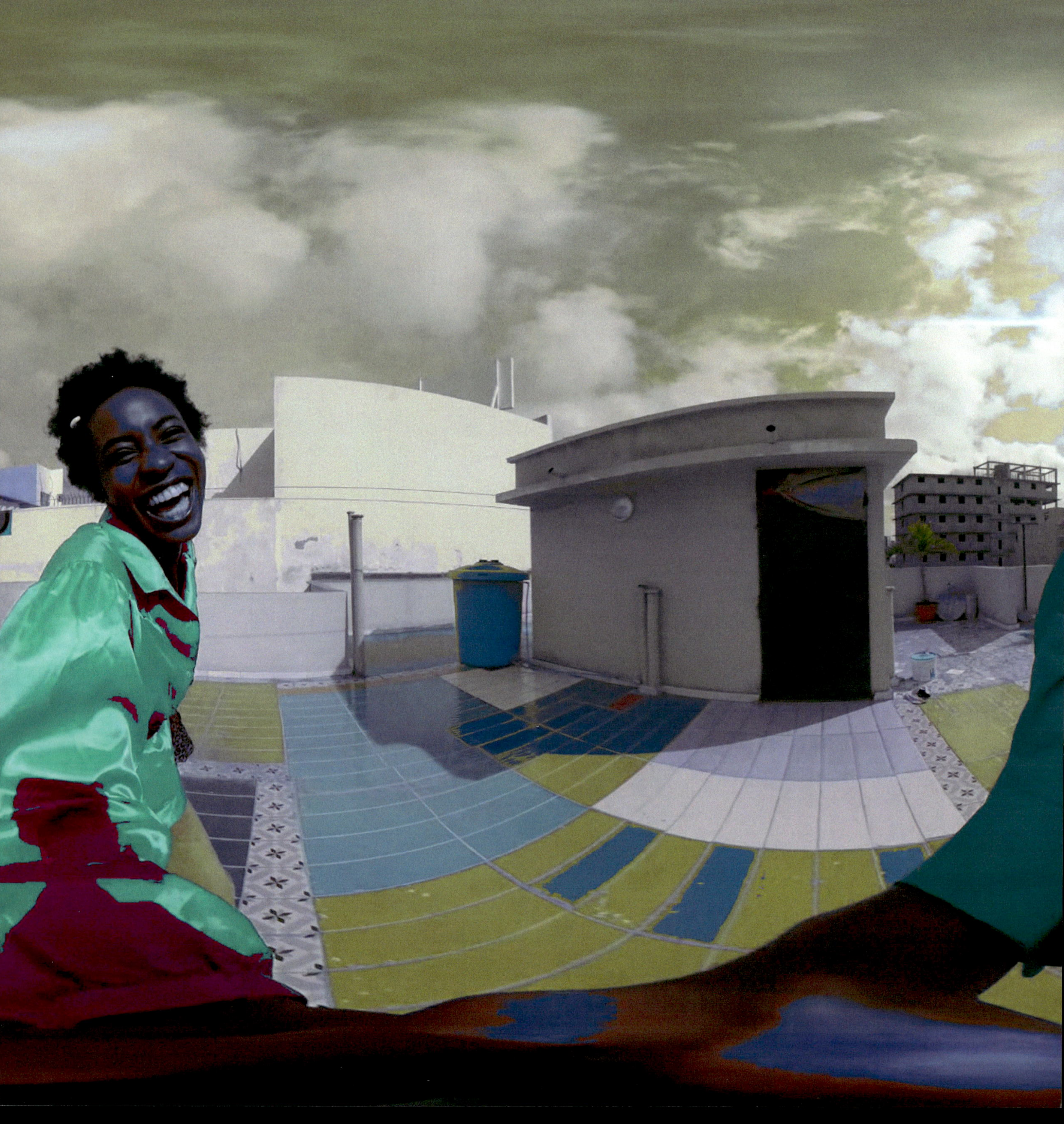

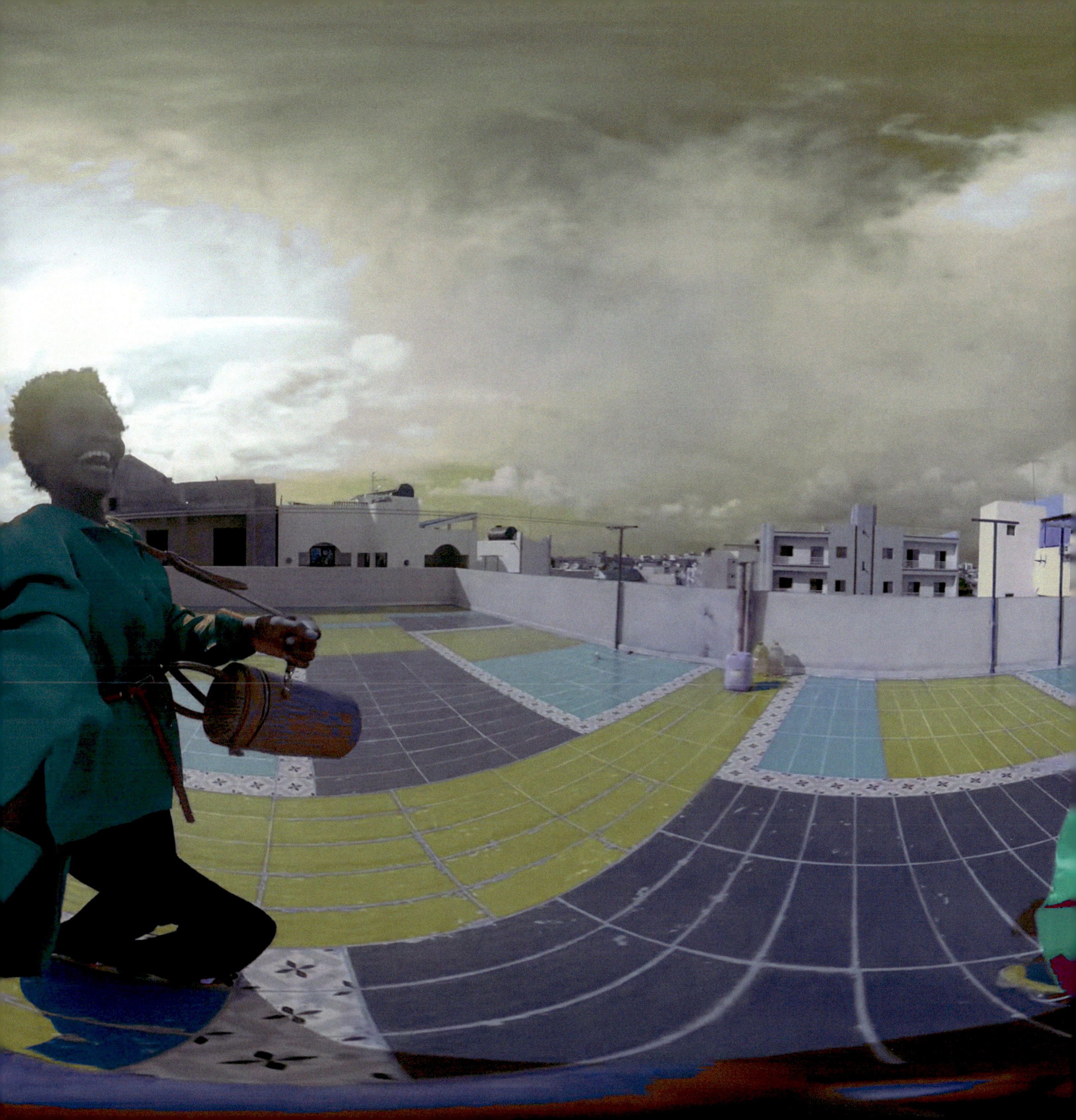

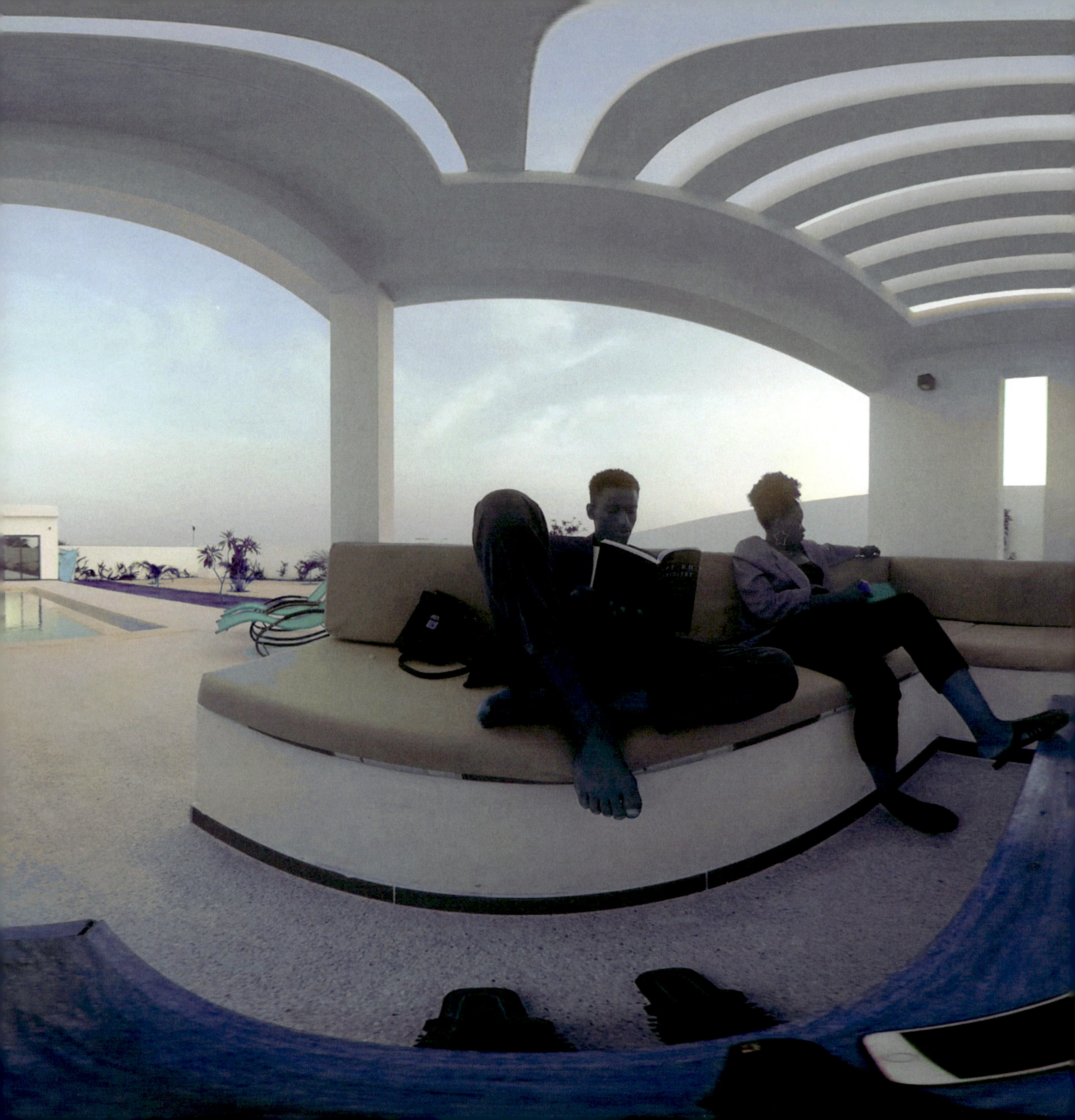

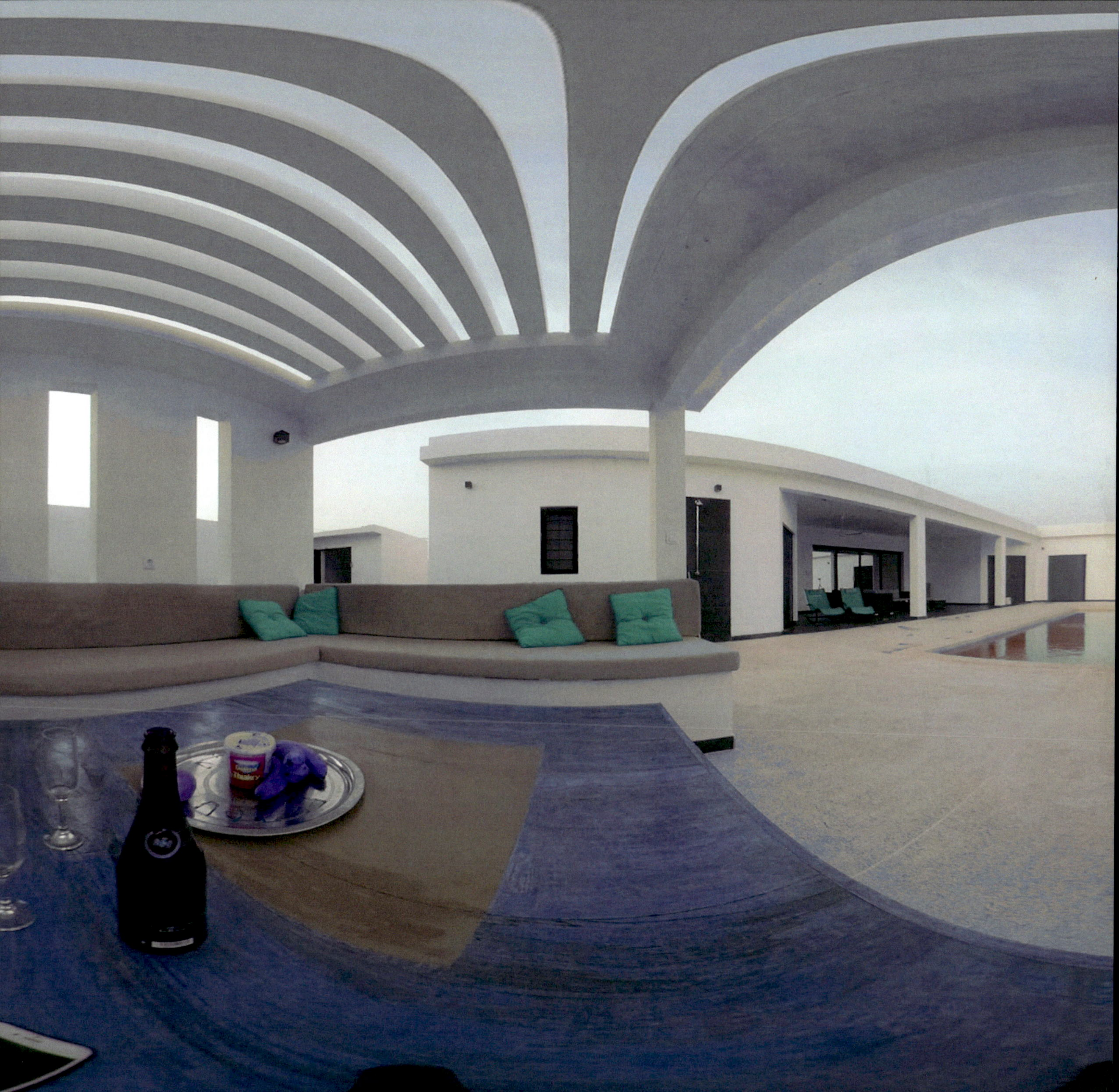

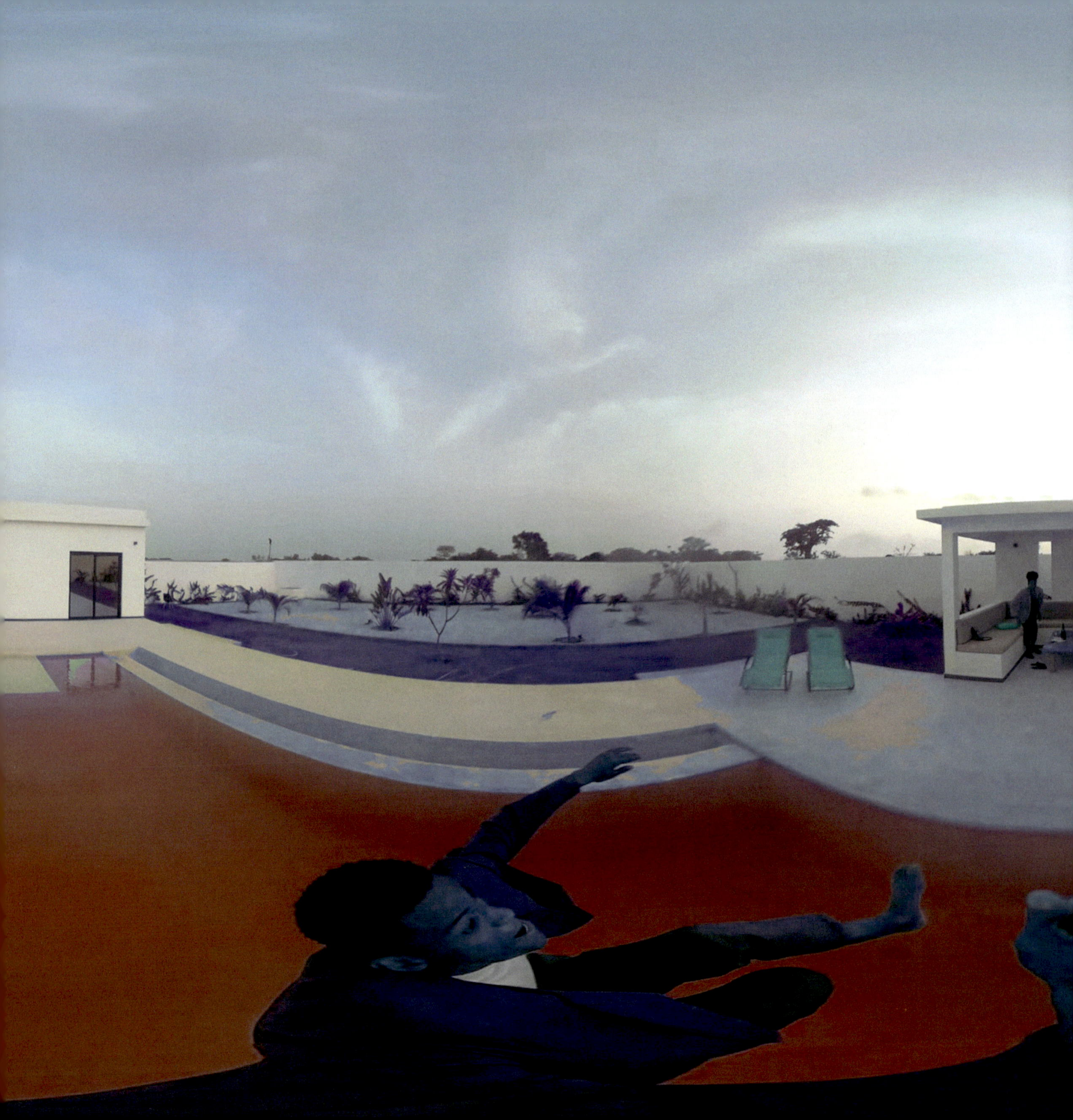

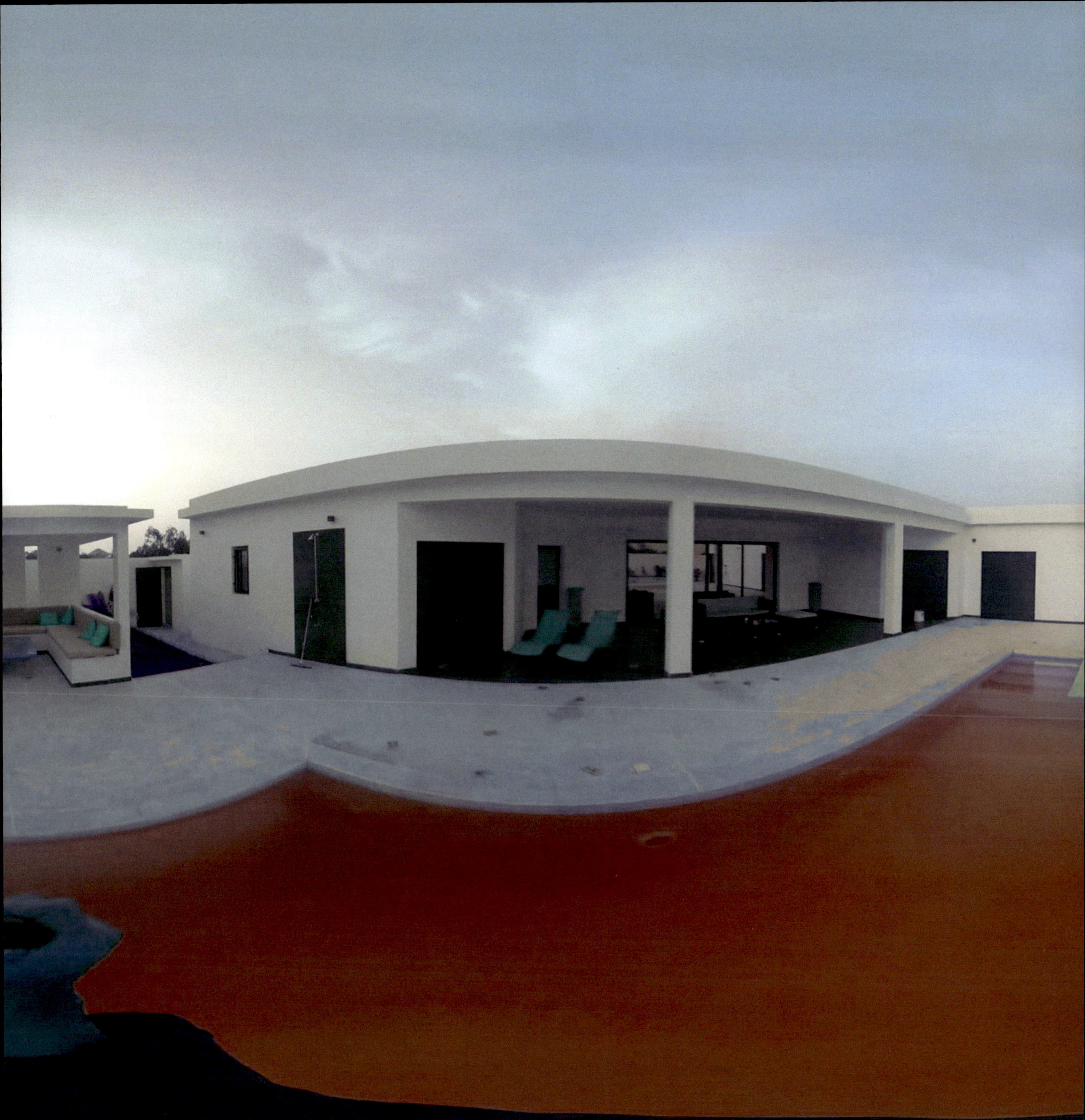

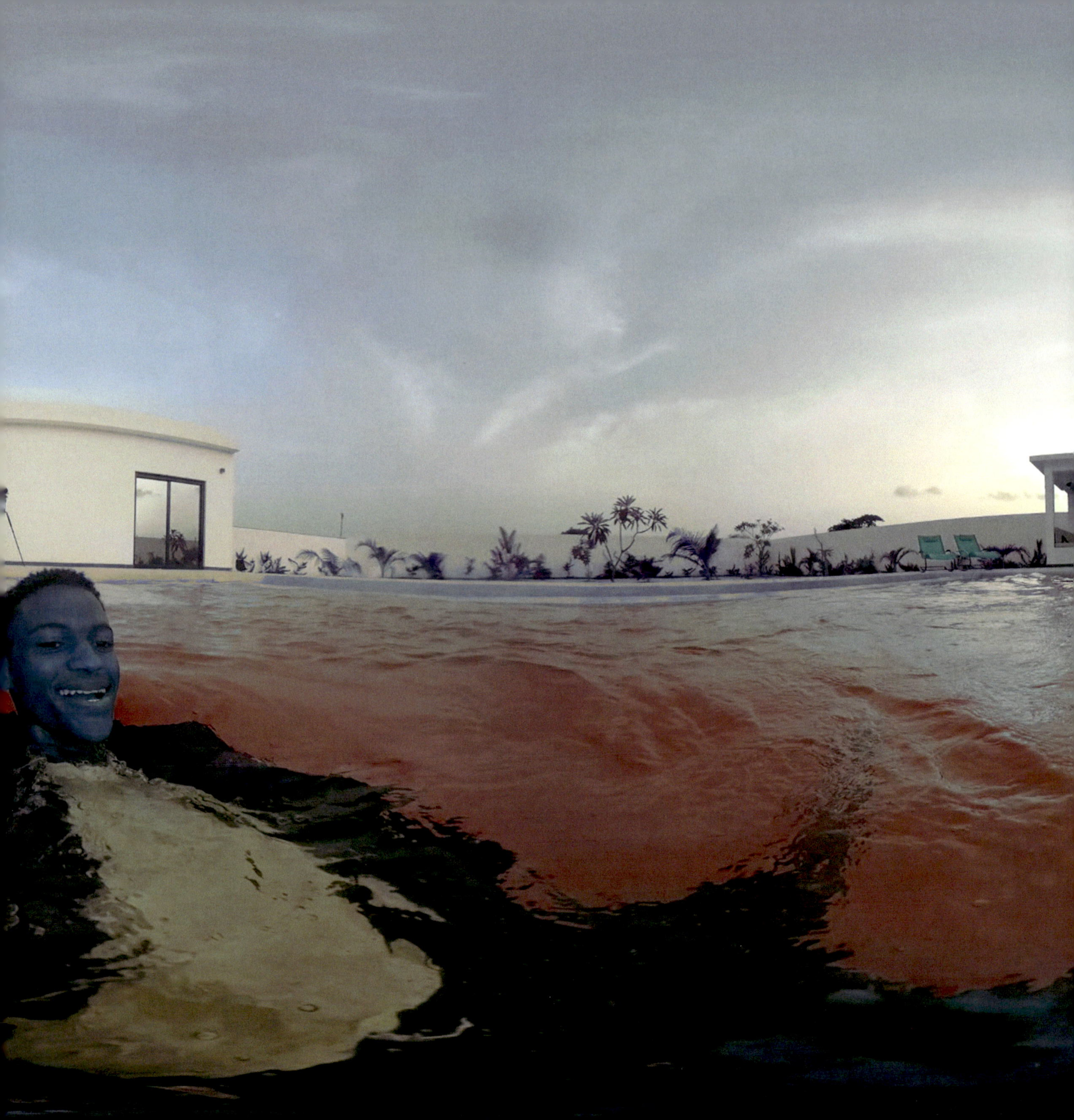

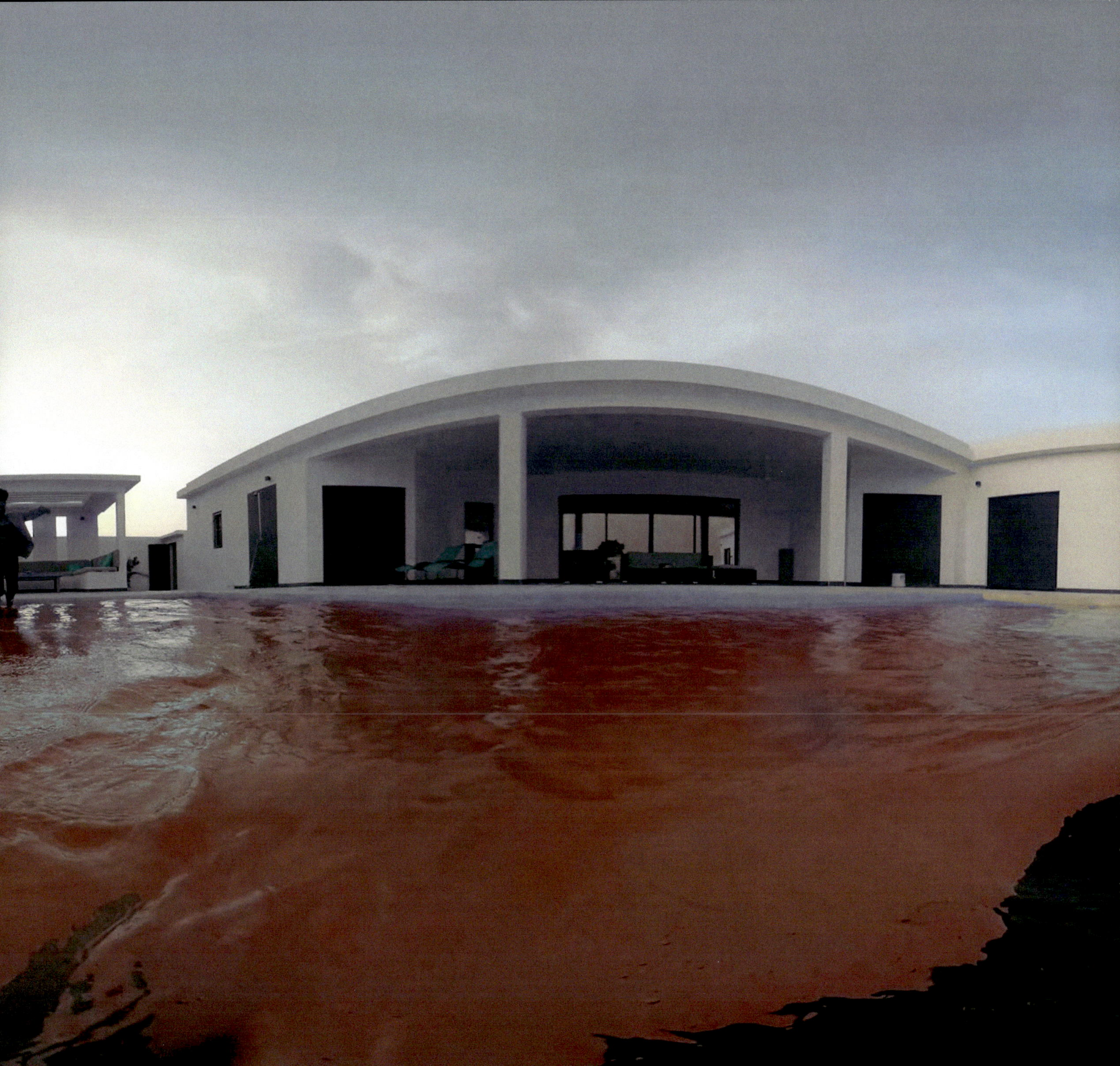

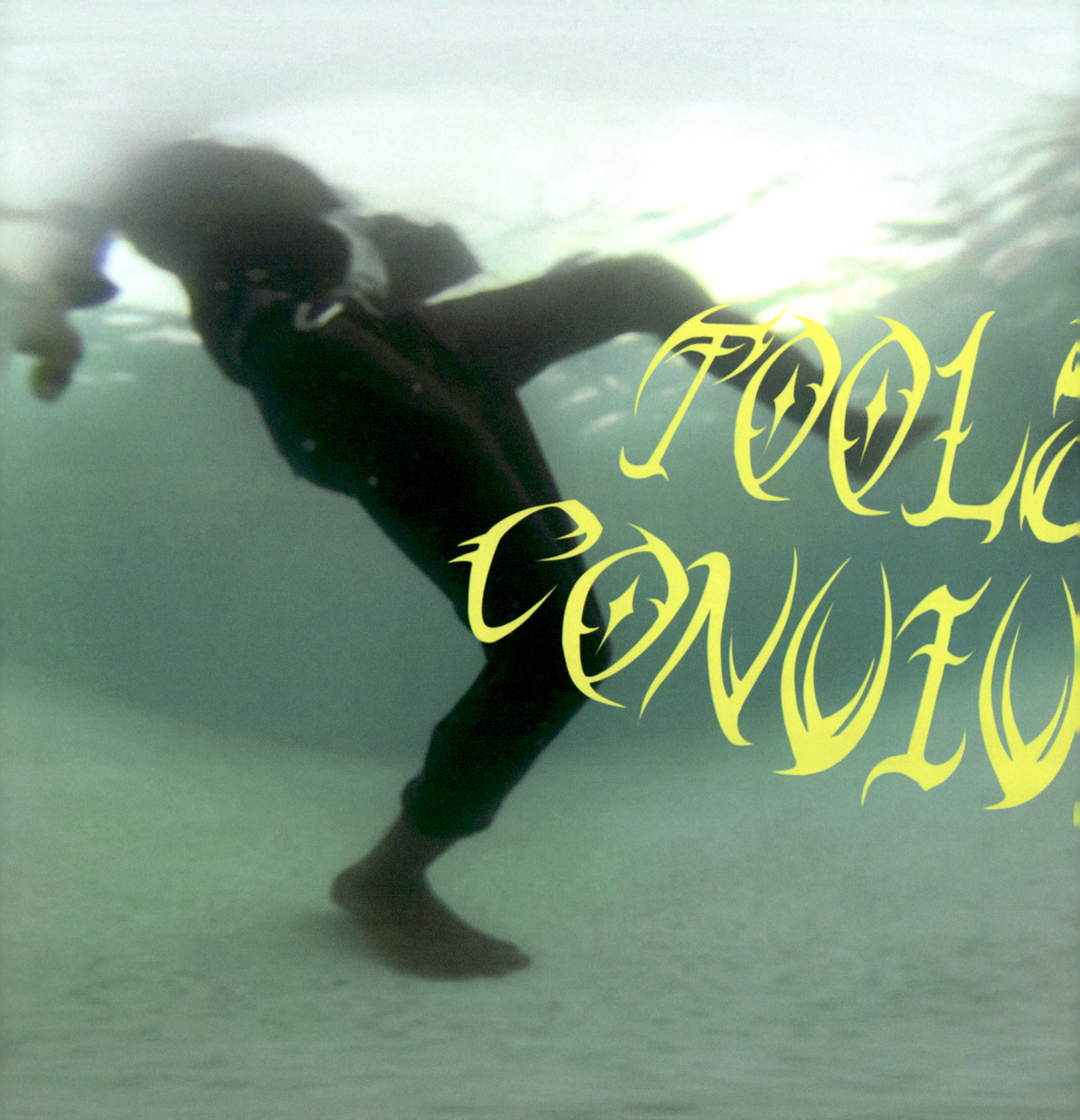
TOOLS
CONVOY

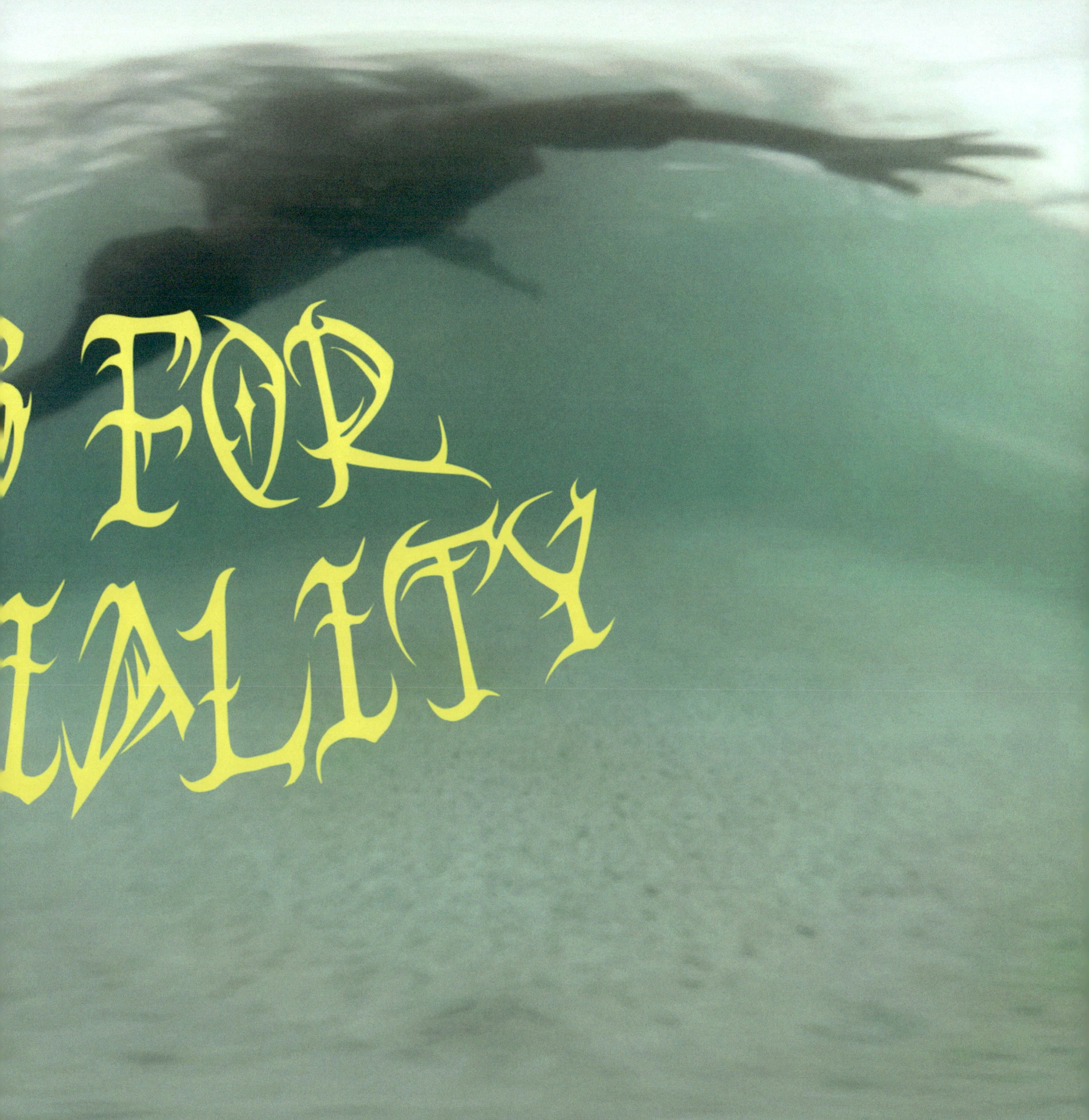
FOR
EALITY

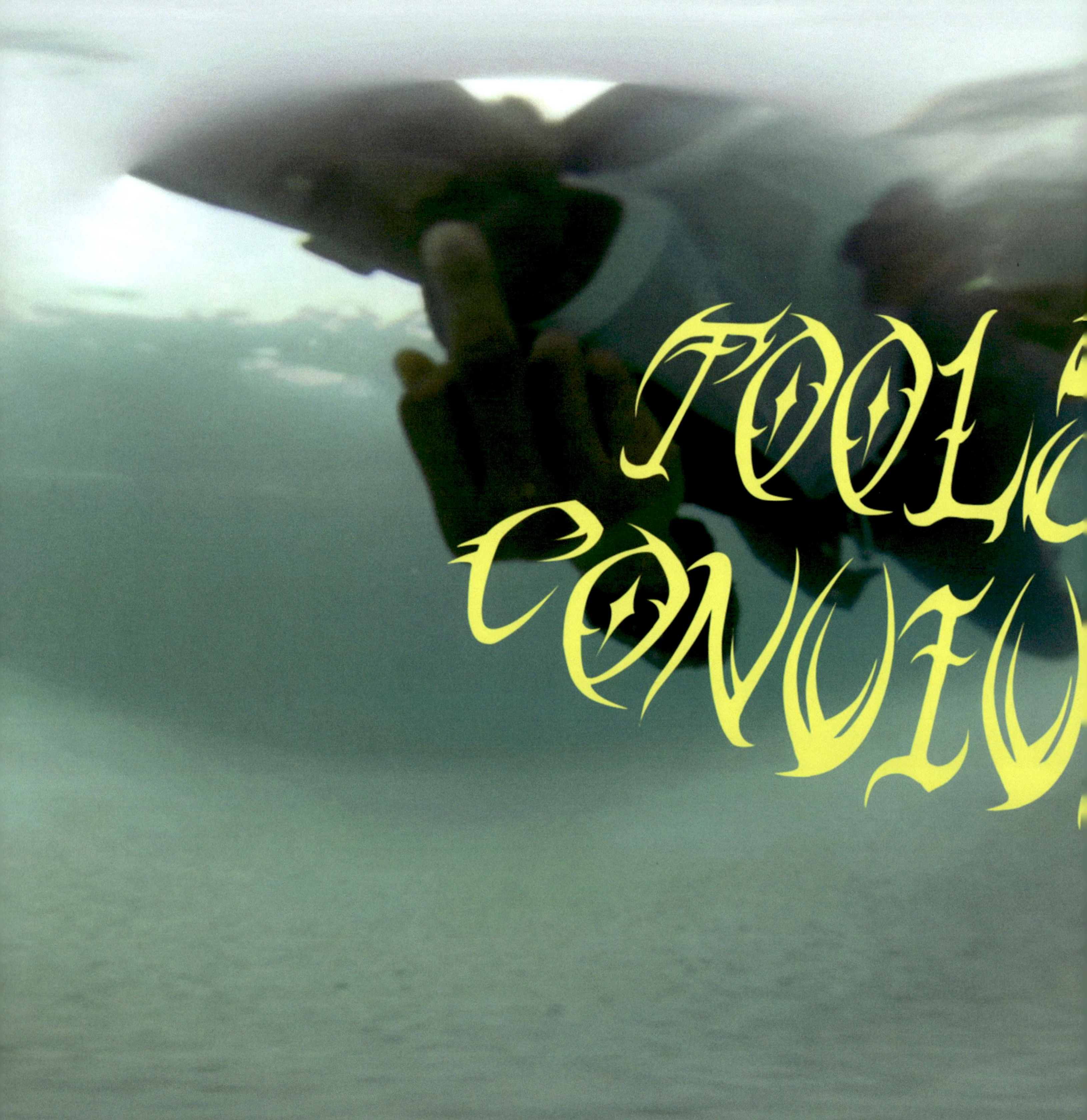
TOOLS
CONVOY

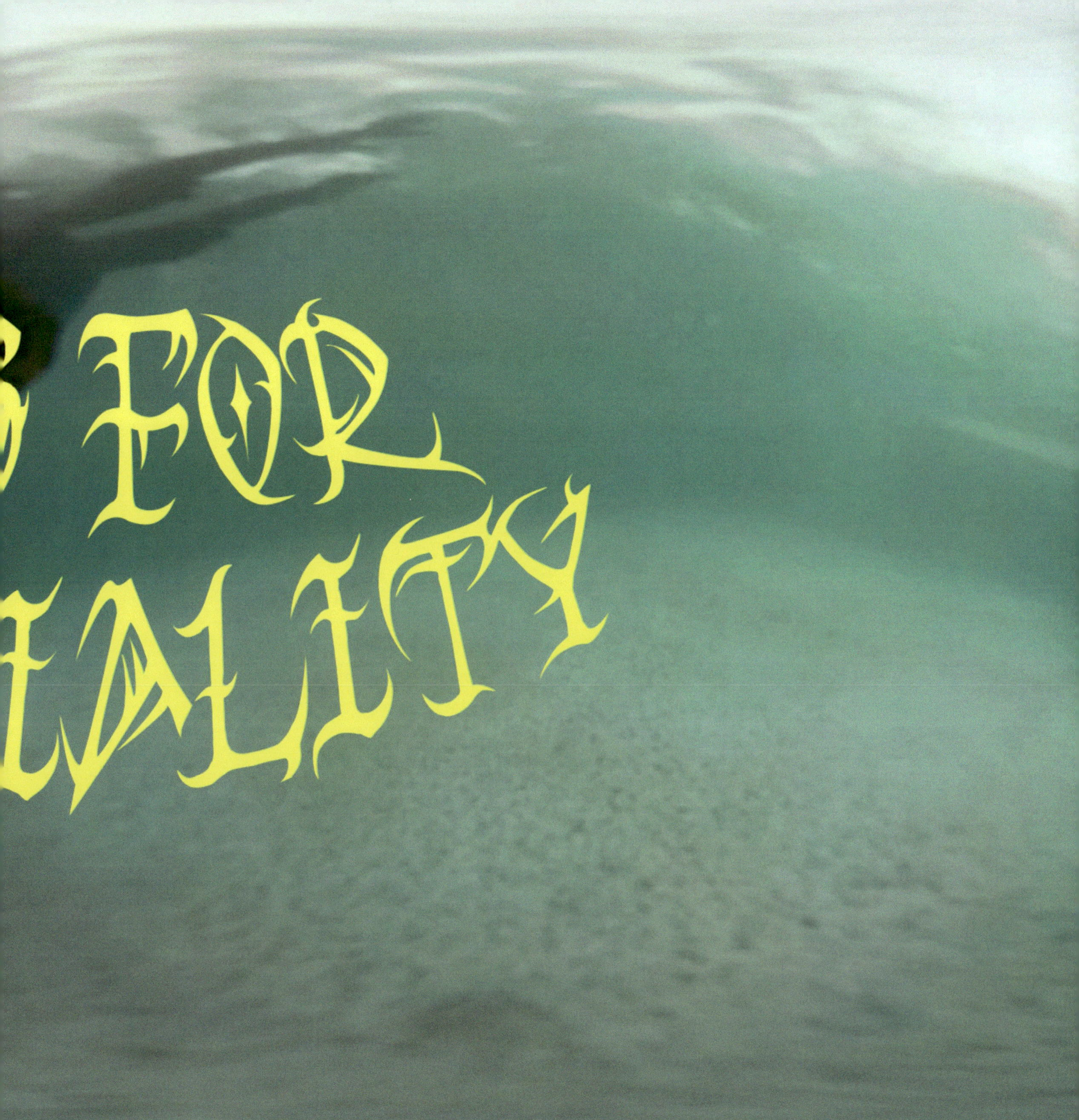
FOR
EALITY

"GROUP CHAT" ☆ 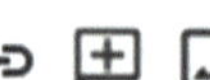 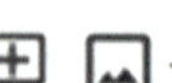

Datei   Bearbeiten   Ansicht   Einfügen   Format   Tools   Add-ons   Hilfe   Letzte Änderung gestern …

GROUP CHAT

Emily Watlington, with Anna Ehrenstein and Saliou Ba, Donkafele (Mandé Mory Bah and Thibaut Houssou), Nyamwathi Gichau, Lydia Likibi, and Awa Seck

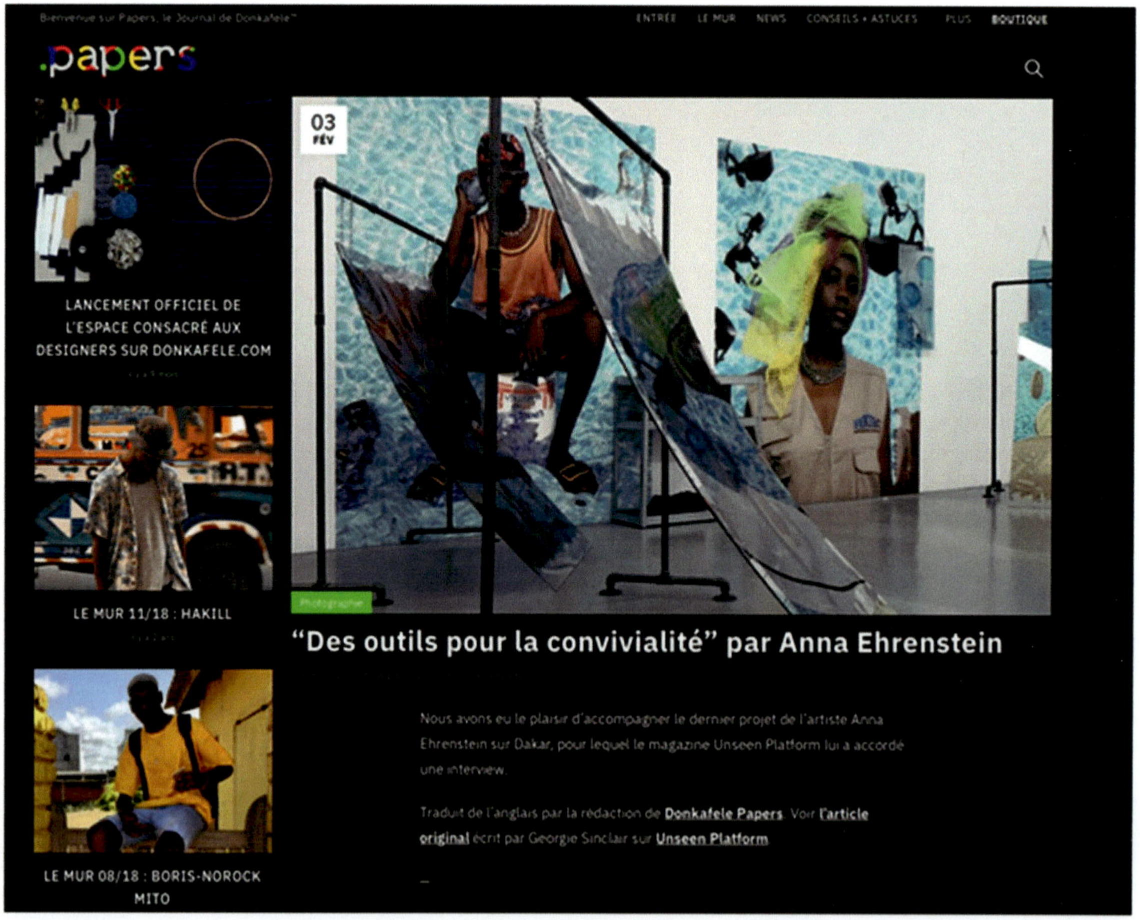

In June 2020 I posed questions to the team behind *Tools for Conviviality* in a Google doc. The document became a digital space for us to commune despite travel restrictions and the coronavirus's quarantine imperatives, and across a range of geographies and time zones. We

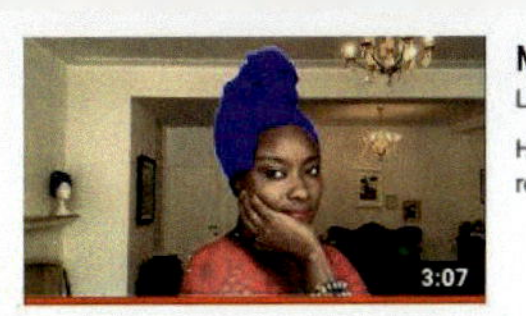
Moussor Tabaski Headwrap
Les Moussors de Awa · 42.448 Aufrufe · vor 1 Jahr
Hello mes belles voici le tuto 1/4 rien que pour vous m. La Tabaski arrive alors choisis: ressemble pour donner à …

3:07

+8 MEHR

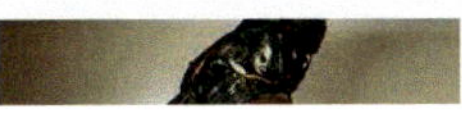
Les Moussors de Awa
Les Moussors de Awa · 47.922 Aufrufe · vor 4 Jahren

Anna 2020-06-21: I am translating with Google for me and Emily, *oui? Merci trop*, Manden <3 Let me know if there is something I and Google don't get right! Anna & google translate: I'm Mandé Mory Bah, twenty-eight years old. Originally from Guinea, I have lived for over ten years in Senegal, where I work as a user experience designer. In addition, I am responsible for a small company that finds and sells products from thrift stores: Donkafele.com.

Thibaut 2020-06-26: (FR) Je suis S. Thibaut HOUSSOU, 26 ans, Béninois, et je vis à Dakar depuis bientôt 11 ans où je fais des études de médecine. Esprit rebelle aux diktats de la société, j'ai commencé à explorer assez tôt mon intérêt pour des choses jugées incompatibles avec ma formation, entre autres en créant une marque de vêtements expérimentale puis en co-fondant une petite entreprise, Donkafele, qui est spécialisée dans la distribution de produits à fort impact communautaire et environnemental.
Thibaut: (EN) Hi! My name is S. Thibaut Houssou. I am twenty-six years old, and I am from Benin. I have been living in Dakar for almost eleven years now, and I'm studying medicine. Rebellious to the diktats of society, I started early to explore my interest in things deemed incompatible with my studies, among other things by creating an experimental clothing brand and then cofounding a small company, Donkafele, which specializes in the distribution of products with a significant community and environmental impact.

Anna 2020-07-12: I spoke to Nyamwathi, and she's quite busy at the moment—but to not leave out her personal work here: she studied psychology, works as a yoga teacher, kinaesthetic and reiki therapist, shaman, and writer. She lived and worked in Dakar for a few years and is currently based in her hometown, Nairobi.

Emily: How did you guys use the photos that Anna took of you in your own work? <If you can paste screenshots from your website or social media below, I'd love to see them!>
Anna & google translate: Comment avez-vous utilisé les photos que Anna vous a prises dans votre propre travail ? <si vous pouvez les coller ci-dessous, j'adorerais les voir ! C'est-à-dire : captures d'écran également du site Web ou des réseaux sociaux>

Lydia 2020-06-24: The photos and videos we made with Anna were posted on social media. Please find below the links:
https://www.instagram.com/lydsdesign/
https://www.instagram.com/lydsdesign/channel/

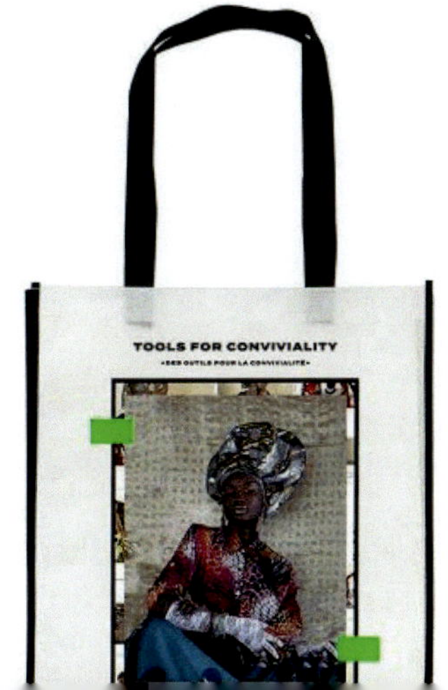

article originellement publié sur le site Unseen Platform sur le
travail d'Anna en le traduisant en français pour le publier sur notre blog Donkafele.com/papers, afin que notre public francophone puisse le saisir. Ensuite, avec Anna, nous avons entrepris de faire de son travail des œuvres ambulantes en les imprimant sur des t-shirts et tote bags (en cours). Anna & google translate: First, we appropriated an article on Anna's work that was originally published on the Unseen Platform site by translating it into French and publishing it on our blog, Donkafele.com/papers, for our French-speaking public. Then, with Anna, we set out to make her works into ambulant works by printing them on T-shirts and tote bags.

Anna 2020-06-26: I love that you use the idea of ambulant works, Manden. I did not fully grasp the parallels until you now said "ambulant"—when you from Donkafele suggested printing tote bags, patches, and shirts. There are so many ambulant vendors in Dakar who, together with the goods they decided to sell, stroll through the city. This combination of taking over urban space, wanderlust, and poetics—love to think of the shirts spreading art this way, too!

Saliou 2020-07-11: The first time I met Anna was in my apartment. I am hosting on Airbnb, and she booked with me. After explaining about what she was doing, she took some nice photos of my loft. They were so nice that I used them and changed the old ones on my Airbnb profile. Here are some of them!

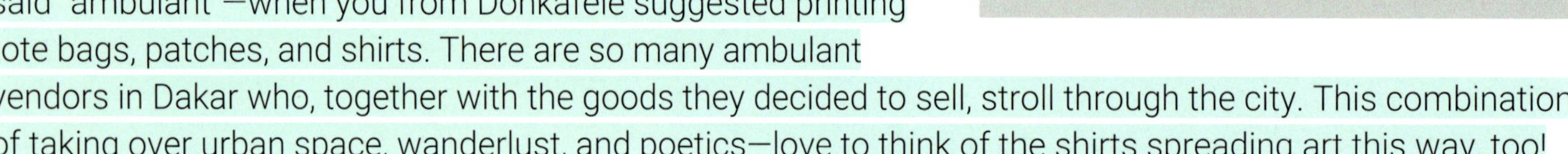

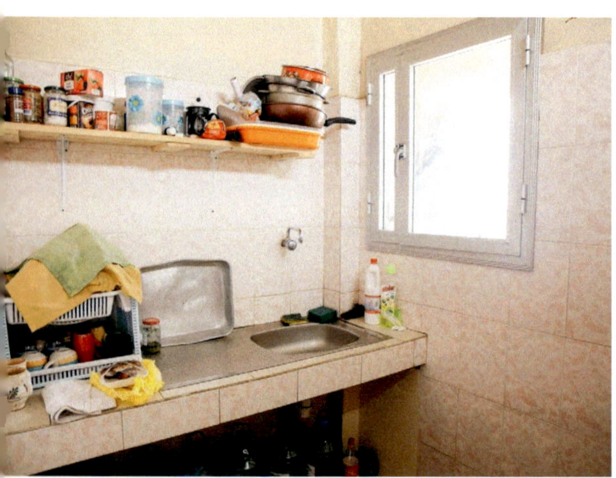

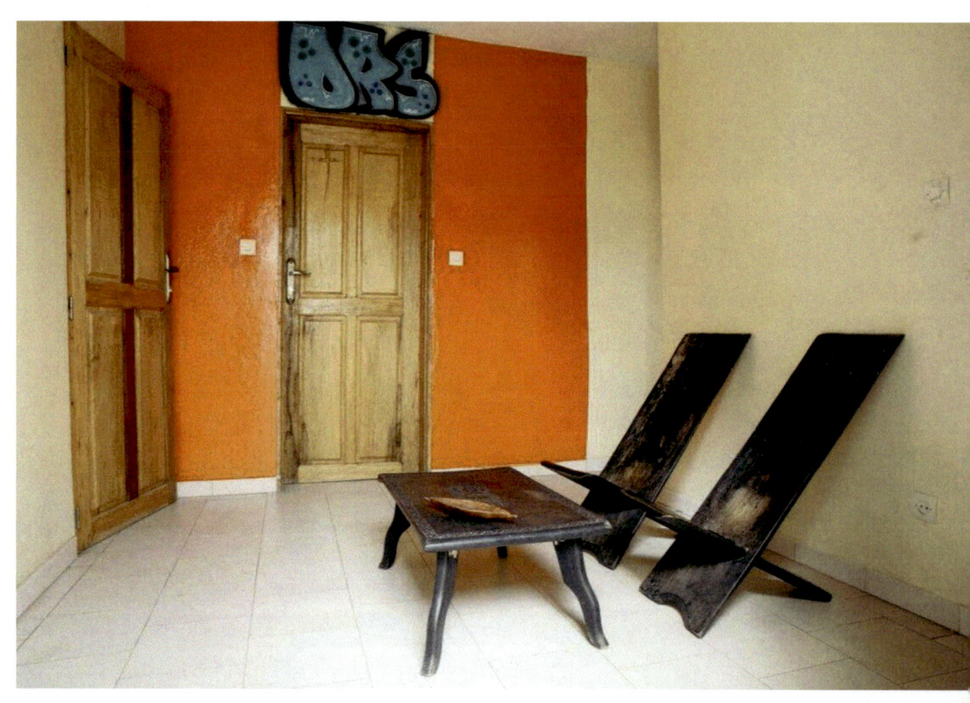

Emily: There's a real sense in the video that the group of you is more or less hanging out. There are scenes in the video where we see Anna. In the fashion show scene, one model hands off the

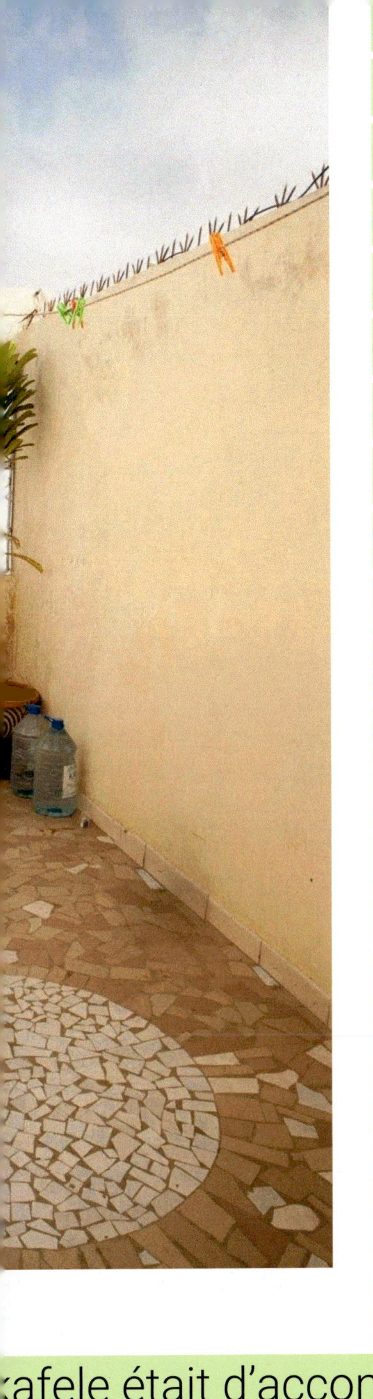

s'amusait est bien réelle. Travailler avec Anna ou même simpl
interagir avec elle, s'est toujours fait dans une atmosphère co
En me parlant de son projet, j'ai découvert le travail de Illich su
convivialité », une critique de la société industrielle à travers u
analyse du capitalisme, non pas sous le prisme de l'exploitatic
l'Homme par l'Homme, mais sous celui de la servitude de l'Ho
des « outils contre-productifs » sous couvert d'avancée techno
Je trouvais que l'approche de Anna, bien qu'abstraite, s'appare
un outil convivial » : un outil qui ne doit pas créer d'inégalité, q
renforcer l'autonomie de chacun et accroître le champ d'actio
chacun. L'application des enseignements de l'œuvre qui lui a i
projet m'a séduit car cela dénotait chez elle une réelle authent
Anna avait une idée bien claire des termes et aboutissements
collaboration et ça n'a pas été difficile de la suivre vu que nous
partagions pleinement sa vision. C'était important pour elle de
embarquer dans un travail mutuellement bénéfique. La 1ère éta
donc de définir ensemble, et en toute transparence nos intérê
ensuite de définir comment les converger. Nous avons co-par
rôles, tout en sachant dans quelle circonstance et pour quelle
fallait se mettre en retrait et laisser la direction.
Concernant notre collaboration vidéo-photographique par exe
afele était d'accompagner une création de contenu en phase avec ses valeurs e
ssus de collab était globalement de l'improvisation structurée. Nous avons tenu
s séances de brainstorming sur le format de la réalisation, la direction, les outils c
ue nous avions collectés ensemble en sillonnant les marchés de la ville. Nous av
e, trouvé ensemble l'endroit idéal pour le tournage hors de la ville, et nous avions

Anna 2020-07-12: It's true, improvisation was a central element of the shooting process in Da
me, it was even more important to not have concrete plans and ideas from the beginning, but t
them on site together with everybody involved. You know, from my side the project started with
moments of fury. Being sick of Western media depicting migration as unipolar. Merely toward
west. As if only imperialist centers in the NATO states had multicultural spaces. At the same tir
hoping that working in a process-based way and in conversation with cultural producers in Dak
support a joyous approach to speaking about these issues through positive and constructive e
Almost ninety percent of migration on the African continent is within. You can work without a v
Its cultural richness makes it an important creative mecca. At the same time it was absolutely
through reading Paul Gilroy, to come across Illich's fifty-year-old critique of tools and how thing
escalated since then. Tech bros are trying to tell us that collecting our data and modifying our
the price we pay for living in the digitized age. Outsourcing our decision-making into algorithms
systems of oppression like race, class, and gender, escalating the pace and density in which th
structured through these systems. What happens when photographic technologies like 360-de
virtual reality become consumer technologies? Because Albanians have been historically racial
rendered as peripheral or Middle Eastern savages and their suffering is currently sustained by t
the Othering of Muslim communities
I cannot personally identify with whiteness. Still, we have the privilege of proximity to whiteness
Let's keep it real—in the West African context I am snow-white, "Caucasian." It was clear to me
only do a project in Dakar through conversation. How can we overcome divisions while acknow
differences? An attempt to challenge the power hierarchies that usually make documentary pra
build the foundation of so many "collaborative" contemporary art projects by people living in Eu
working on the African continent. Many projects critique structures that they actually reinforce
they work.
In the harsh context of a world order based on extractivism, white supremacy, and capital and
the dependent French colonial legacy in which West Africa and its young creatives are trapped-
abusive power structures of art production were something I really wished to disrupt. I contacte
people whose amazing work I saw online through social media or mail. As I said, it was importa
have a fixed concept from the beginning, but to just meet and listen to the ideas of the collabor
develop parts together, and see how my work can also serve their personal projects. Everyone
engaged in enacting sociopolitical change in their personal work through a very diverse usage
creativity, teaching, and entrepreneurship. I'm their biggest fangirl! We all come from multifacet
backgrounds, and I don't even speak French.
The first years of working as a visual artist are very precarious if you don't come from generatic
and only possible through working within imperialist nations. I had a ridiculous budget for the p
if your budget is twenty times larger, it is much easier to exploit your surroundings to do an eve
spectacular project. And my chosen precarity is in itself a massive privilege. Some people cry a
to fill out too many documents in the hope of getting arts funding, yet others don't have access
water. The duality is that generating power also means having more power to share. A constan
of access and barriers. Work within the arts is so based on hierarchies and heroes, trying to wo
young position leads to a balancing act, and everything is always far from perfect. With barriers
on this planet LOL . . . space, language, time, money and while trying to be aware of how we are
was central to prioritize having a good time together!! Instead of trying to hide the barriers make
visible within the work.
As for Nyamwathi, she and I haven't been in the same physical space yet—so she sent me to he
self-love places in Dakar, and it was magic. Saliou showed me the best *thiéboudienne* spot in M
Donkafele team constantly reinvents our collaboration, celebrates life with me on FaceTime or
on top of rental cars, Lydia introduced me to amazing young femmes in the city, and Awa and I
time when she worked in Berlin. I learned and unlearned loads while working with the team and

iou 2020-07-11: She came to my place during the Biennial, but it doesn't mean a lot to me if it is held in
city or not. I am sorry—I don't pay close attention to the Biennial.

dia 2020-06-24: Anna and I met two years ago when she came to Dakar for the first time for the
nnial. We spent a lot of quality time together, talking about our dreams and entrepreneur life. When she
ne again in 2019, we decided to create more fabulous moments by doing photo shoots in the streets of
kar. The Biennial is such a great platform for local creativity. People come from so many countries to se
talented artists.

ibaut 2020-06-26: (FR) J'ai rencontré Anna il y a deux ans à l'occasion de son passage à Dakar pour la
nnale. Elle m'avait sollicité sur les réseaux sociaux pour un de ses projets photographiques. Nous avion
t de suite sympathisé et déjà à l'époque, nous parlions de sujets divers et variés (entrepreneuriat,
ppolitique et relations internationales, mode, art...), en s'échangeant nos vécus, expériences personnelle
s et analyses. Pour ma part, l'ouverture d'esprit indispensable pour un(e) artiste fait de lui/elle une
sonne idéale chez qui on peut espérer trouver le regard le moins biaisé sur le monde. C'est pour cela,
pir cet événement, une des principales manifestations d'art contemporain africain avec sa renommée
ernationale, est quelque de très positif pour l'émancipation et l'affirmation du continent. Je me sens
connaissant que la biennale ait permis notre rencontre. Ce fut très enrichissant.
ibaut: (EN) I met Anna two years ago when she came to Dakar for the Biennial. She had contacted me o
cial networks about her photographic project. We immediately hit it off and, even at that time, we were
king about various and varied subjects (entrepreneurship, geopolitics and international relations, fashion
. . .), sharing things about our background, personal experiences, opinions, and analyses. I think that
en-mindedness is essential for an artist. That makes the artist an ideal person with whom we can hope
find the least biased view of the world. This is why having this international event, one of the main
pressions of contemporary African art, is something very positive for the emancipation and the
irmation of the continent. I feel grateful that the Biennial allowed us to meet . . . it was very rewarding.

na 2020-06-26: @Thibaut and Saliou. It's crazy, but I feel you both. I am actually surprised and a little
esmerized by Thibout's faith, and simultaneously it feels important to recognize the many good reasons
y the world of biennials looks so dull and dry.
e Western / European art canon has constructed an elitist and Eurocentric narration of modernity and
e arts. It makes it very difficult for many people to relate to something so elitist and whitewashed. The
th of the Western art canon ignores actual history and reciprocity. How things have been inspired and
rally been stolen from cultures outside of the West. Even in many "progressive" art circles colonialism,

difficult to cycle, so they are surprised to see me so carefree and let off steam with this machine in the streets when they are in their car. It must be said that cycling is often very practical.

Thibaut 2020-06-26: (FR) Je répondrai pareil que Manden et ce n'est pas surprenant haha. Nous utilisons le vélo comme moyen de transport dans la vie de tous les jours et ce n'est peut-être pas surprenant aussi nous en avons fait le moyen de livraison de l'entreprise de Donkafele.
Thibaut: (EN) I will answer as Manden, and it is not surprising haha. We use the bicycle in everyday life, so is not surprising that we made it the delivery method of the Donkafele company.

Anna 2020-06-25: @Emily, screens from photos I took with Lydia on her channels:

Anna 2020-06-26: Haha, REALLY forgot about this photo of me with the bag you gave me as a present when we met the first time @lydia. It's in front of my old building in Berlin :) Also I love the first photo from the shoot we did at the Marché Tilène, I remember it was so much fun even though it was Ramadan—your muse and model was fasting properly in the heat, and I had to fly back the same evening!

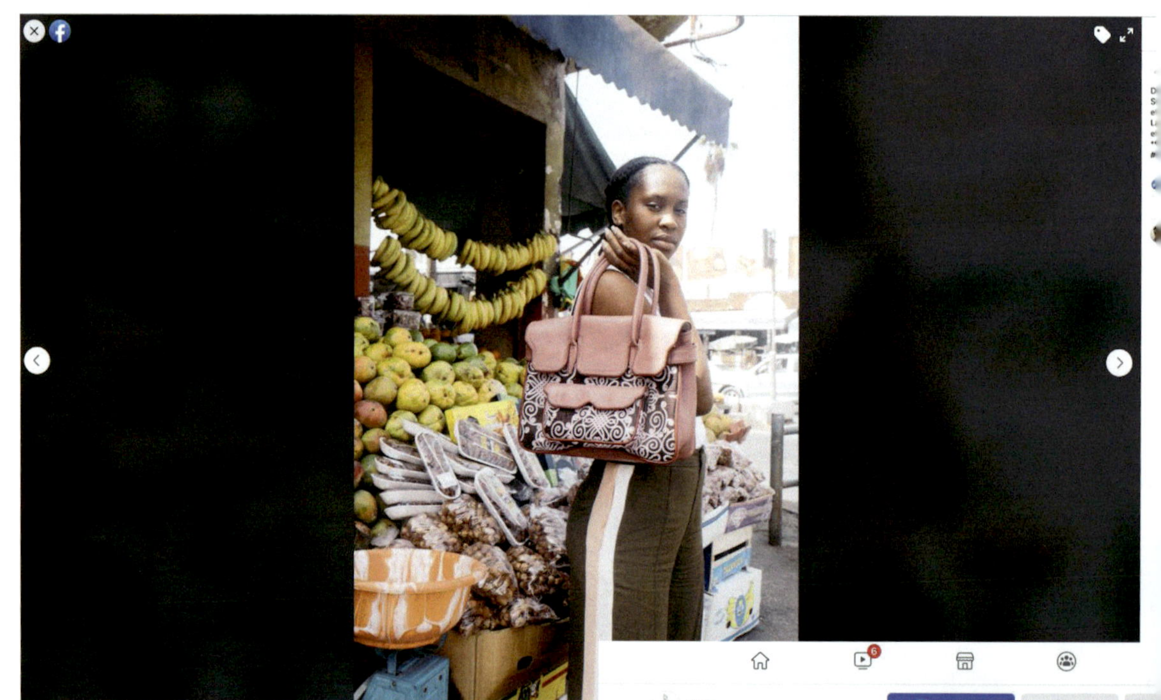

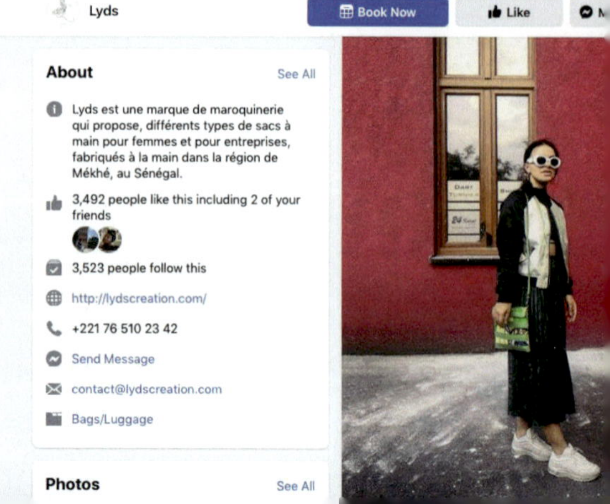

Emily & Anna: @Saliou, could you please translate our conversation to Wolof?

Saliou 2020-08-24: Ci weeru 'juin' 2020, dama laaj ay laaj mboolo mi nekk ci ginaw "Tools for conviviality" ci benni 'Google doc'. "Document" bi dafa mujjee nekk barabu juntukaay yu bees yi tax ñu deggo ñun ñëp, donte tere neñu dem bi ak dikk bi ndax xeexu Coronavirus bi ci dëkkuwaay yu yaatu ak waxtu yi niñu wute wee. Waaye tamit ci ay juntukaay ak mankoo leñu weeru ngir sotti sunu xalaat ci ay kallaama yu bari te wute: waxtaan wi bokk na ci ñu dëkk wala cosaano Senegal, Belgique, Amerique, Allemagne, Albanie, Benin, Republique de Congo, Gambie, ak Guinee. **Emily: Mbooloo mi ñoo ngi leen di ñaan ku nekk ci yeen wax ñu mooy kan ci ay kaddu yu gatt. Saliou:** Maa ngi tudu Mamadou Saliou Ba, am lijaasu Master Anglais, etudes Americaines, maa ngi yëngu ci firi kallaama nasaraan, ak jaayum wotir, aki dalal ay gan ci Airbnb. Nitt bu ubbee ku laa ci aduna bi, bëgg lepp ci lu jëm ci weccoo xalaat ak cosaan aki lepp luy begël doomi adama ci kaw suuf. **Awa:** Man Awa Seck laa tudu, man maa taxawal "Marque" musooru bopp "Les Moussores de Awa". **Lydia:** Mangi tudu Lydia Likibi. Mangi bawoo ca Congo, dëkk fi ci Senegal ci jamono 2001 ba leegi. Maa taxawal "Lyds Design" te man maako Jiite, ñu ngi yëngu ci walum Design ak defar saaku yo xamni loxo leñu ko defaree fi ci Afrik. **Manden:** Maagi tudu mande Mory Bah, amnaa ñaar fuki at ak jurom ñet, bawoo ca Guinee. Bima dëkkee Senegal ak leegi matna fuki at. Fii lay ligeeyee, di yëngu ci walum design boole ci di topatoo benni "societe" buy yëngu ci walum fëgg jaay: Donkafele.com. **Anna:** Maagi koy firi ci Google ngir man ak Emily, waw? Jërëjëf, su fekkee juum naa ci firi bi rek Manden jappalema ci. **Thibaut:** Maagi tudu S. Thibaut Houssou, amnaa ñaar fuki at ak jurom benn di jang kaarange. Dama teela xeex yenn aada yi ak dikle yi ci biir dëkkuwaay-yi, tambali yëngu ci yoo xamni mengoowul ak lima jang. Bokk na ci taxawal "marque" yere ak bokk taxawal ab "societe" Donkafele buy yëngu ci walum seddale ay yëf yu am njëriñ ci nit yi ak dëkkuwaay yi. **Anna:** Waxtaan naa ak Nyamwathi, wante dafa japp fimu toll nii waaye ngir baña baayi walam ci ligeey bi ni: "Psychologie" la jang te mi ngi yëngu ci jangale "Yoga", "Kinaesthetic" ak "Reiki therapist", "chaman" ak bind. Mongi dëkkoon Ndakaru di ligeeyee fii ci ay at yu neew wante leegi dellu na dëkkam, Nairobi. **Emily: Naka ngeen jëfandikoo nataal yi leen Anna mësë jël ci sen ligeeyu bopp? Su fekke ni mën ngeen def "capture" ci seen "siteweb" wala "reseaux sociaux" taf ko fii dinama neex loolu ma gis leen fii. Lydia:** Nataal yi ak wideo yi ma jota jël ak Anna ñungi leen fësaloon ci "reseaux sociaux" yi ci suuf nii: https://www.instagram.com/lydsdesign/ https://www.instagram.com/lydsdesign/channel/ **Manden:** Dañoo njikk jël benn ci "article" yu Anna fësaloon ci benni site internet bu tudu "Unseen Platform", ba noppi firi ko ci nasaraan fësal ko sunu blog, Donkafele.com/papers ngir nit yi ñuy gëstu tey laqq nasaraan. Ba pare ñu deggo ak Anna ci sotti ligeeyam yi ci ay ligeeyu ambulant, maanaam imprimer ko ci ay yere ak ay saaku. **Anna:** Ni nga xalaatee ligeeyu ambulant bi beg naa ci Manden. Gisee wuma ko woon noonu ba ni nga ko waxee "ambulant" (yeen waa Donkafele bi ngeen xalaatee imprimer ko ci ay saaku, an bandoo ak yere). Jaay kat ambulant yi bari nañu loolu ci ndakaru te ñoom ak seeni bagaas deñuy wër dëkk bi yëp. So xoolee niñuy feesalee tali bi di doxantu, neex lammin tek ci, loolu yëp soo ko boole wee (suma xalaatee ni yere mën na tasaare noonu art bi, dama ciy beg)! **Saliou:** Bimay njikk xam Anna sama kër la woon. Damay faral di dalal ay gan ci Airbnb, ci loolu la ñëwee sama kër. Bi ñu waxtaane ci lumy yëngu ba noppi ci la jël ay nataalu kër gi yu rafet sax. Ma contaan ci loolu ba ci noonu laa dindi wee yi nekkoon sama "profile" def ci yu bees yi. Maagi leen di sedd yenn yi ci suuf ni! **Emily:** Ci biir wideo yi amna luy xawa wone ni ñenn ñi ci mbooloo mi deñu daan and di genn. Amna ay "scenes" ci wideo bi buy wone Anna. Ci "Fashion show" bi, gis neñu benn ci model yi di joxe GoPro bi keneen ñu koy aawante ci xall yoon bi. Ñoo gi leen di ñaan ngeen wax ñu tuuti ci sen jokkalante ci walum art wi ak wideo yii? **Saliou:** Jotnaa am wërsëgu ligeey ak moom bimu doon am ay laaj yimu doon laaj jaaykat yi ci marse ba. Mbekte bu am solo la woon ci jangat. Dama nekkoon di firi ci wolof wante fulla ak jom bi Anna defoon ci ligeey bi def ma mujjee yobbaale ba mënuma woon def leneen ludul fullal ko def ci jom bu bari. Loolu mo nekkoon sama jangat bu gën mag, te ci laa xamee cosaanu marse gambie ba ca Kolobaan. **Thibaut:** Reetaan! Loolu dëgg la. Daawoon neñu genn di foo. Ligeey ak Anna wala di jokko ak moom kesse mbekte la saa su ne. Bi mu ma wonee projet wam ci laa rañññee ligeeyu Ivan Illich teere bu tudu *Tools for Conviviality*". Ñu ciy ñaxtu ci "societe industrielle" yi ci kaw gis-gis boo xamante ni capitalism moo ko lal, baña doon loo xamni nitay njariñoo moroomam, waaye mu doon gis-gis bu laloo ci ni ñuy njariñoo doomi adama yi di leen mingale ak juntukay yu bees yi and ak jamono te duñu sonn. Jotnaa ci jangat daal ni Anna fimu ko tënkee daal xawna niru ak *"Tools for Conviviality"* (bepp yëf mbaa jëf bu mën dab sa banneex): loo xamni dafay tollole, lo xamni daal dafay yokk ku nekk. Limu jota jangat ci teere bi tax mu toppaat tank yooyu, bëg ko dëggël ci projet wam bi taxna ma nawko. Dëggu kesse la wone foofu. Anna

gallankoor yi ci ligeey bi moo gën ñu leen di nëbb. Lu jëm ci Nyamwathi moom, man ak moom sunu jëmm yii tasantee ngu ñu. Wante jotnama wax barab yi mou gënoom bëgg Ndakaaru te bama demee foofu mbekte kese laa fa jëlee. Saliou moo ma won ku gën safle ceebu jën ci Medina. Wa Donkafele ñoom jogewuñu ci yeesal seeni jokkalante ak man, ñoo ngi may begee ci "facetime" bi ak ay fecc ci kaw wotiru luas, Lydia boole na ma ak ay ndawu jigeen yu baax, man ak Awa moom dundu nañu lu neex bimu daan ligeeyee Berlin. Sama ligeey ak mbooloo mi jang naa ci lu bari te baayi lu bari boole ci di am mbekte saa su ne. **Emily**: Yeen ñëp ci Biennale Ndakaaru bi ngeen xamantee, may lajte xew bu ni mel naka ngeen ko dundee sen biir Dëkk? **Saliou**: Jamonoy Biennale sama kër la Anna daloon wante lu biennale xewee sama dëkk tekkiwul lu bari ci man. Maagi jeggalu waaye duma baayi xel ci lu jëm ci ay biennale. **Lydia**: Man ak Anna ñoo ngi xamante ñetti at ci ginaw, bimu ñëwee woon ci biennale bi. Dundu neñu lu bari man ak moom, di waxtaan ci sunuy gint ak bëgg-bëgg, ak ci sunu dundinu "entrepreneur". Bimu ñëwaate ci atun 2019, ci lañu tambali di jël ay nataal yu amul fenn ci mbeddu ndakaaru yi. Biennale bi buntu bu mag la ci ndawu reewmi yi bëg "créer". Nit yi fepp ci aduna bi leñuy joge ngir gis sunu artist yu xarañ yi. **Thibaut**: Ñaari at ci ginaw laay soga xam Anna bimu ñëwee woon ci biennale ndakaaru bi. Mi ngi doon jokko ak man ci "reseaux sociaux" yi xamal ma "projet" jël ay nataal bi. Ci saas yi leñu deggo te jamono jooju ñu ngi doon waxtaan ci lu bari te yaatu (entrepreneuriat, geopolitique ak realtion internationale, fashion, art) di weccoo ci sunuy cosaan, jaar-jaar, xalaat ak gis-gis. Gëm naa ni moom, Artist dafa wara am xalaat bu yaatu, mo ëpp solo ci moom. Loolu dana tax Artist bi doon nit koo xamni dara duko jomm ci aduna bi. Looloo tax am yëngu-yëngu bu ni mel, bu ëpp solo ci luy wone art wu doomi afrik yii, am solo loolu ndax dey dëggël te jëmël kanam "continent" bi. Maa ngi dello njukkël biennale ci li mu taxee ñu xamante Teranga kesse la! **Anna**: @Thibaut ak Saliou neexul gëm wante degg naa leen. Kollore bu Thibaut wone bett nama te xawma jaaxal tuuti, waaye itam dafa am solo ñu nangu li baax li waral adunay biennale bi xawa geey. Ligeeyu art wa Amerik / Europe deñoo dem ba gennee ay kallaama ndaanaan ak feetee woo leep lu jëm ci soppite bu baax ak art. Loolu tax na mu xawa jafe ci nit yu bari, ndax liñu waree bayi xel ni lepp luñuy defar wara ndaanaane aki tubaabe. Liggeeyu art wu nasaraan yi limuy magg yëpp soorale wul xew-xewu tay ak wecco bi. Amna ligeey yu bari yo xamni ci cossaanu jambur yu bokkul ci nasaraan leñu ko saccee wala foofu leñu ko jëlee. Boy seet sax lu bari ci art yi jëm ci jamono bu tubaab yi doon nangu dëkku jambur yi ba tay, deñu ko masa soofal jappe ko yëfi demb. Duñu masa nangu ni ñoo tooñ. Nit yi daal ci sen doxalin japp neñu ni cosaan dëkku tubaab yi la joge dem ci ñeneen ñi. Benn tallal kesse. Loolu du dëgg. Yëf yi doxeewul noonu te cosaan nekkul noonu la tasaaroo wee. Nit yii noonu leñu sonnee ca Albani ndax nu njiit yi ci reew ma mayee doole gënante bi laloo ci nit gën moroomam ndax xeetam, wante fii ci Berlin maagi begee ci dëkk bu doon jay doole di nangu dëkku jambur yi. Barina ay nit fi ci Berlin yu jappe sen bopp ay nit yu moom sen bopp, feetee cammoñ mënë njaxtu, yu yaakaar ni waa afrik saw-jant daal luñu gis waa New-york def ci Gram bi moom leñuy def. Cosaan bu melni "luñu luxusee feneen". Ñu ci bari musuñu tek sen tank ci "continent" Afrik bi te duñu deglu lu nit yi joge afrik di leen nettali. Munuñu nangu ni woy yi ñuy deglu jappee ko "western wala digital aesthetics", lu ci bari ci woy yooyu wala art wu ngistal bi ak taar, ci waa Afrik saw-jant leñu ko jëlee. Ci misaal, doomi Afrik saw-jant ñoo dem Angleterre taxawal woyu Grime foofu. Drake woykatu rap bi ca Canada sacc Grime. Woykatu Grime bu magg bi Stormzy mi nga xamni dafa boole deretu Ghana ak Angleterre neena jërëjëf; gisna dooley maggal cosaan. Amna ci ay xalaat yu joge ci tubab yi ñu jappee jaam batay, yu japp ni wa afrik saw-jant deñoo jëli "Insta Aesthetic". Demeewul noonu (Dafay wër te cosaanu Afrik saw-jant moo leen ko xamal). **Emily: Yeen mbooloo mi ban yëf bu kenn dul xalaat la ku nekk ci yeen di jëfandikoo ngir wone nekkin wu rafet (ngir dab banneex ak dundu ci mbooloo)?** **Saliou**: Sama xalaatu nekkin wu rafet ci sama diine Islam laa ko tibbee. Te suma naroon tann benni yëf, yar bima jangat ci diine te diko jëfandiko ci bimay magg lay doon. Maanaam ci gattal, luma gënë muna begël te dima jox mbekte moodi dimbali ñeneen ñi wala gis leen ñu contaan, rawatina newji doole yi. **Lydia**: Fimay fësëlee sama ligeey ci sama biir kër. Dama bëg di am gan dalal ko foofu di naan bisaap di waxtaan ci nuñuy def ba soppi aduna bi ahhhh. **Anna**: Cey yalla @Lydia munumaa gëm ni naanu ma bisaap boobu ba leegi! Contaan naa ci "lien" bi, dinaa fësël benn "capture" bi man tamit. **Manden**: Sama welo (reetaan)! Waaw sama welo! Loolu la nit yima bokkal ligeey dul xaar ci man. Tali Ndakaru yi deñoo metti ci kuy dawal welo mootax deñuy jaaxle suñu nekke seeni wotir dima seen may dawal ak sama ñaqqaay di nuru ku saalit. Deñoo wara wax ni dawal welo saay su nek luy njariñ la. **Thibaut**: Damay tontu ni Manden, te dara waruleen bett (reetaan). Bes bu nekk welo leñuy dawal motax buñu demee ba di jël welo def ko juntukaayu Donkafele

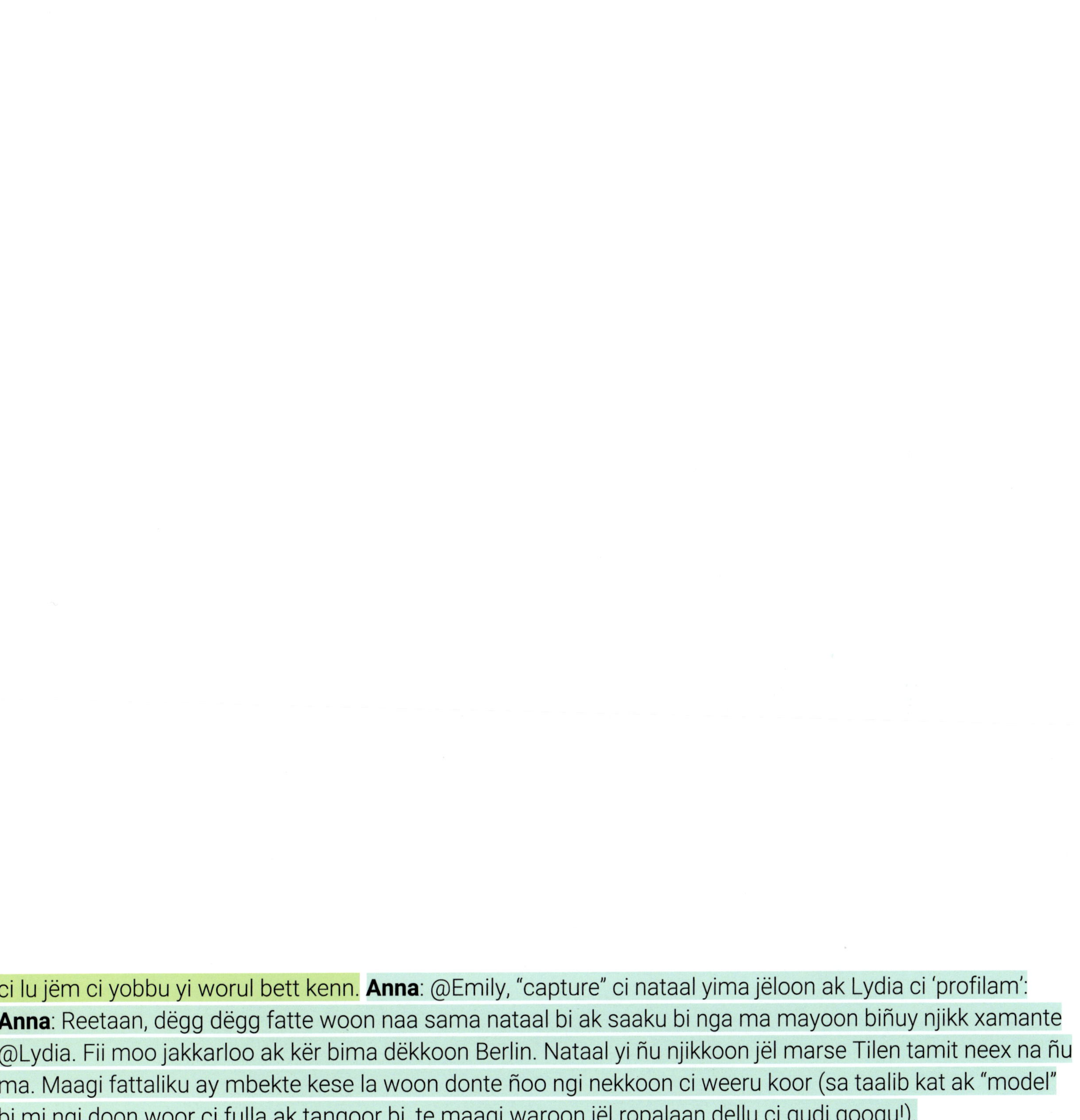
ci lu jëm ci yobbu yi worul bett kenn. **Anna**: @Emily, "capture" ci nataal yima jëloon ak Lydia ci 'profilam':
Anna: Reetaan, dëgg dëgg fatte woon naa sama nataal bi ak saaku bi nga ma mayoon biñuy njikk xamante @Lydia. Fii moo jakkarloo ak kër bima dëkkoon Berlin. Nataal yi ñu njikkoon jël marse Tilen tamit neex na ñu ma. Maagi fattaliku ay mbekte kese la woon donte ñoo ngi nekkoon ci weeru koor (sa taalib kat ak "model" bi mi ngi doon woor ci fulla ak tangoor bi, te maagi waroon jël ropalaan dellu ci gudi googu!).

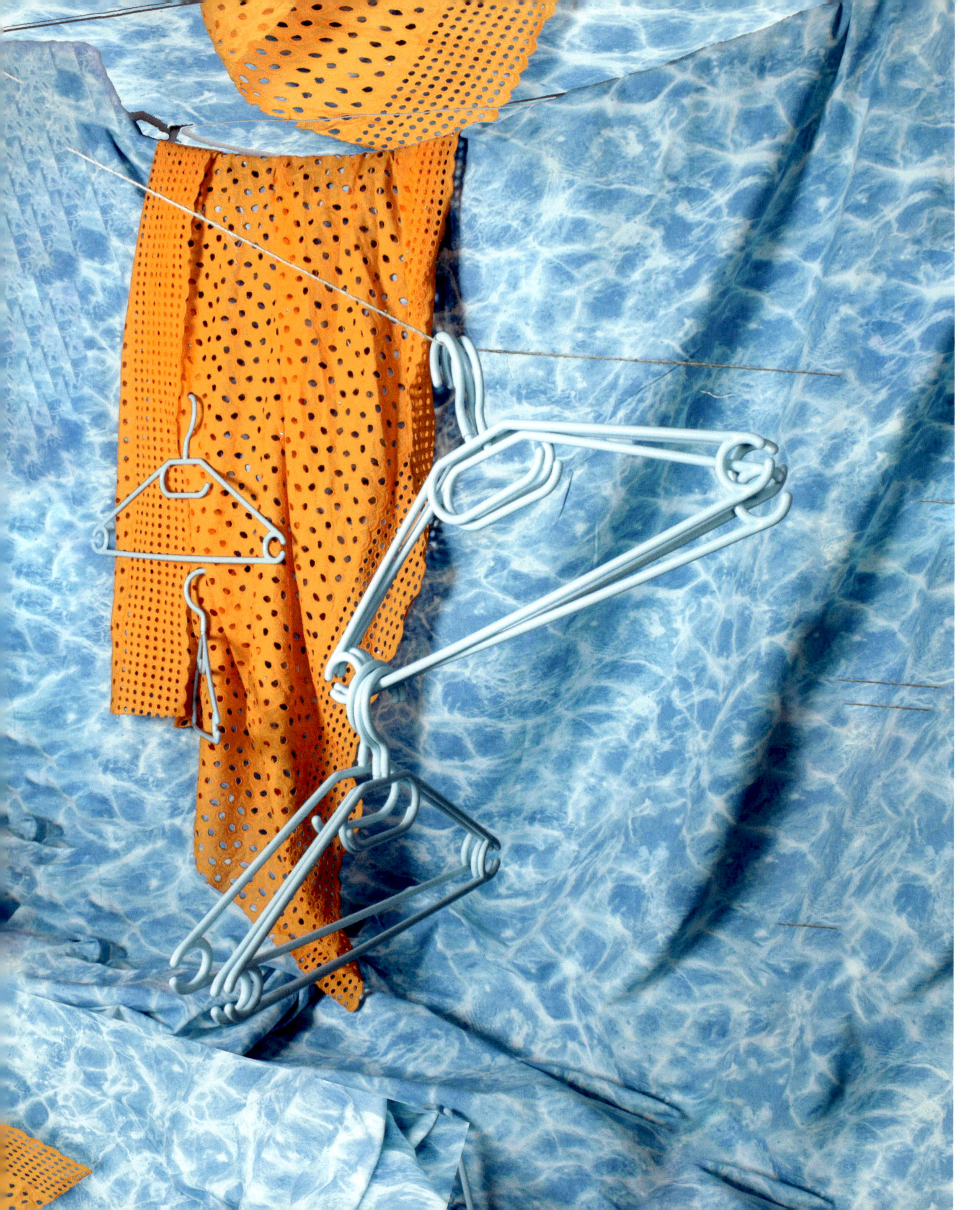

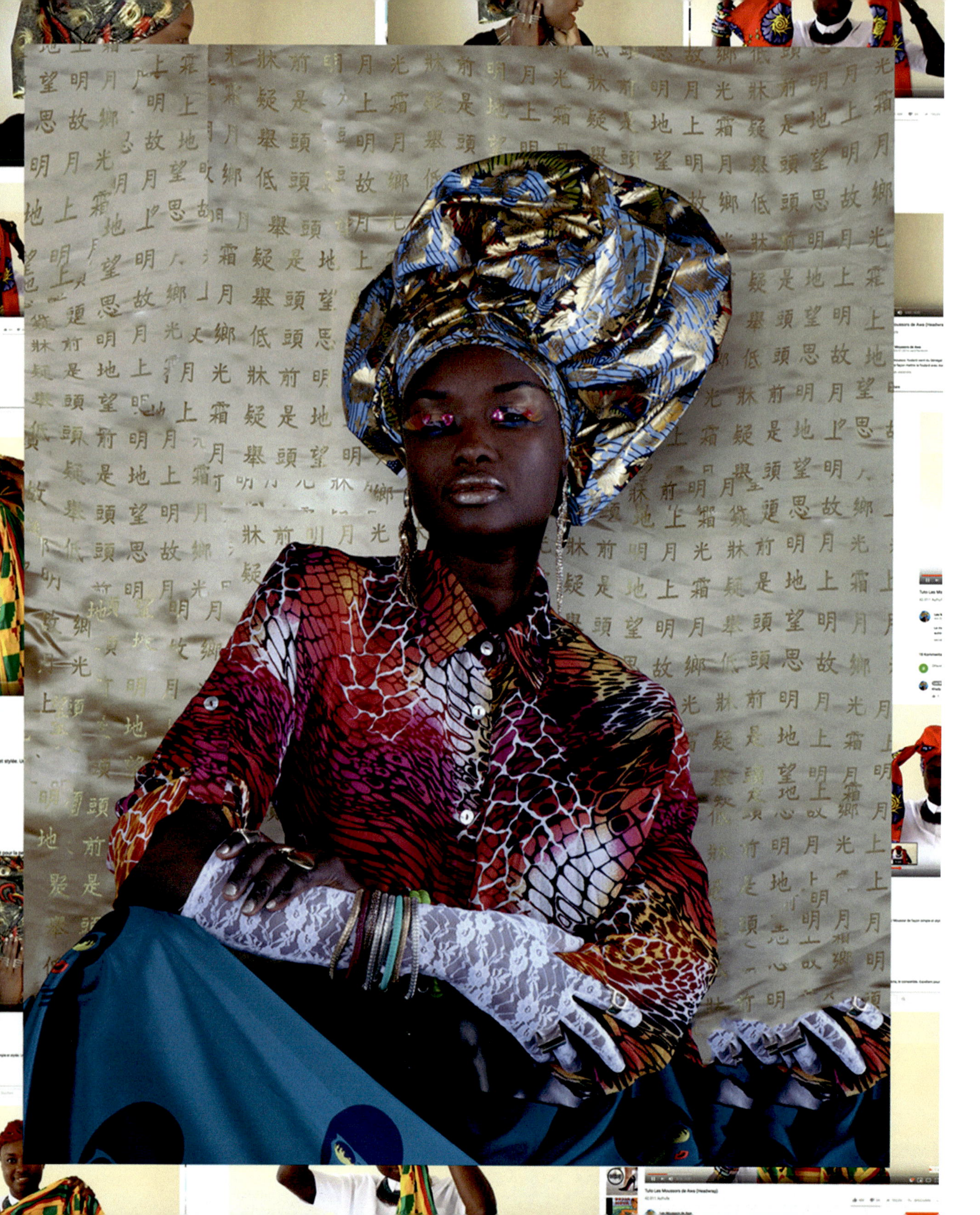

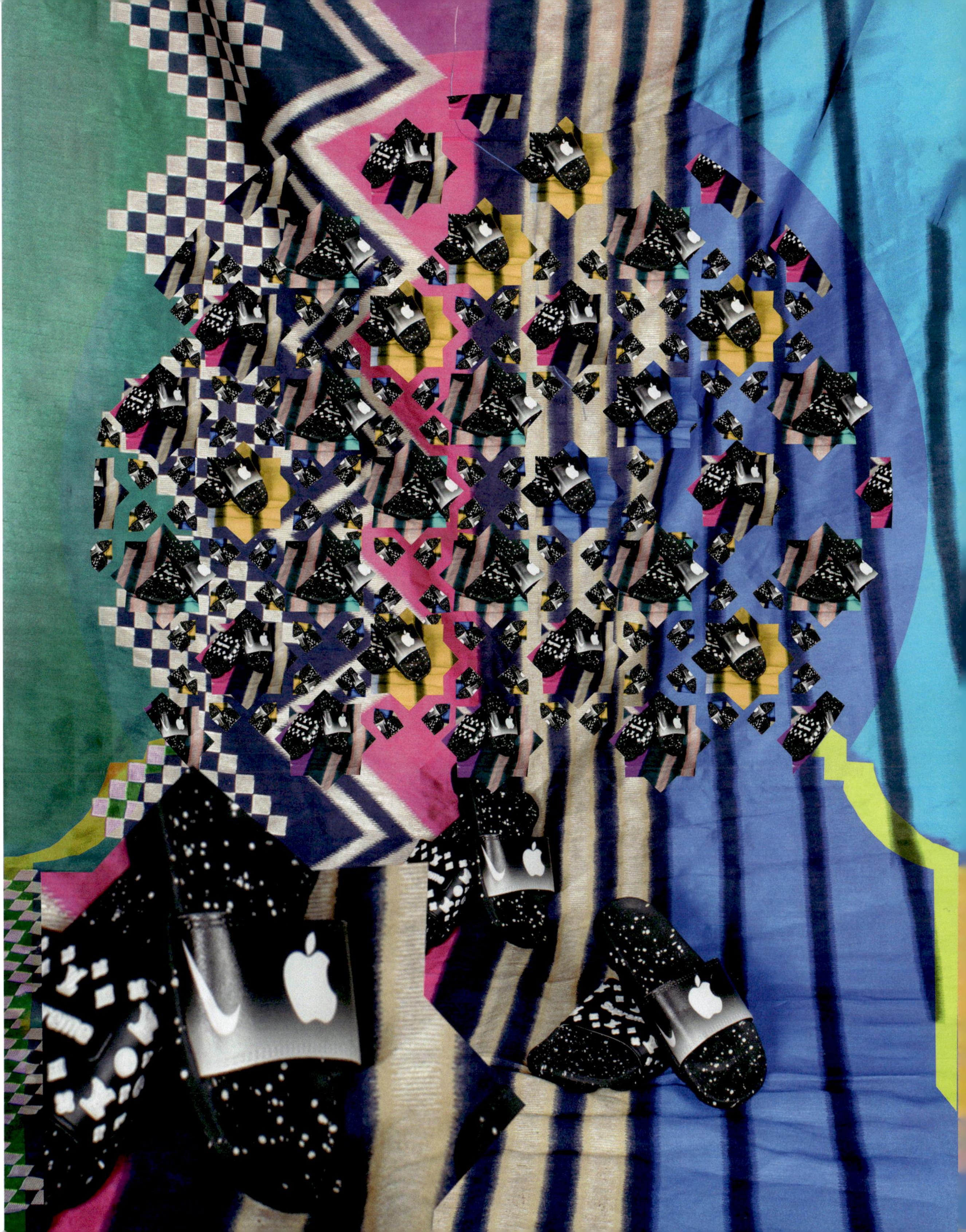

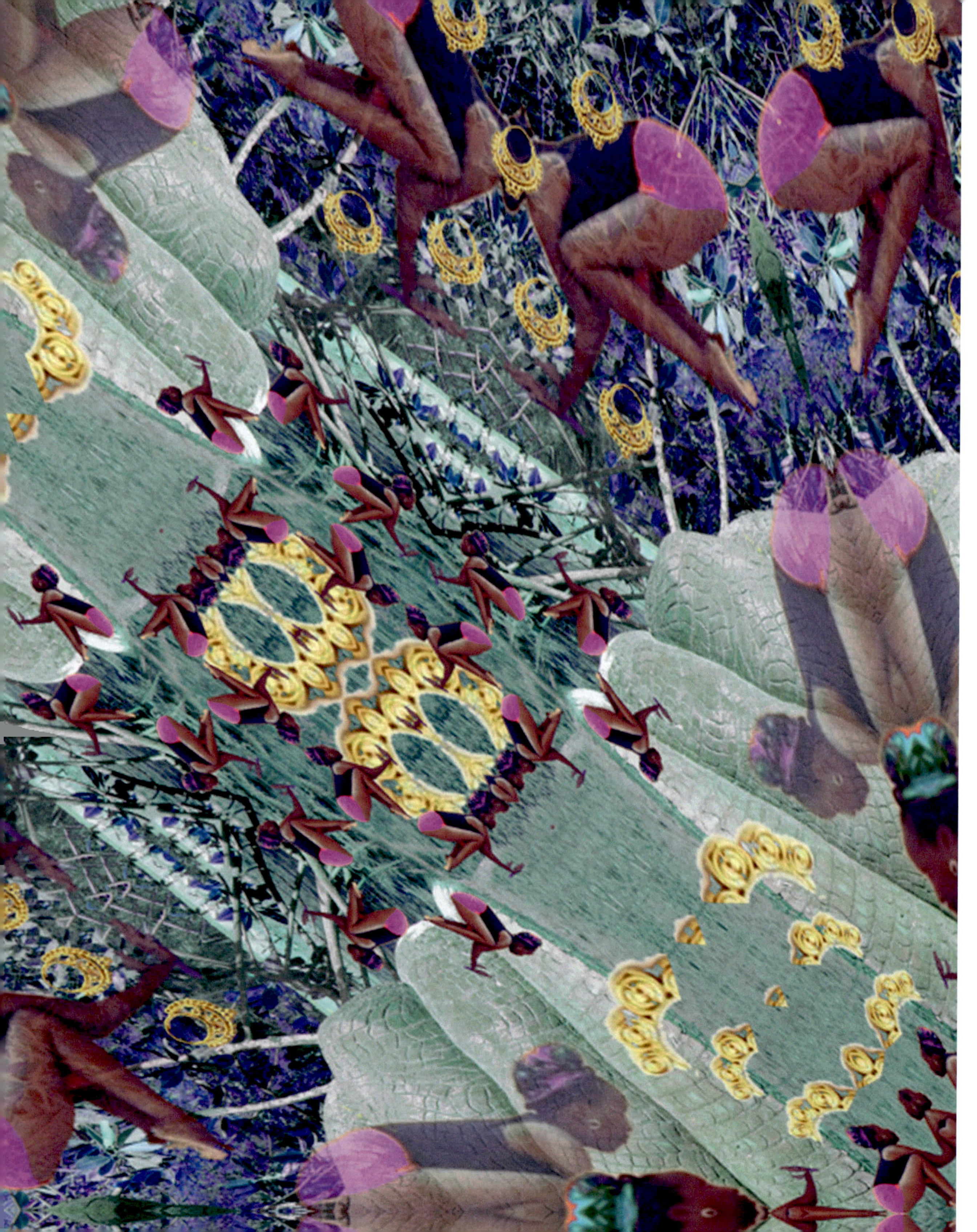

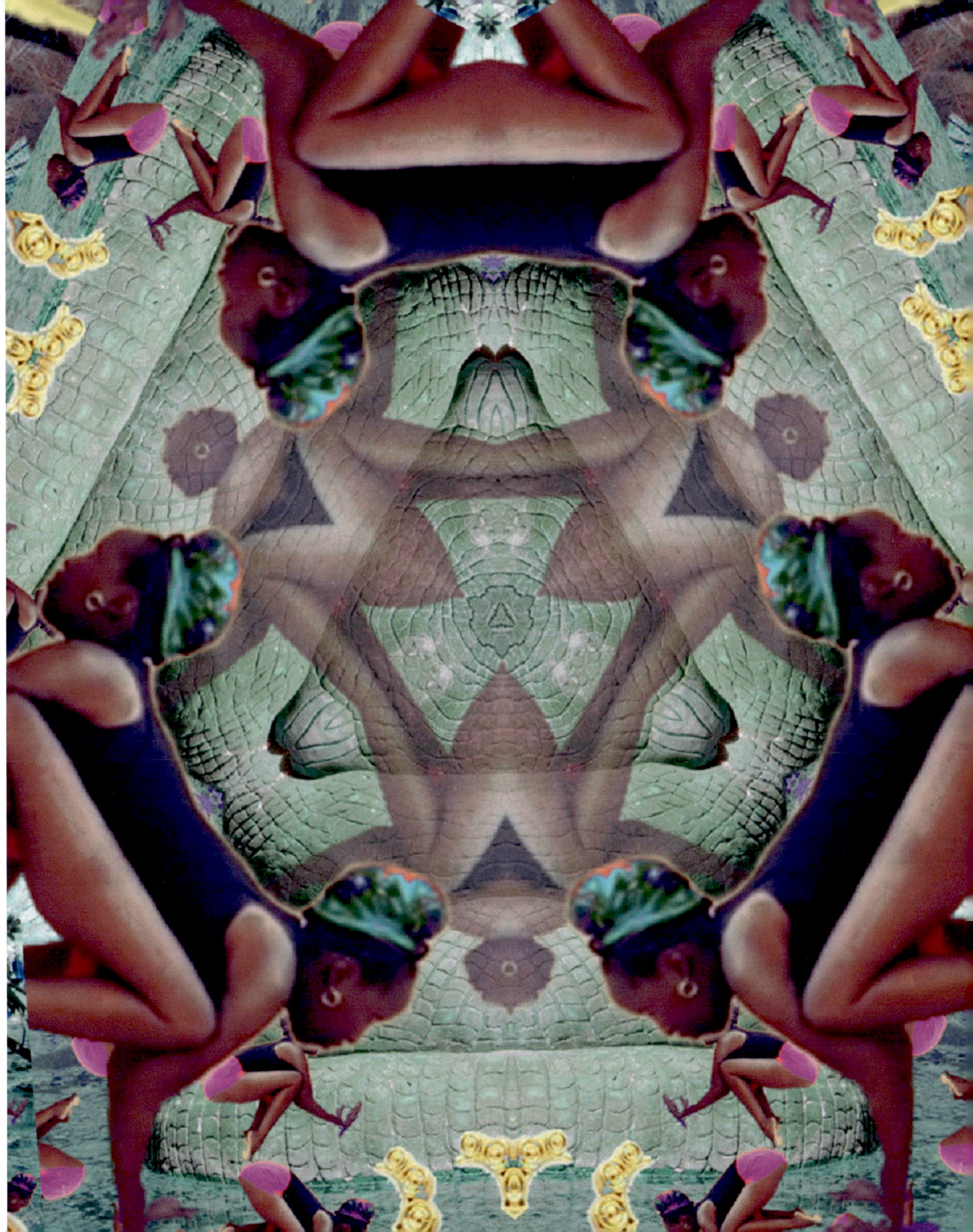

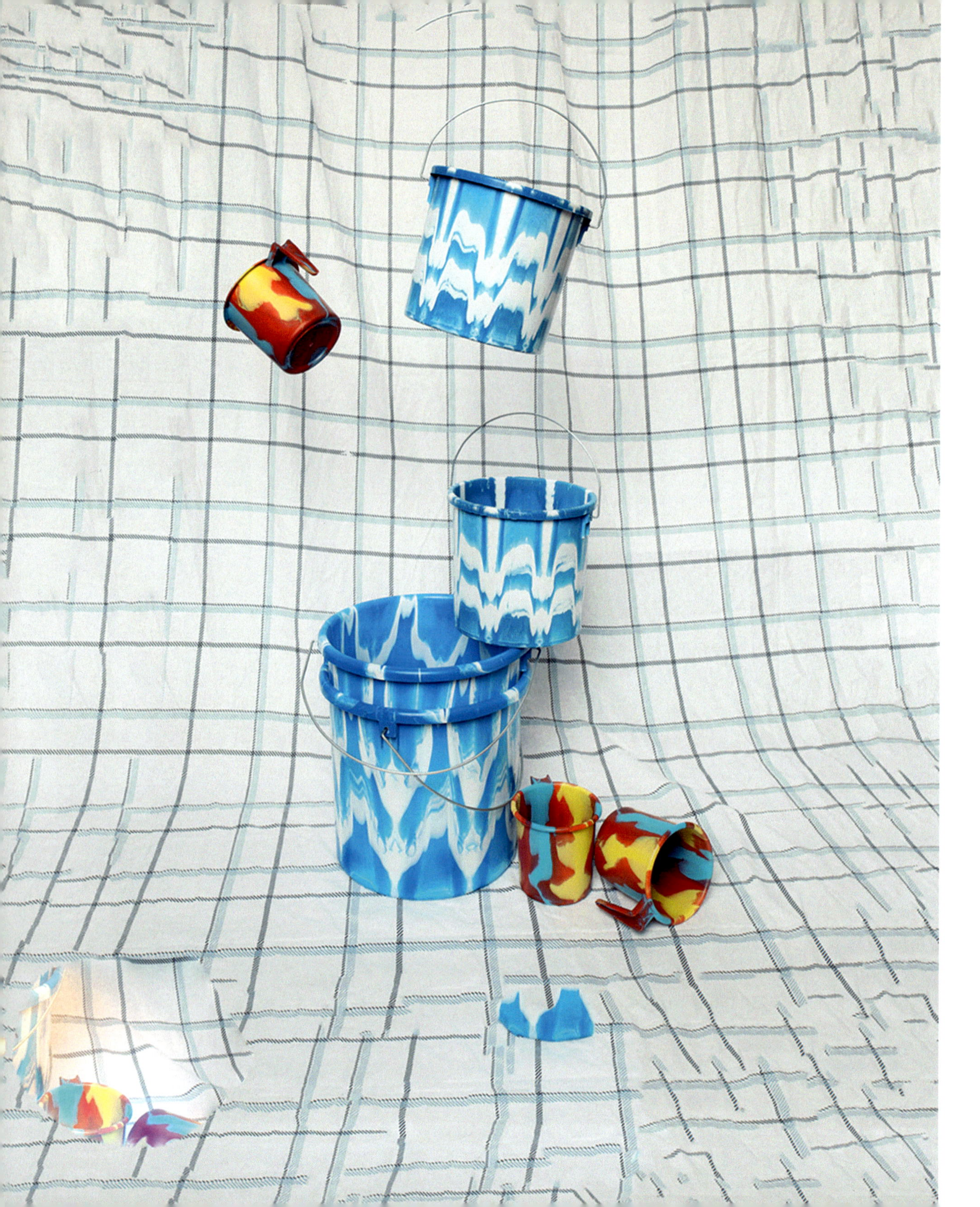

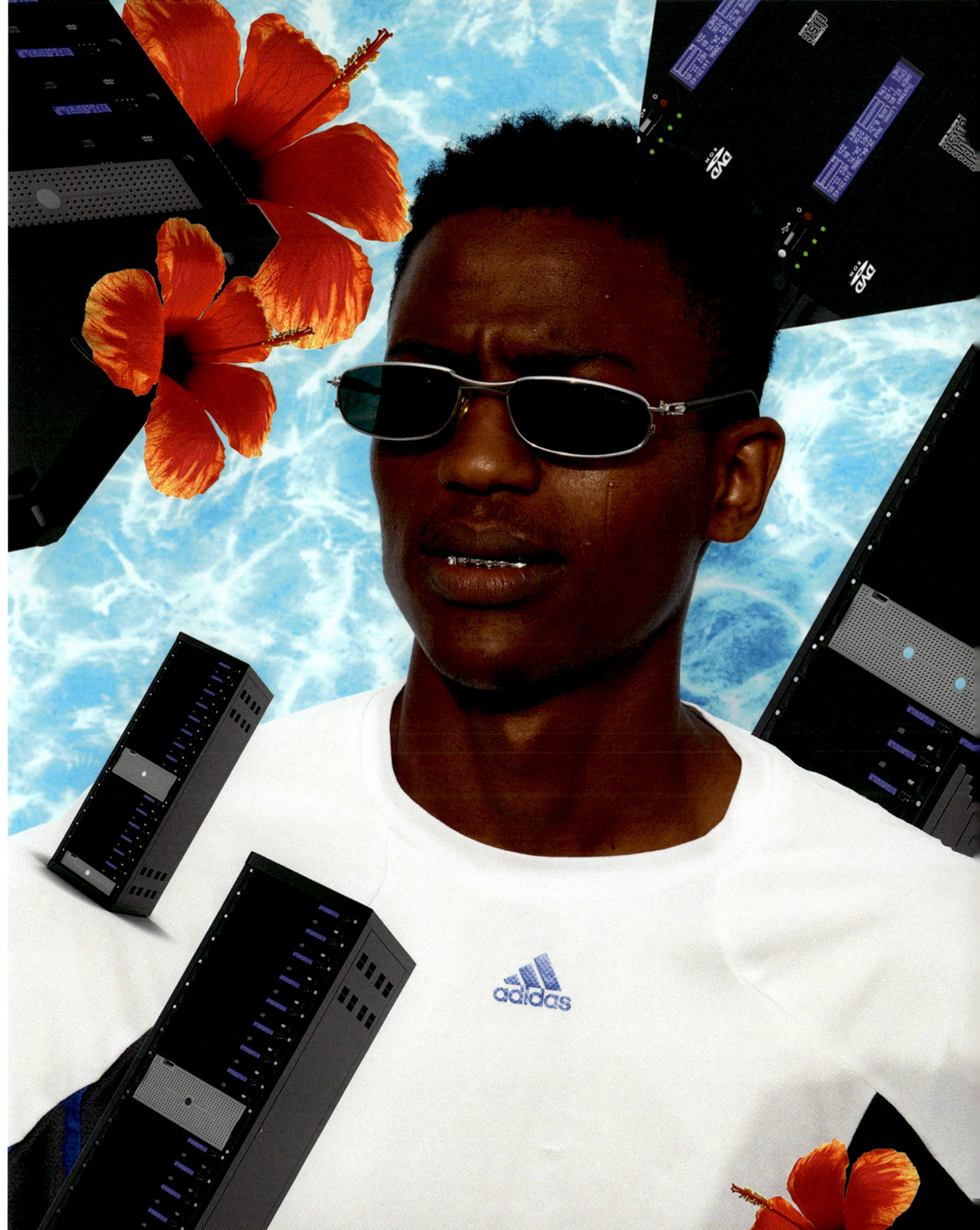

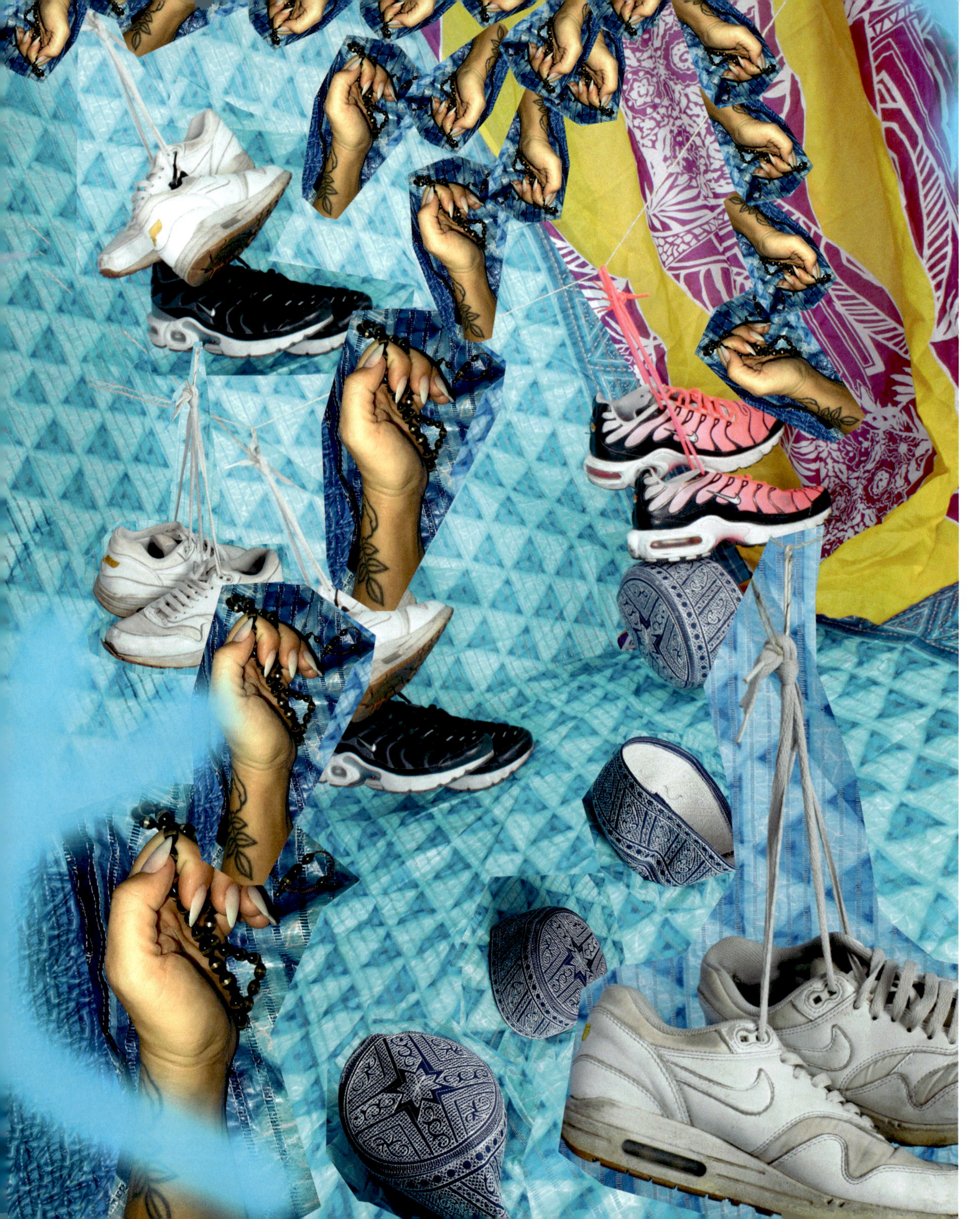

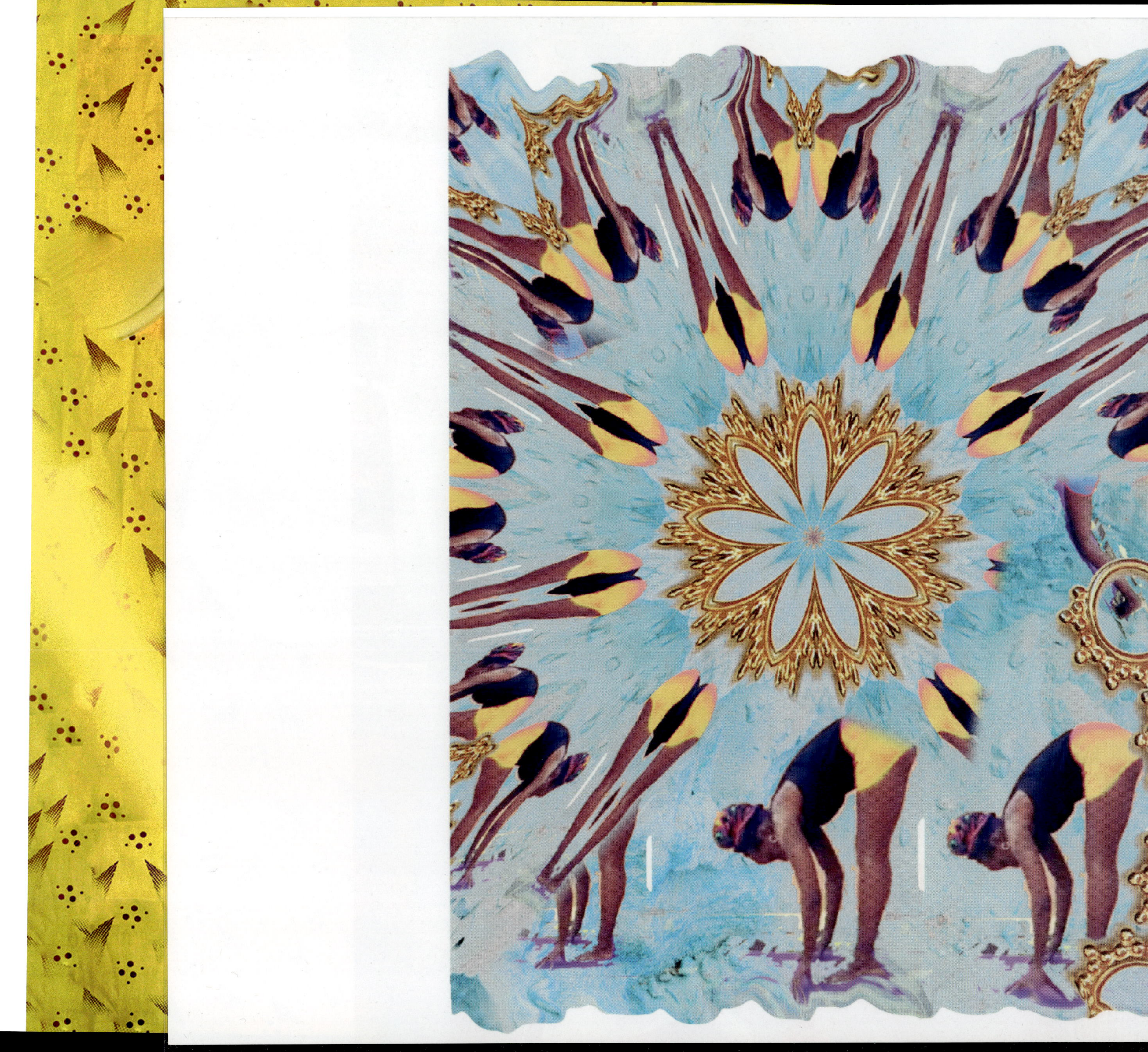

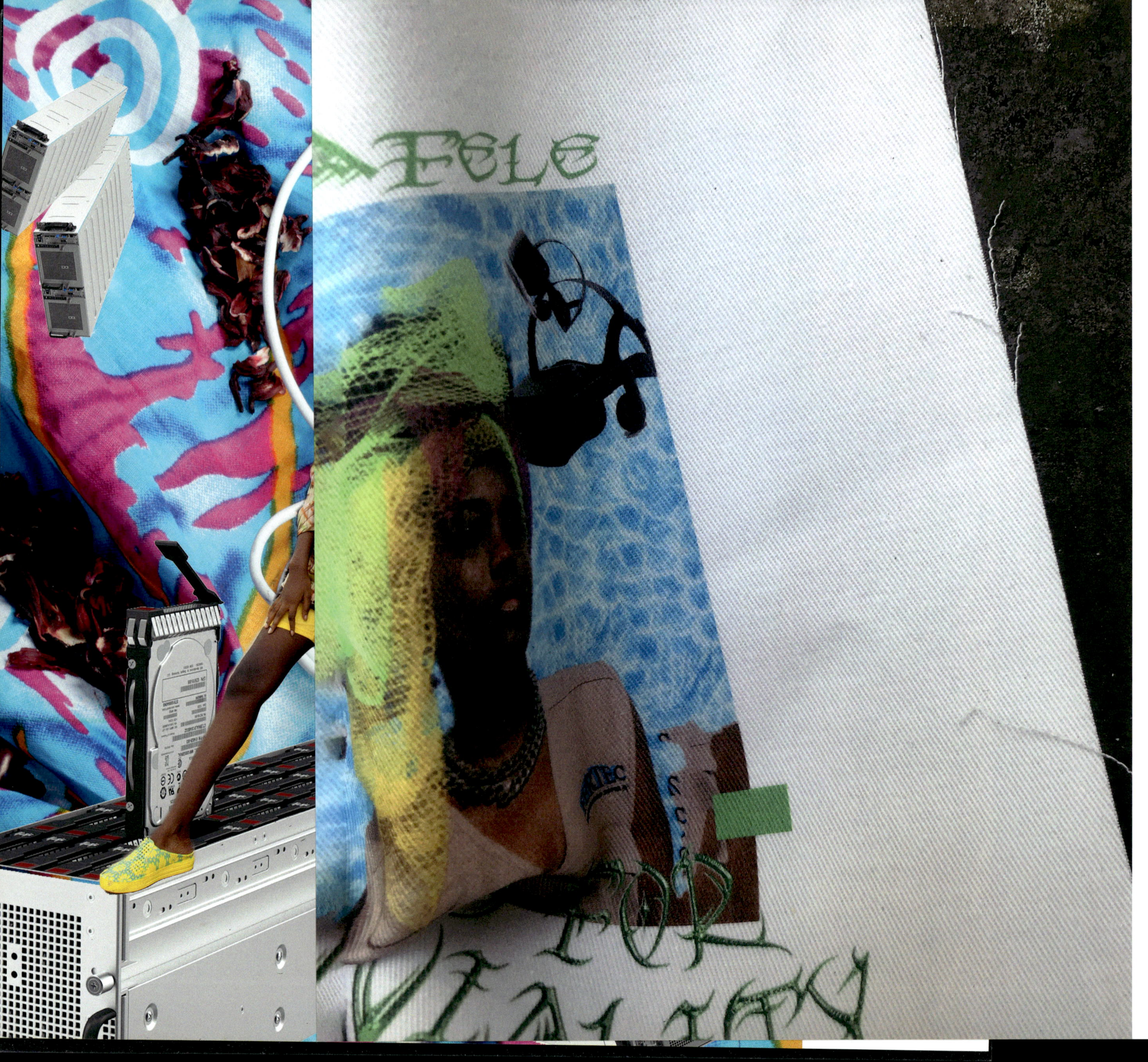
FELE
FOR

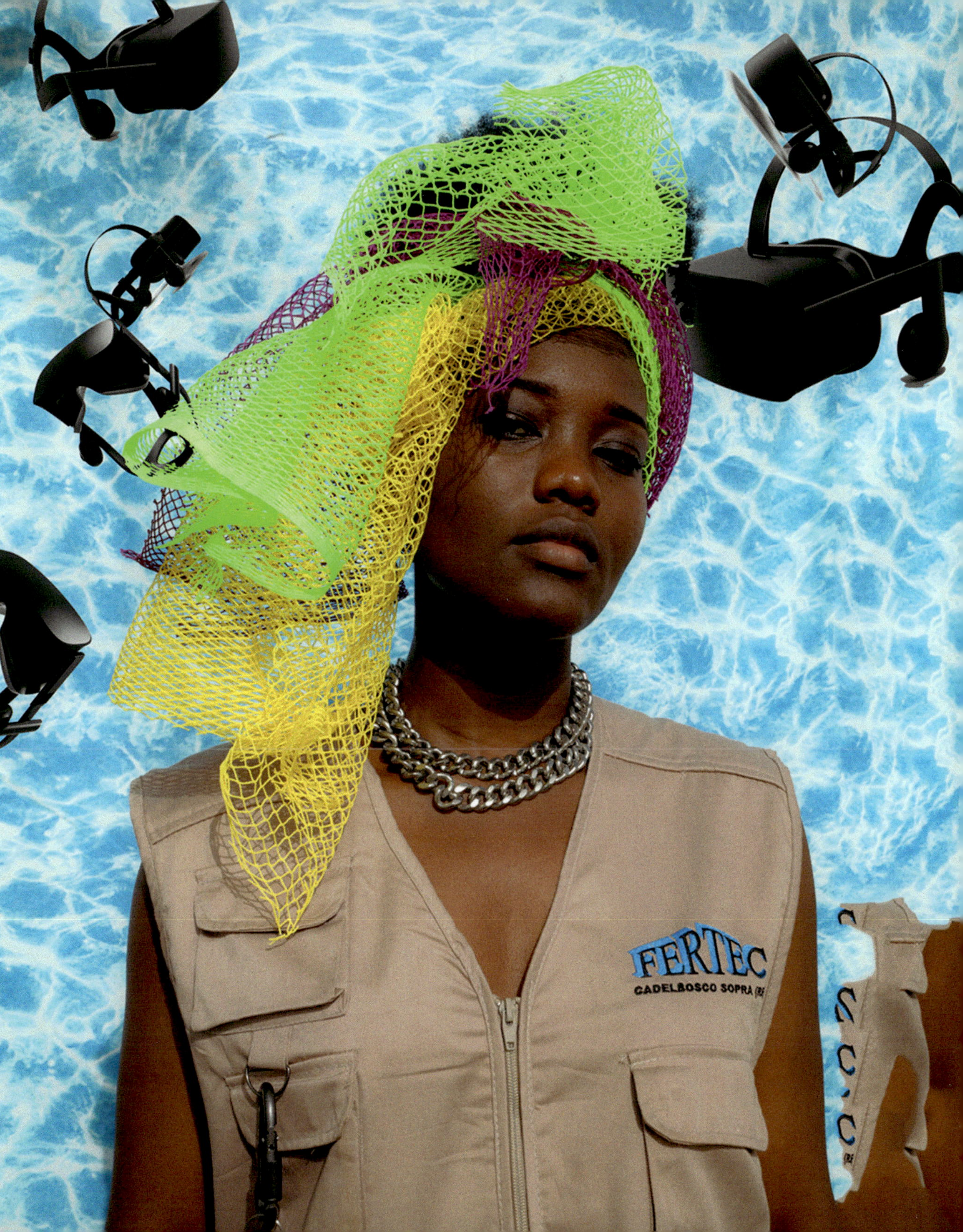

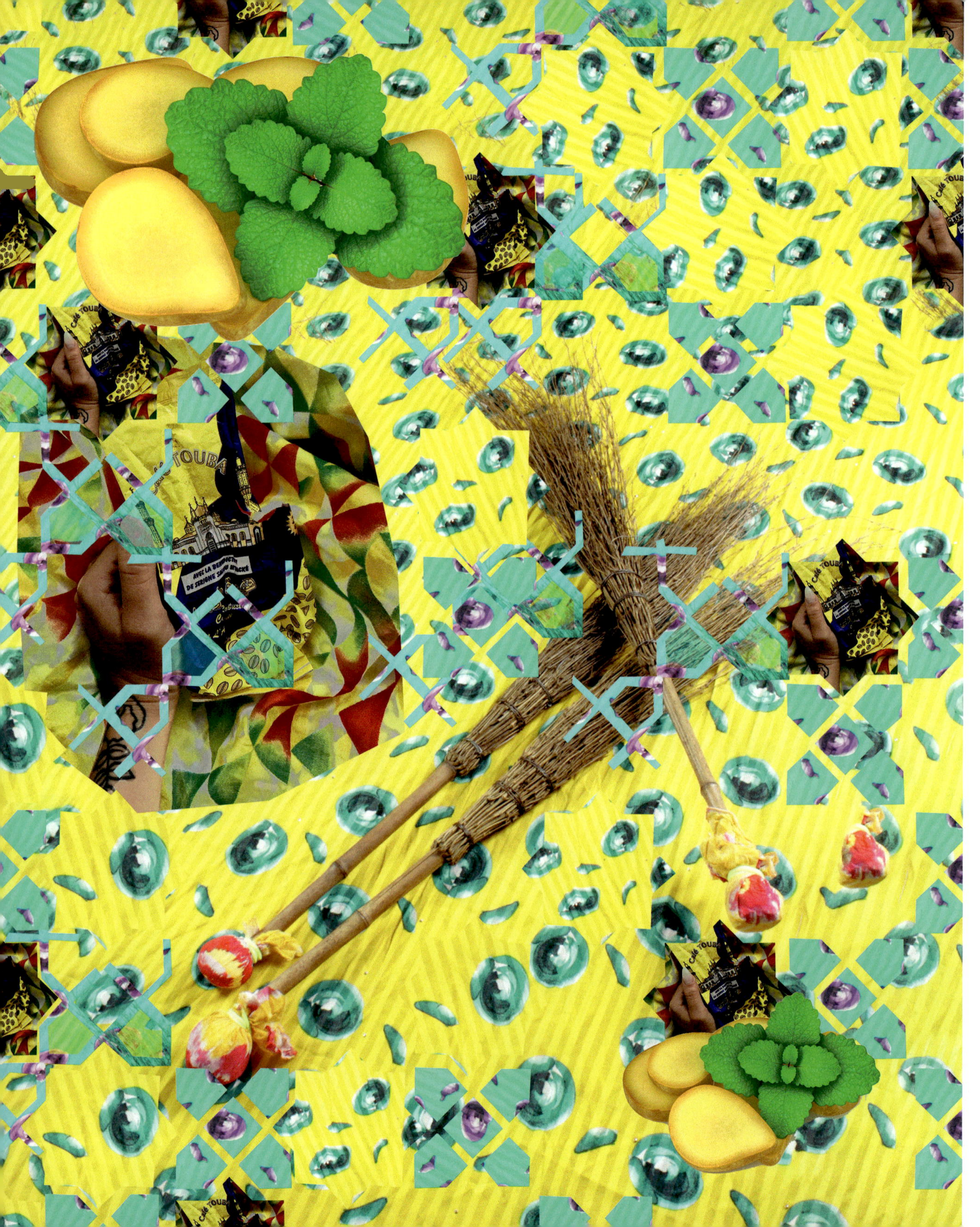

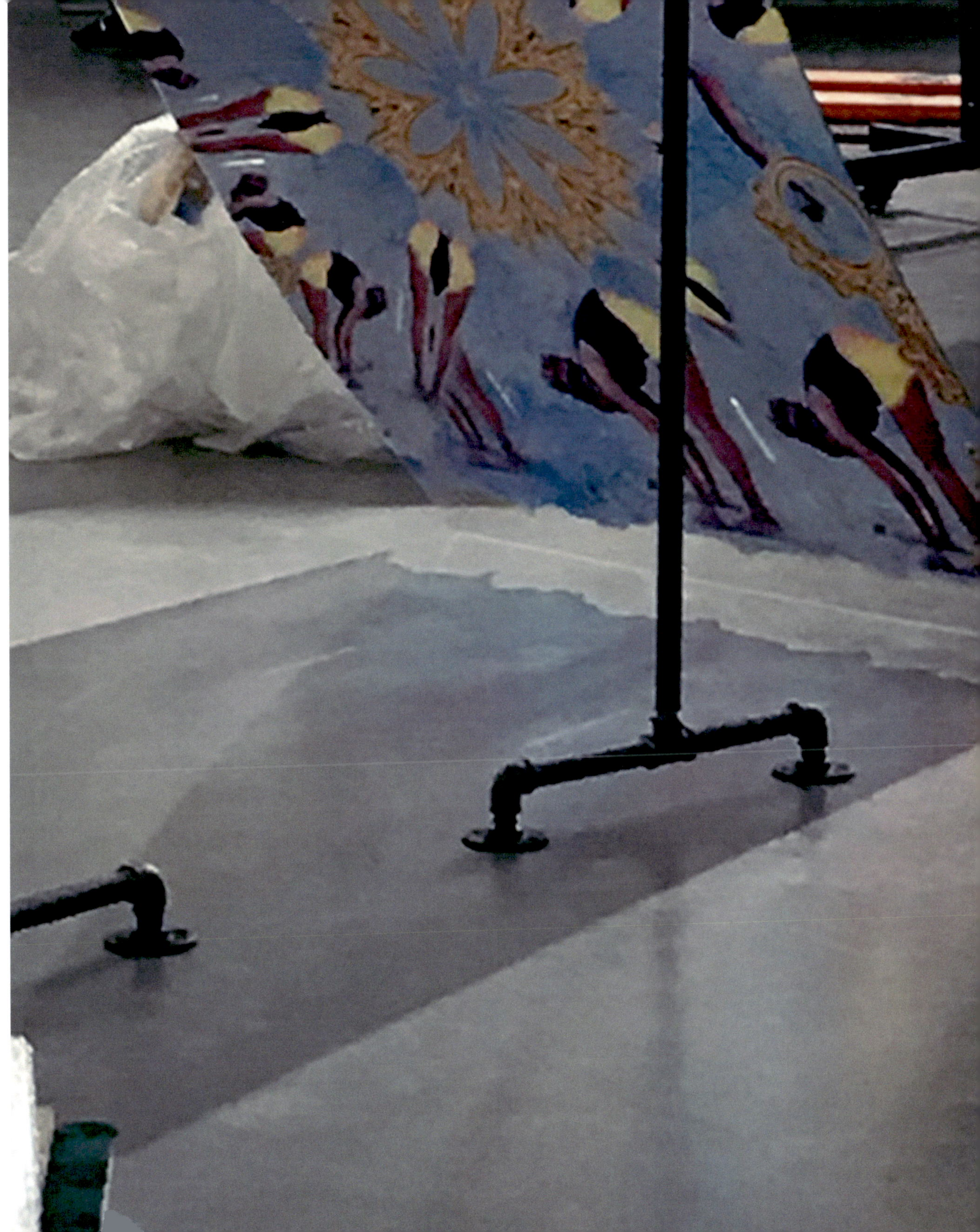

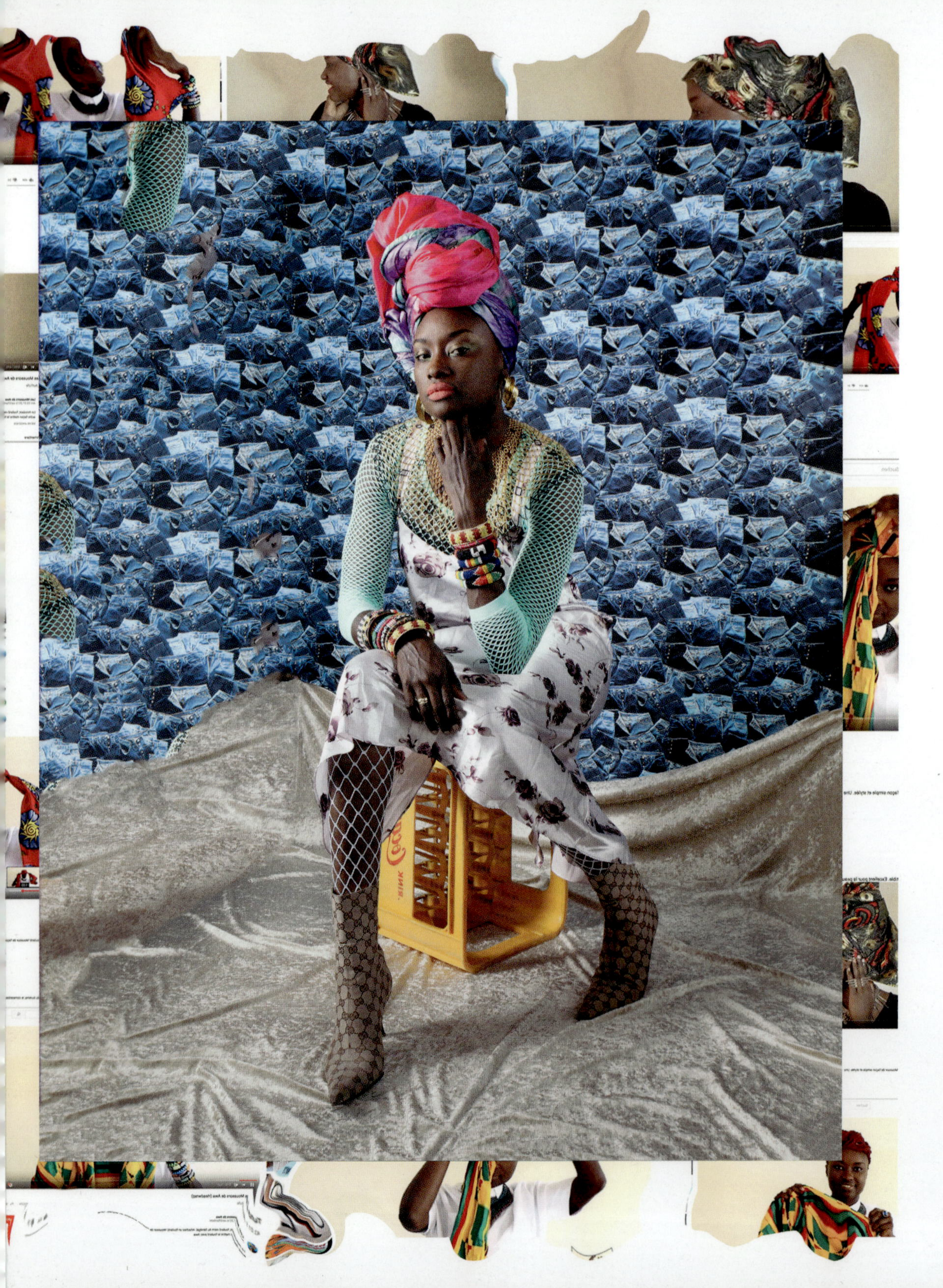

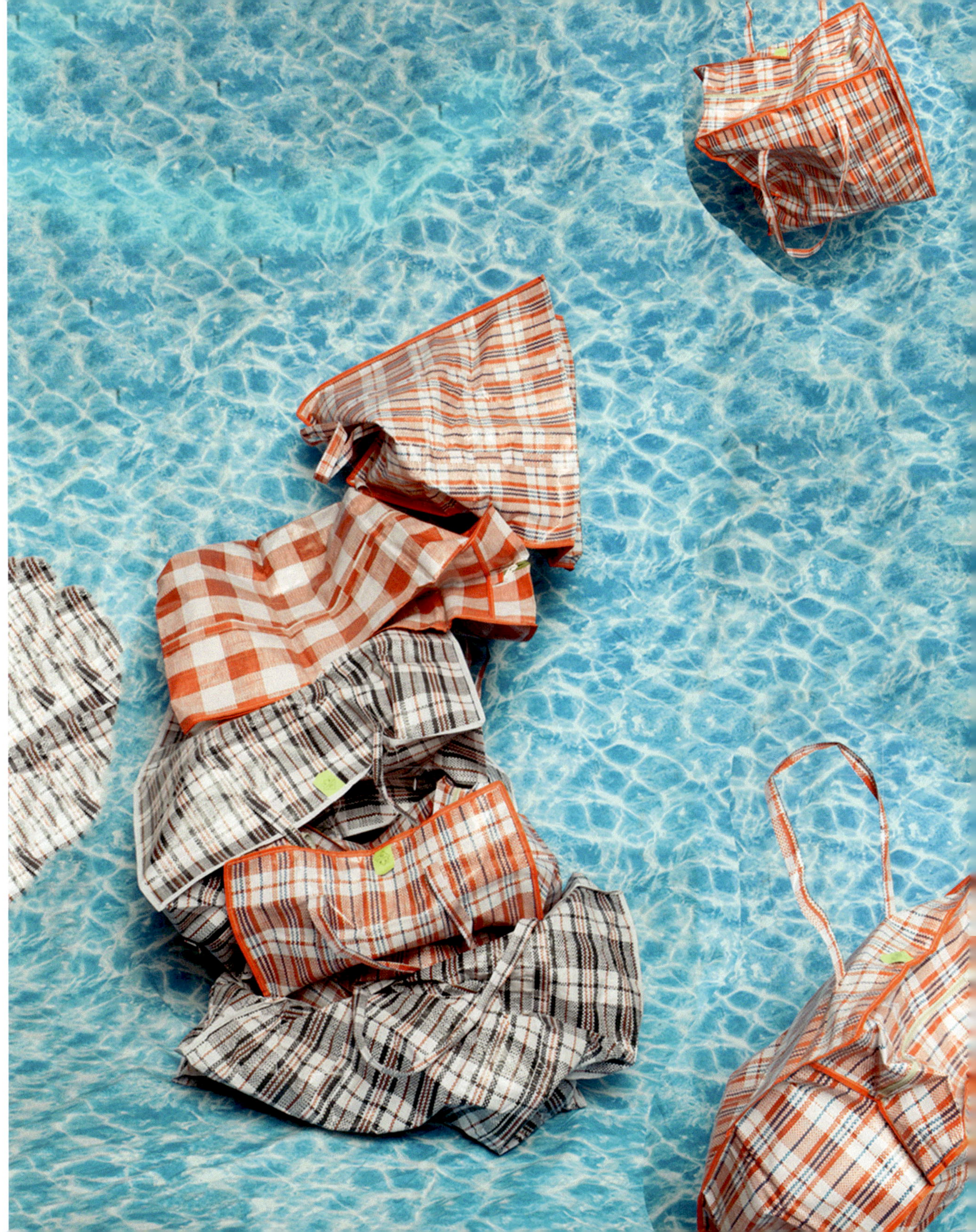

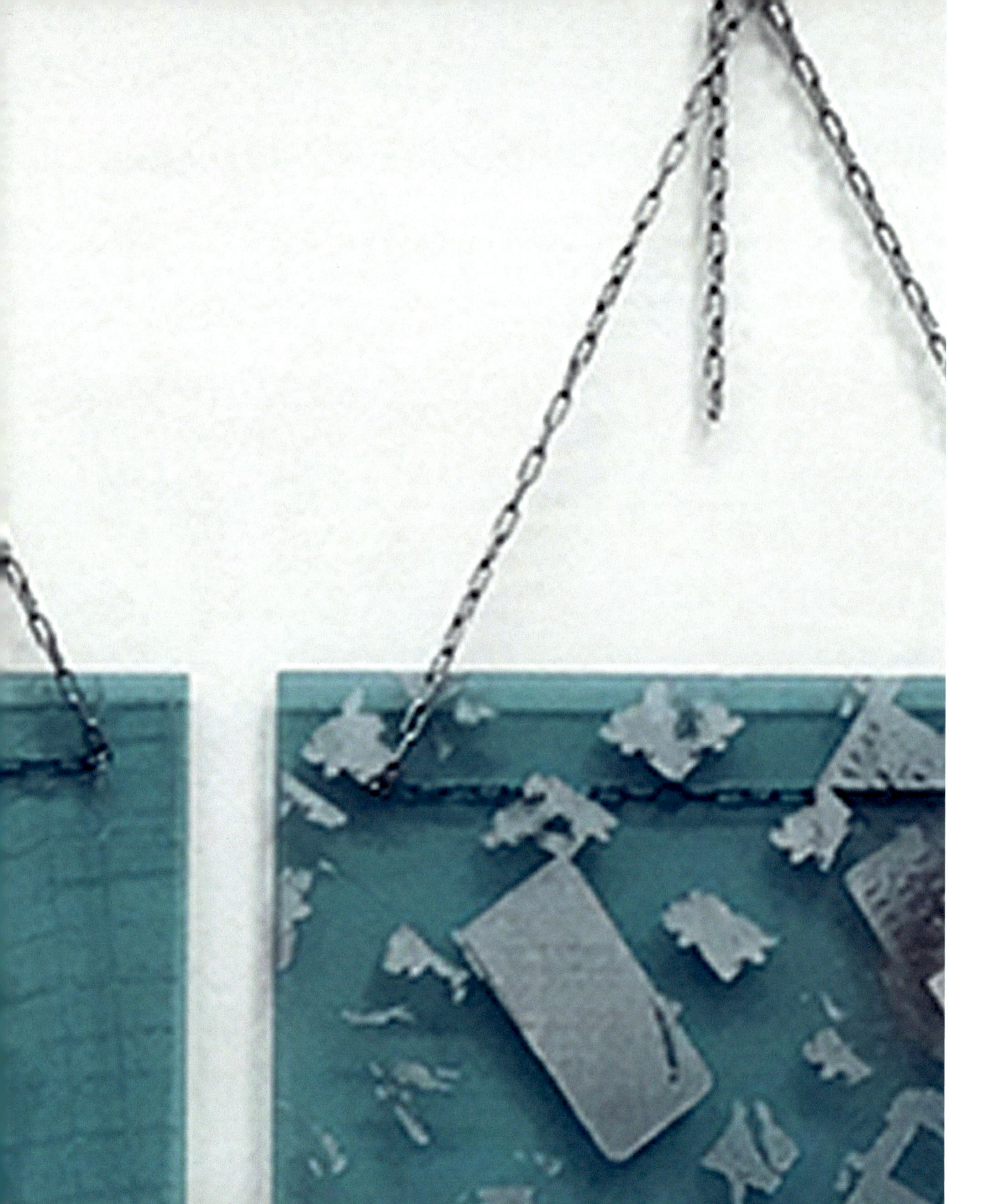

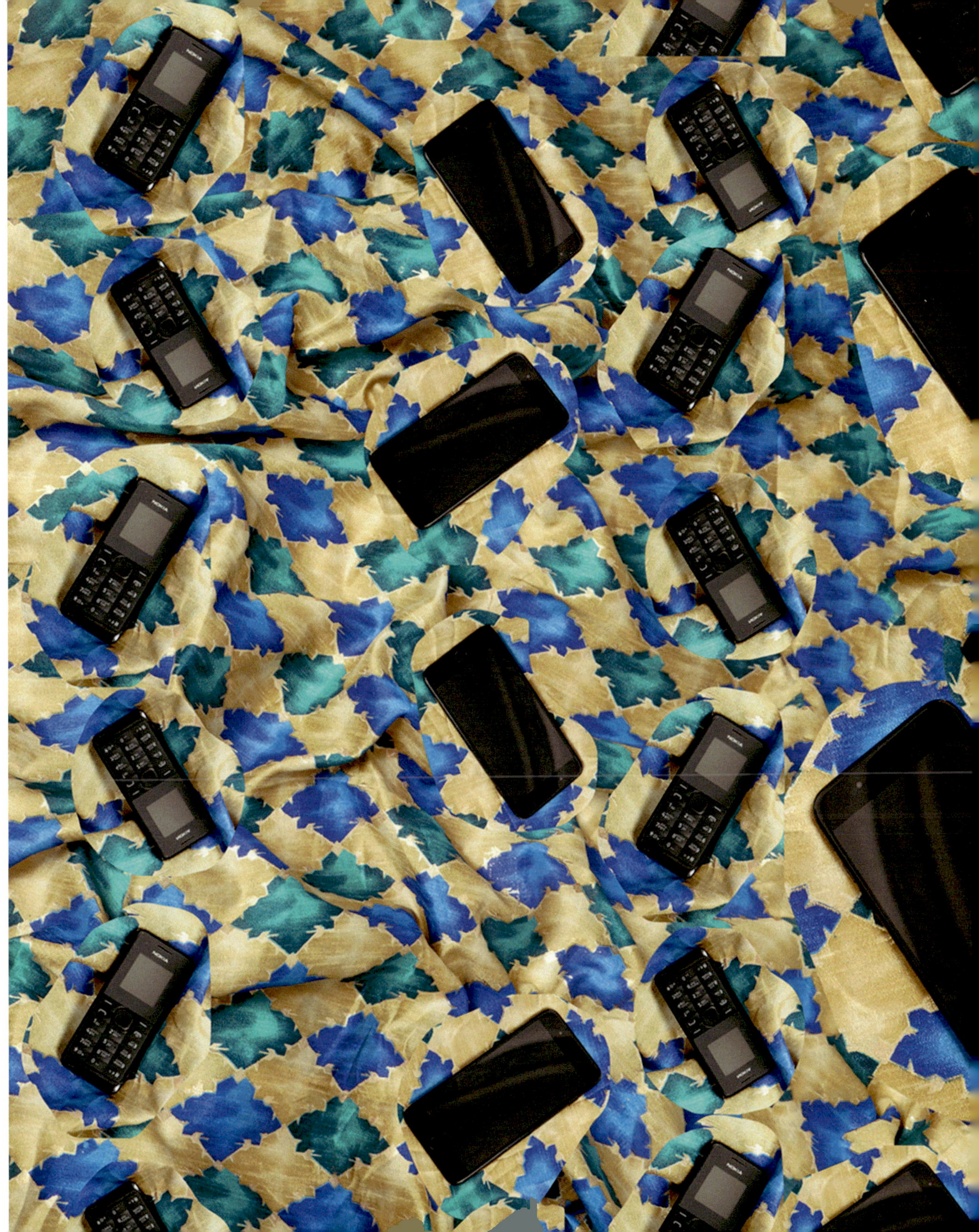

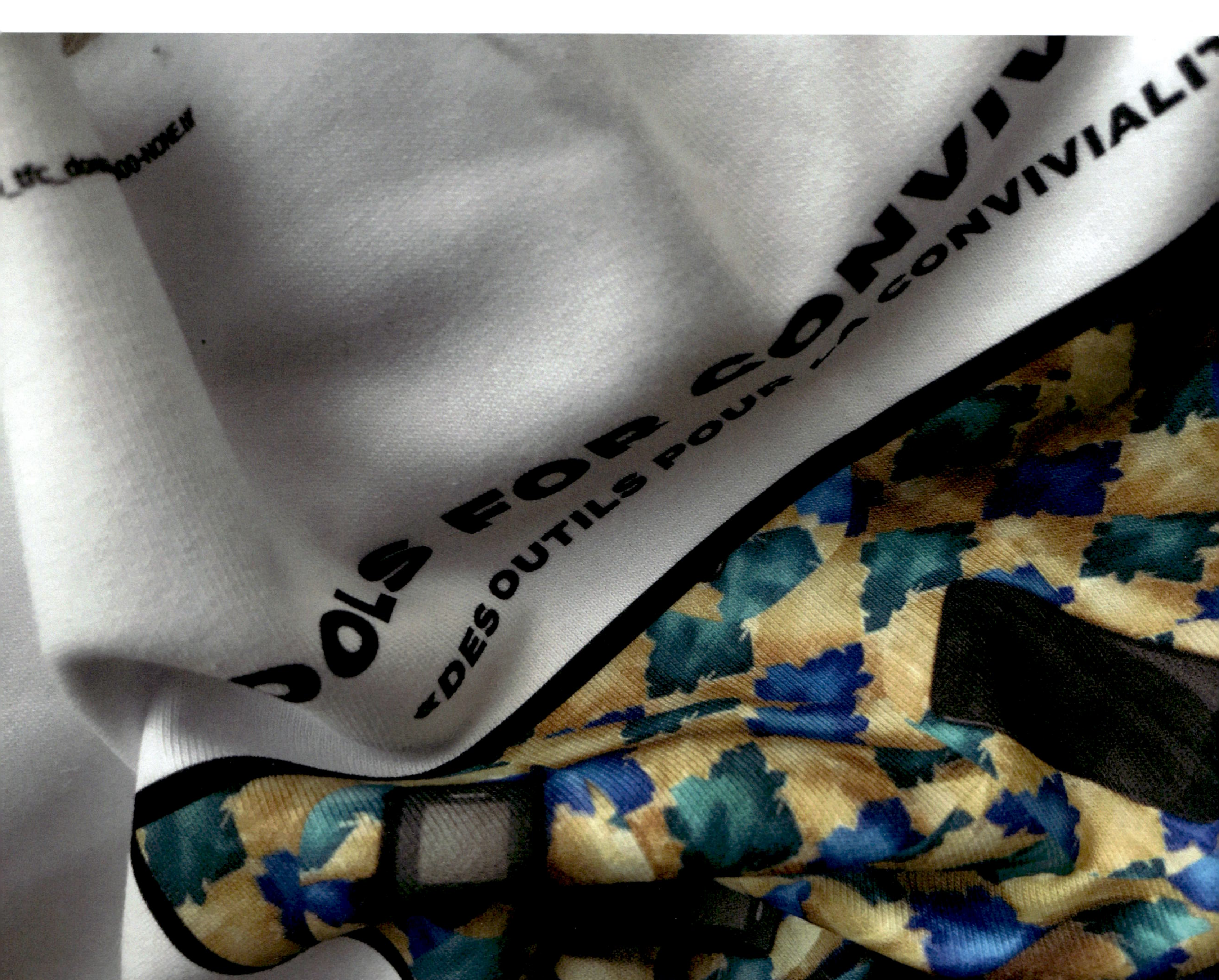
OLS FOR CONVIV
DES OUTILS POUR LA CONVIV
CONVIVIALIT

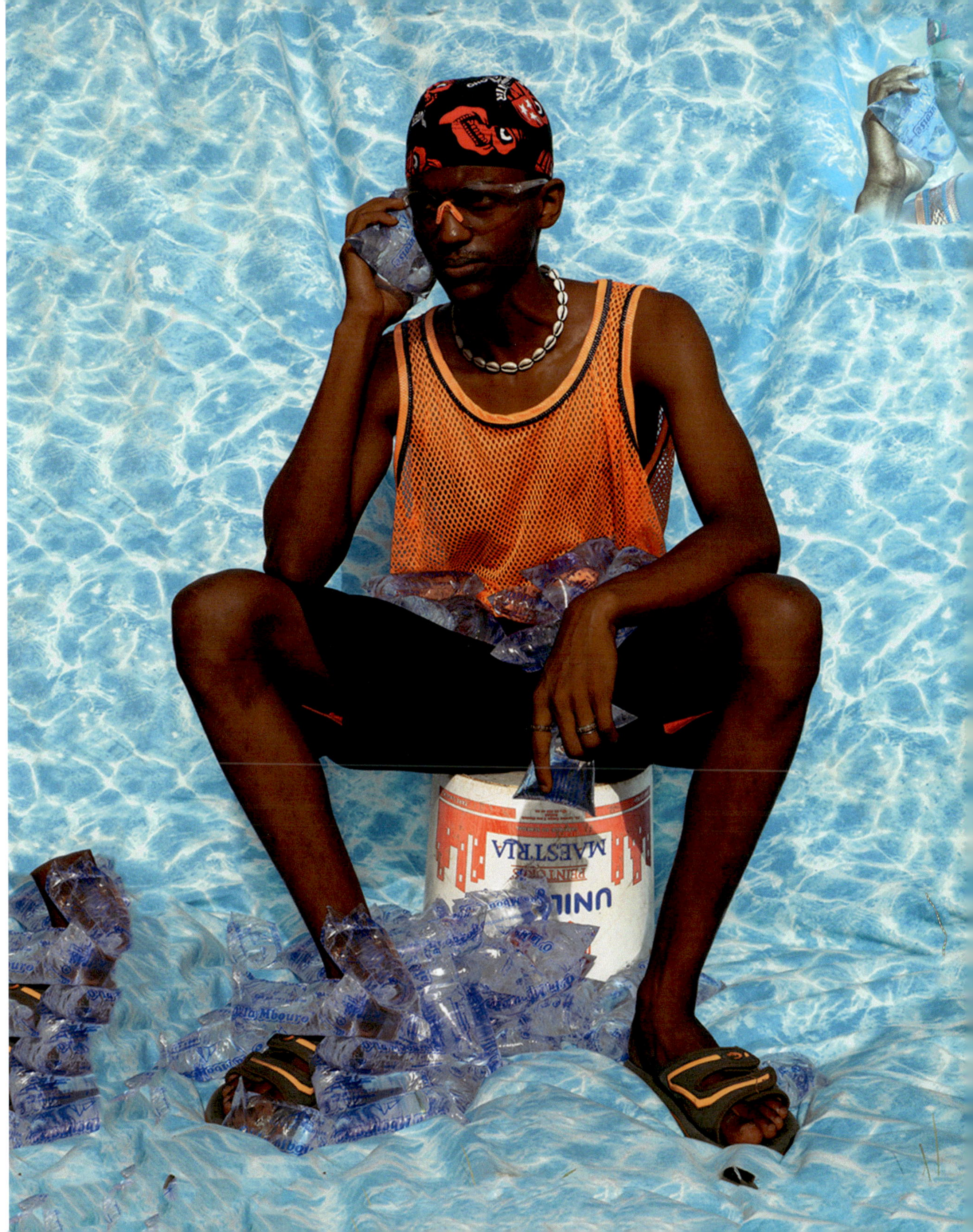

MAESTRIA
PEINTURES
UNIL

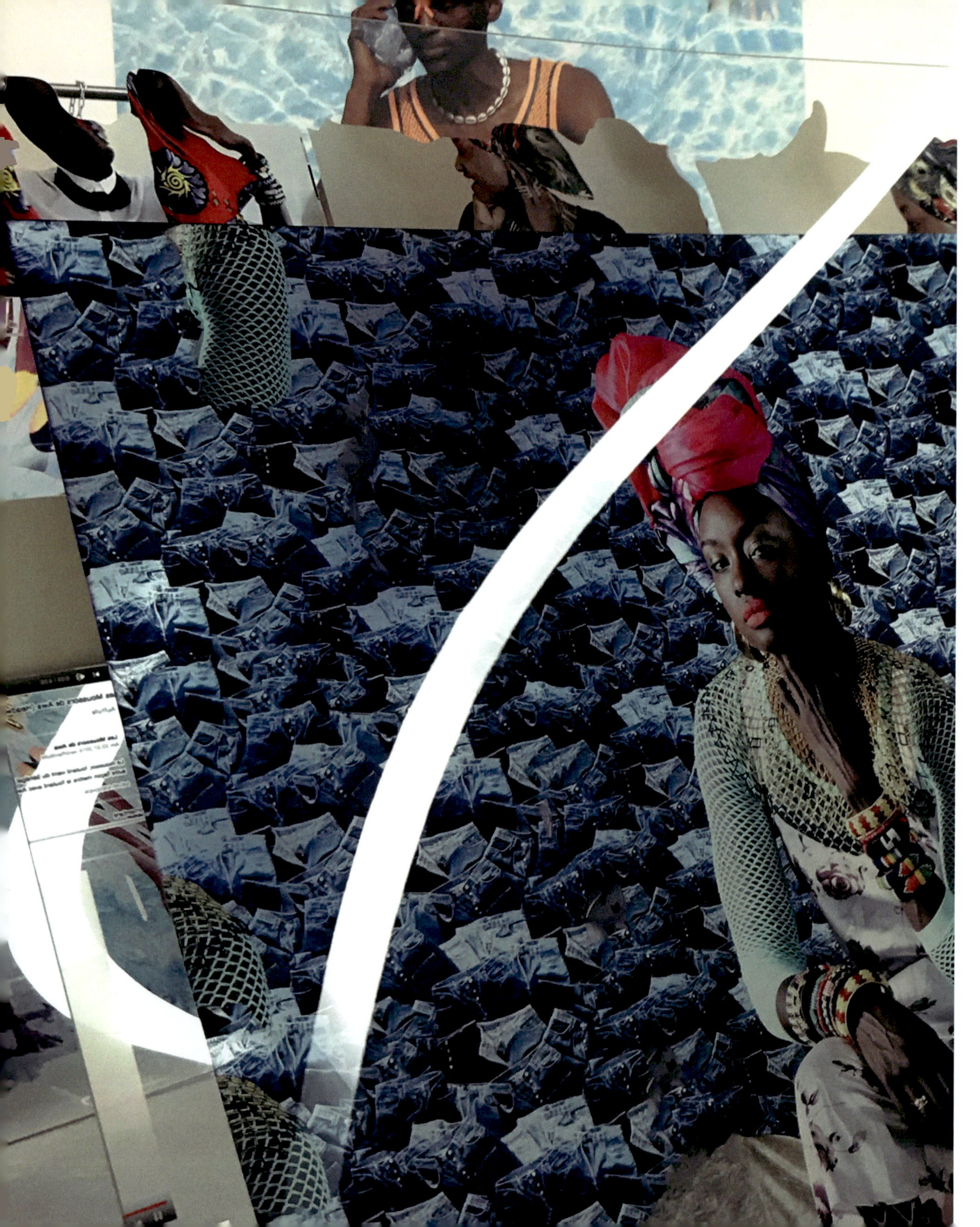

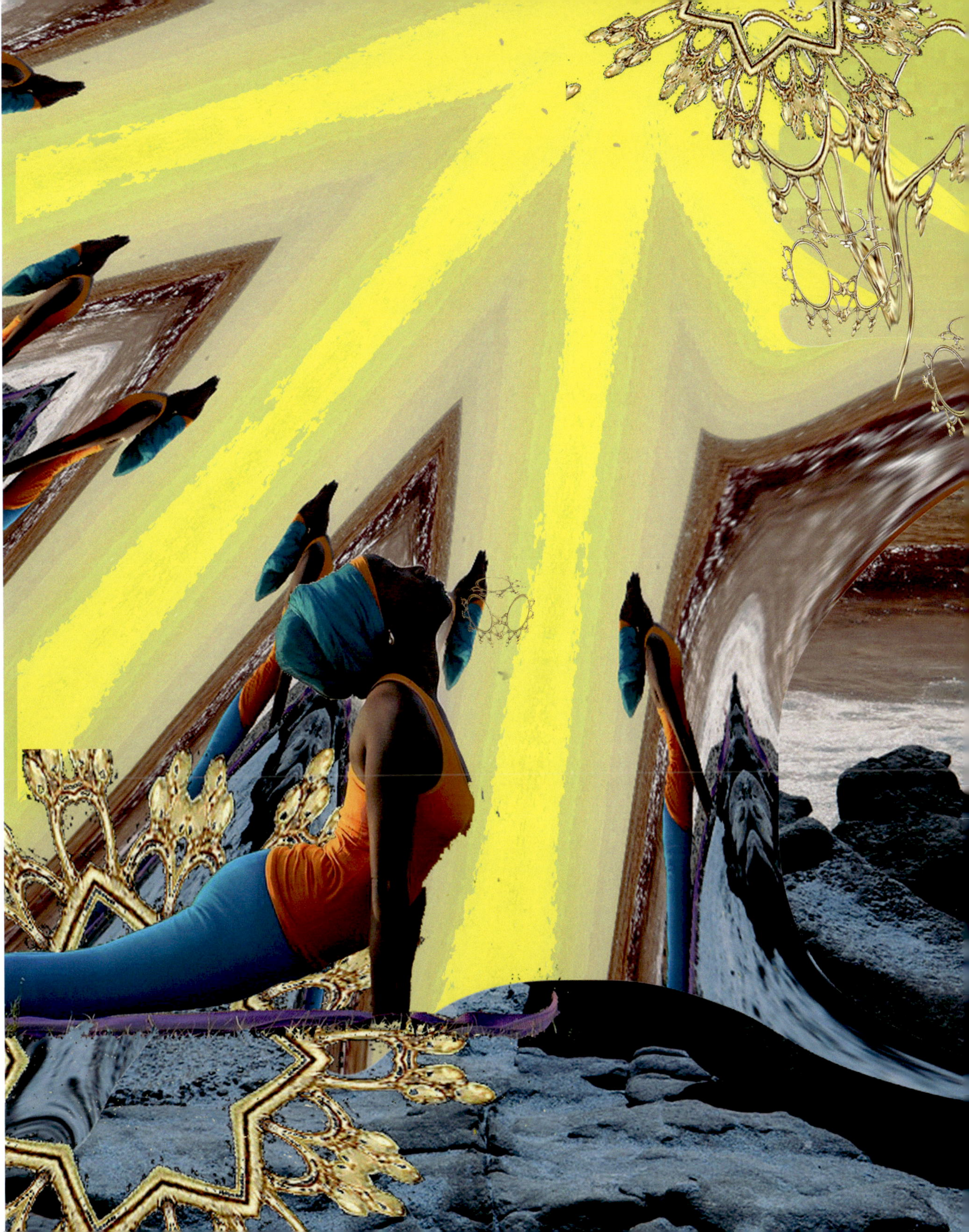

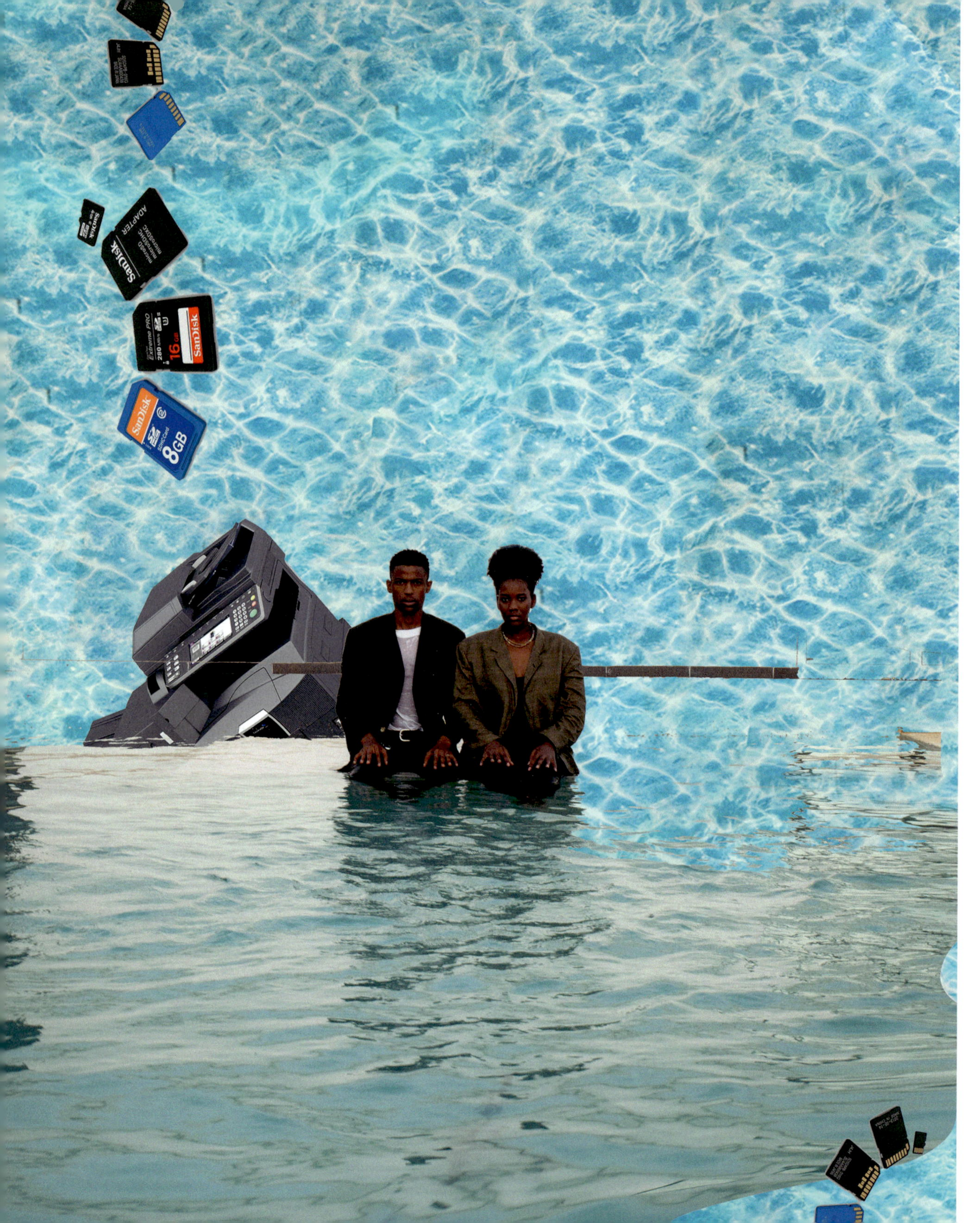

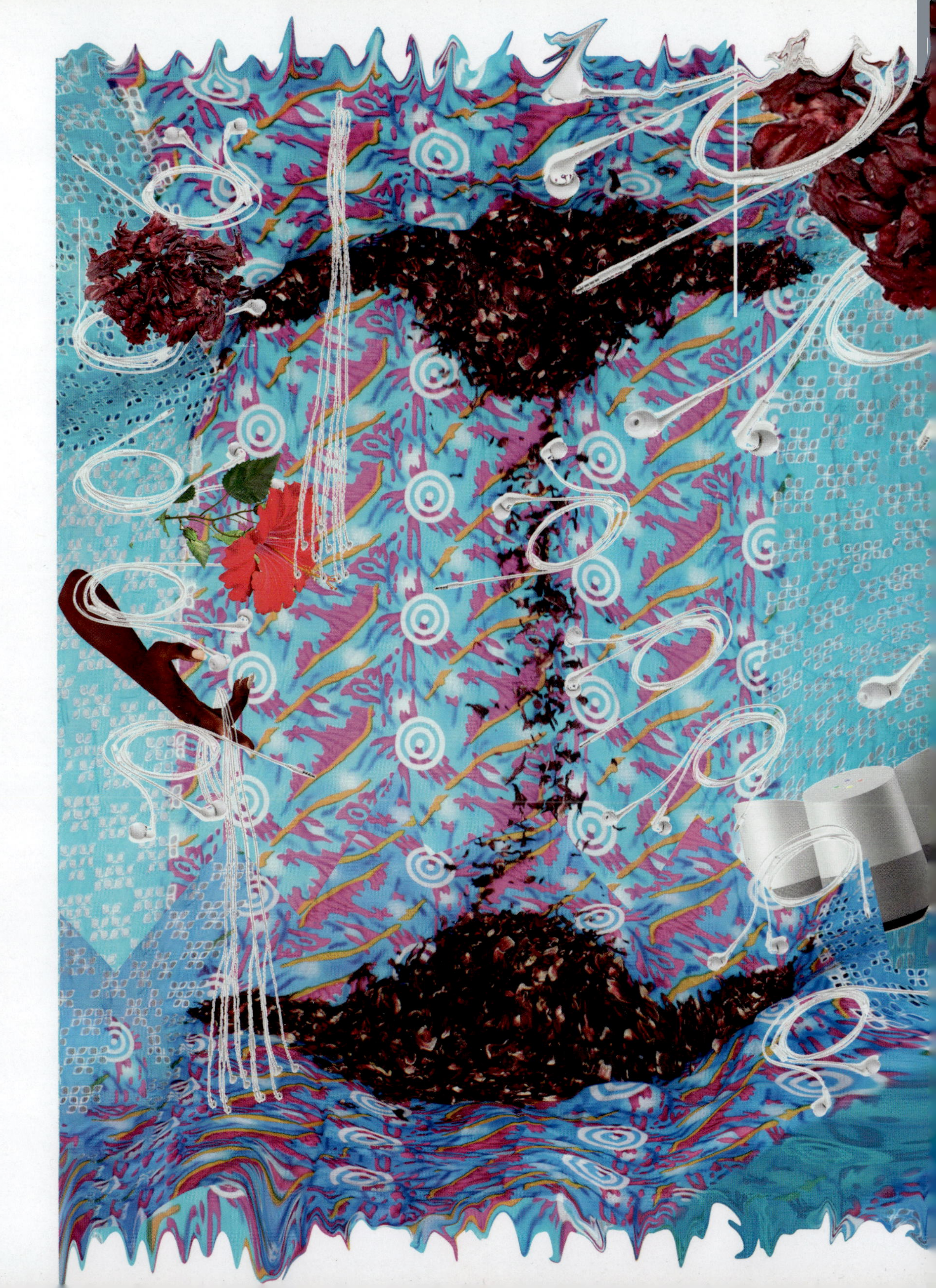

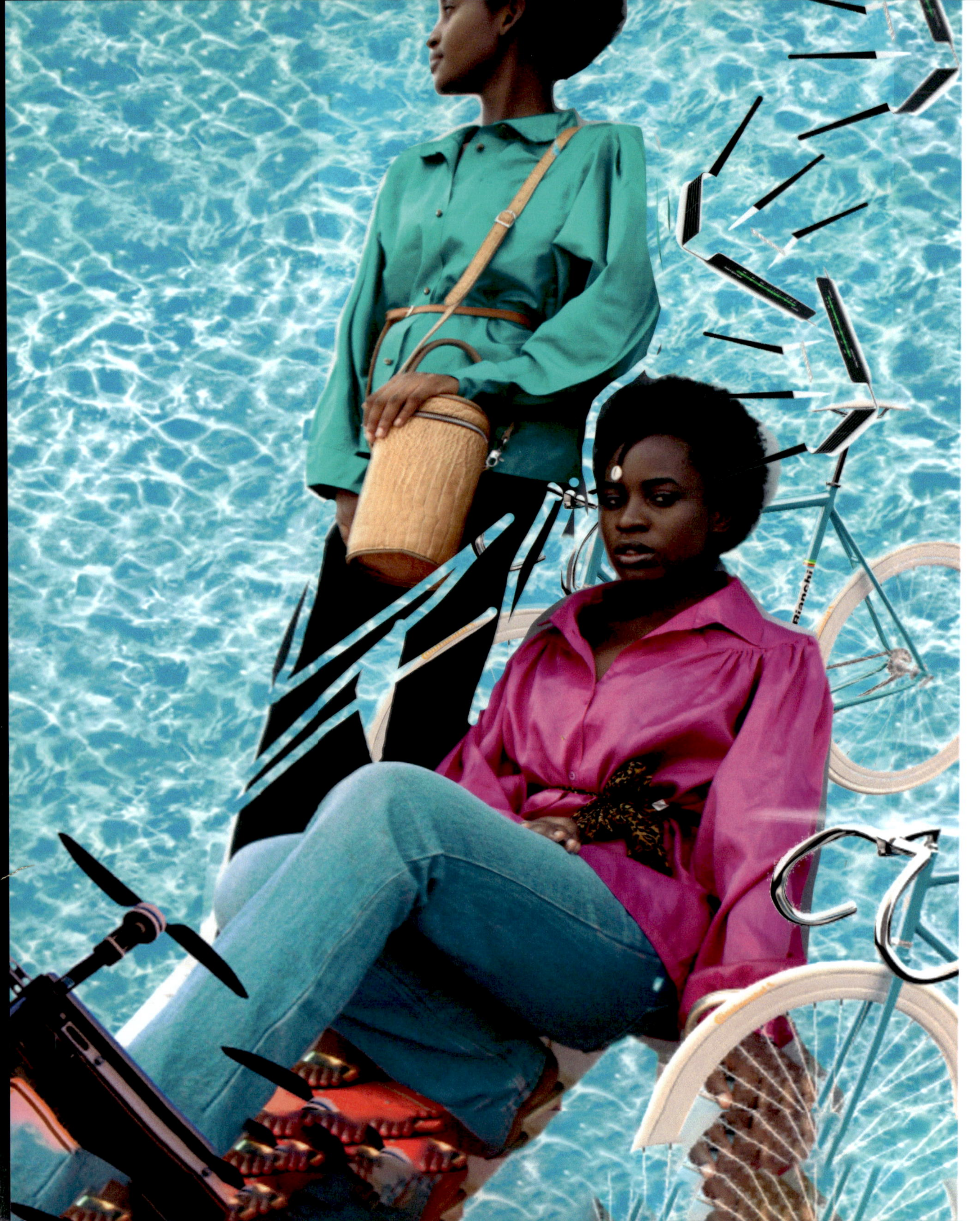

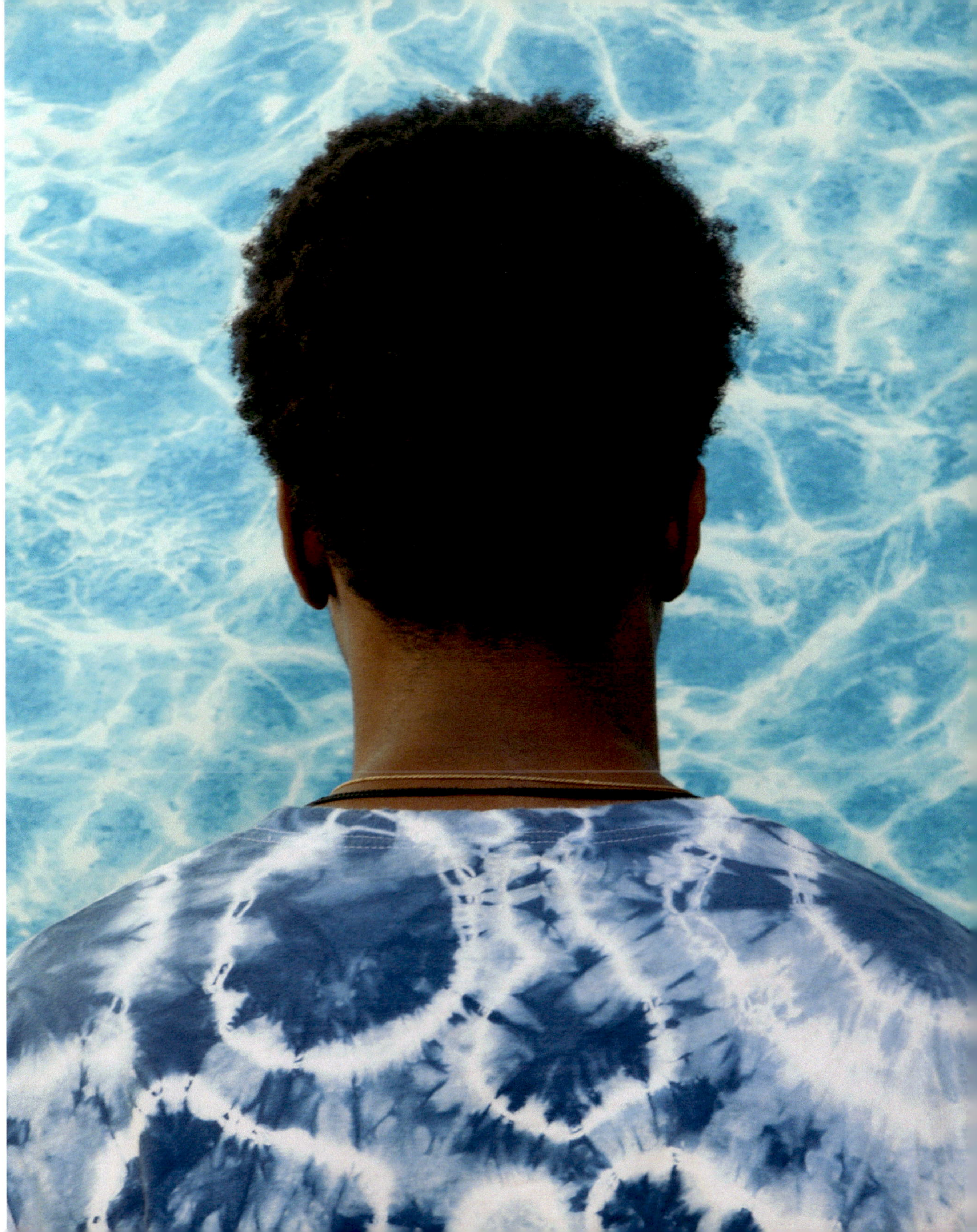

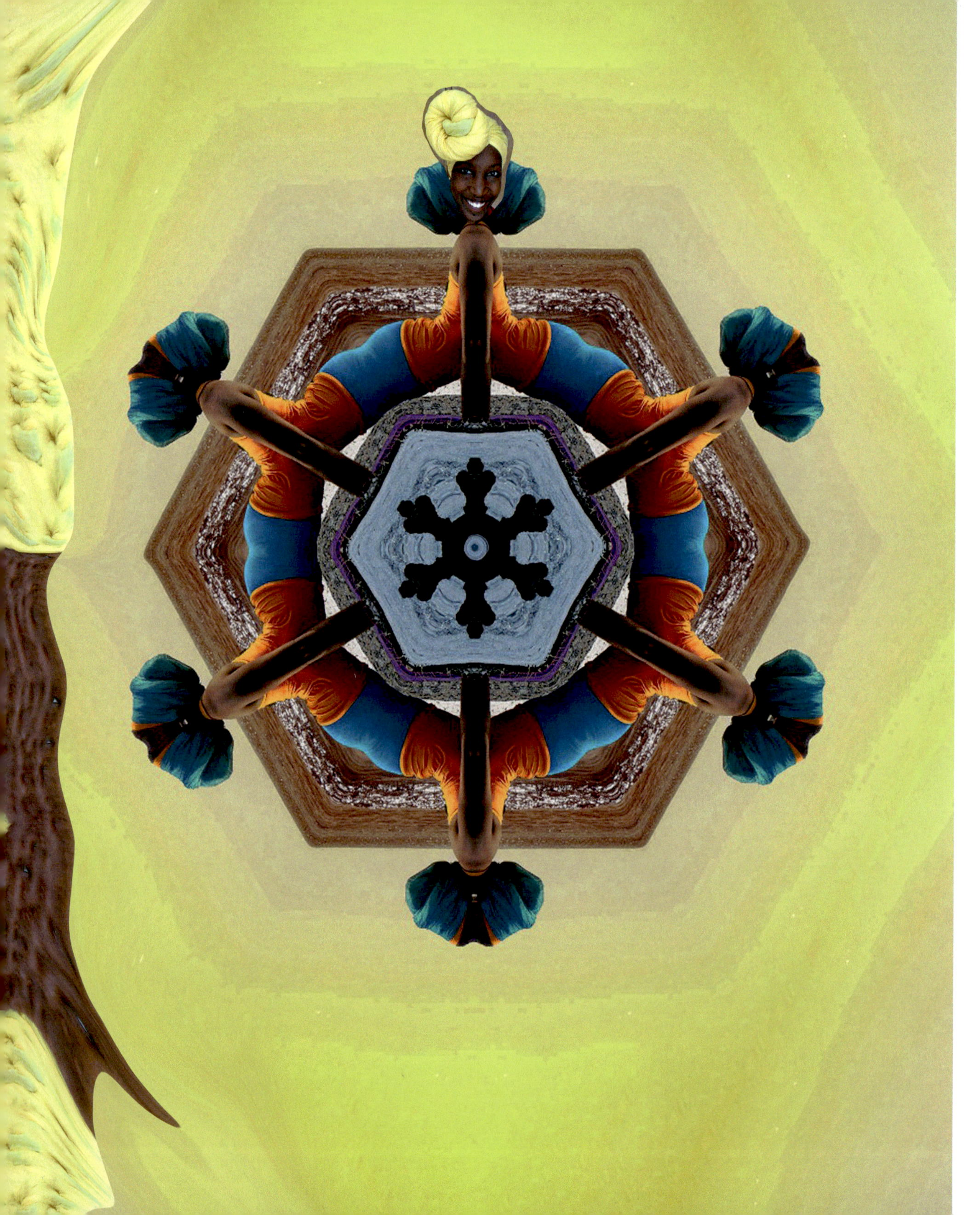

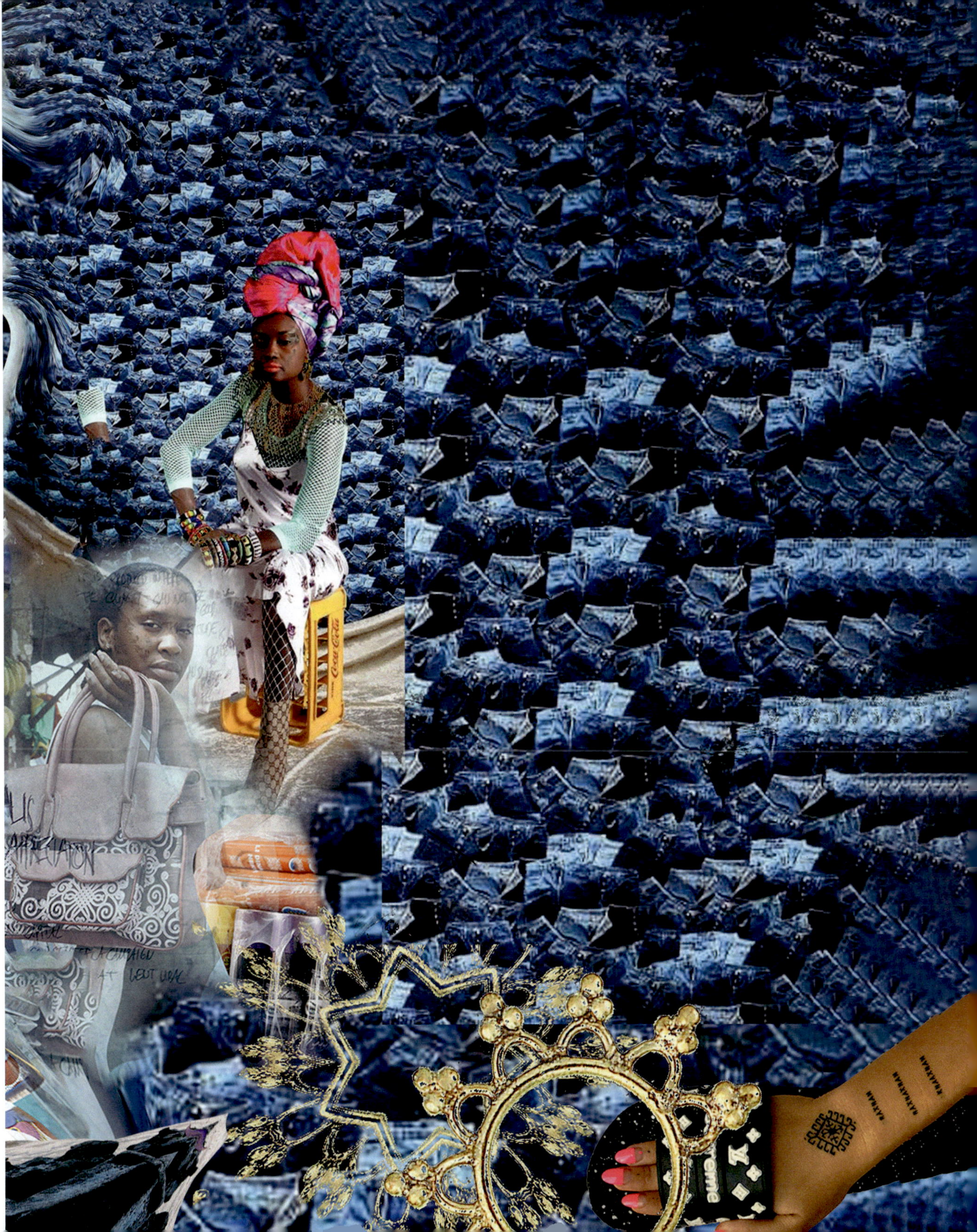

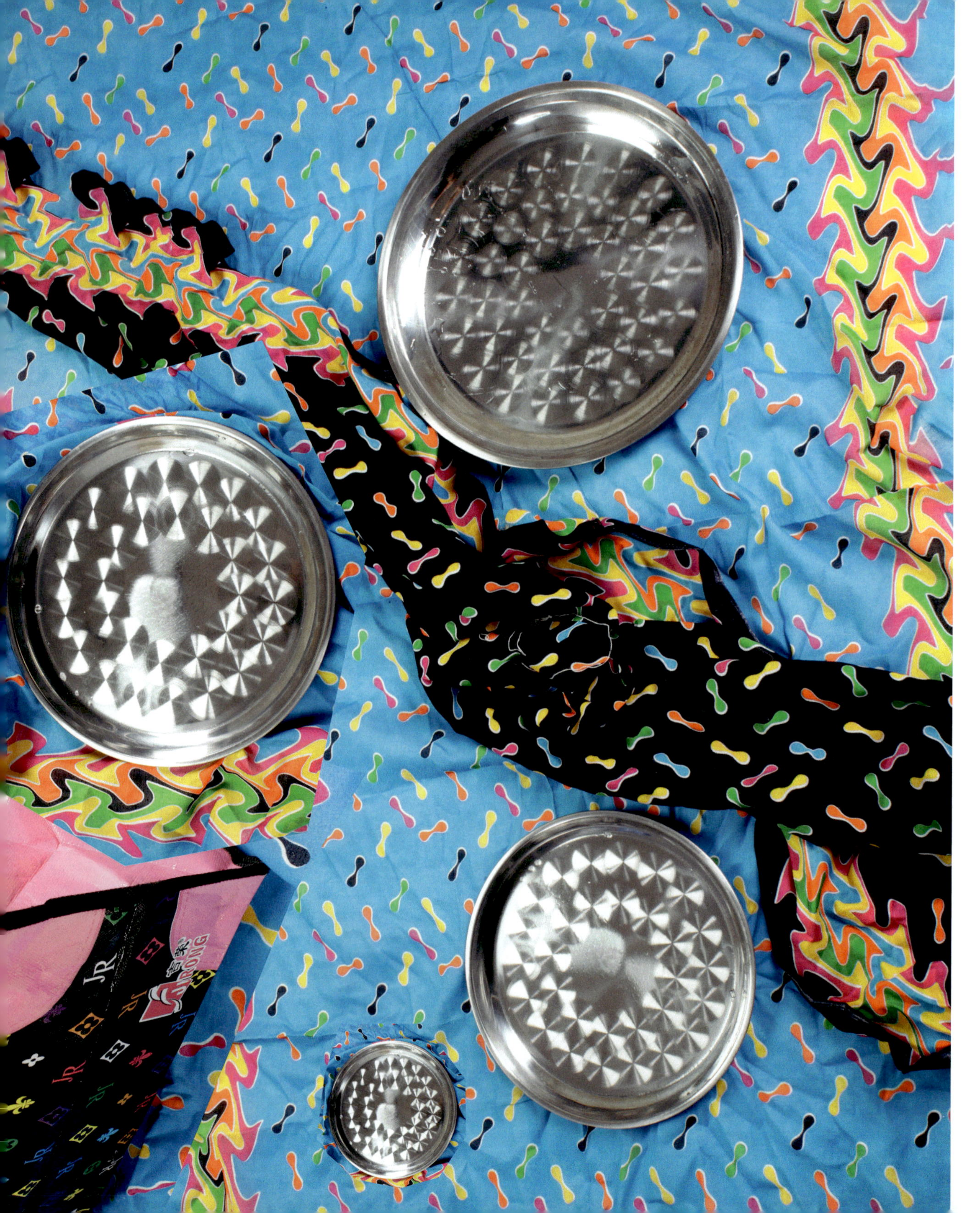

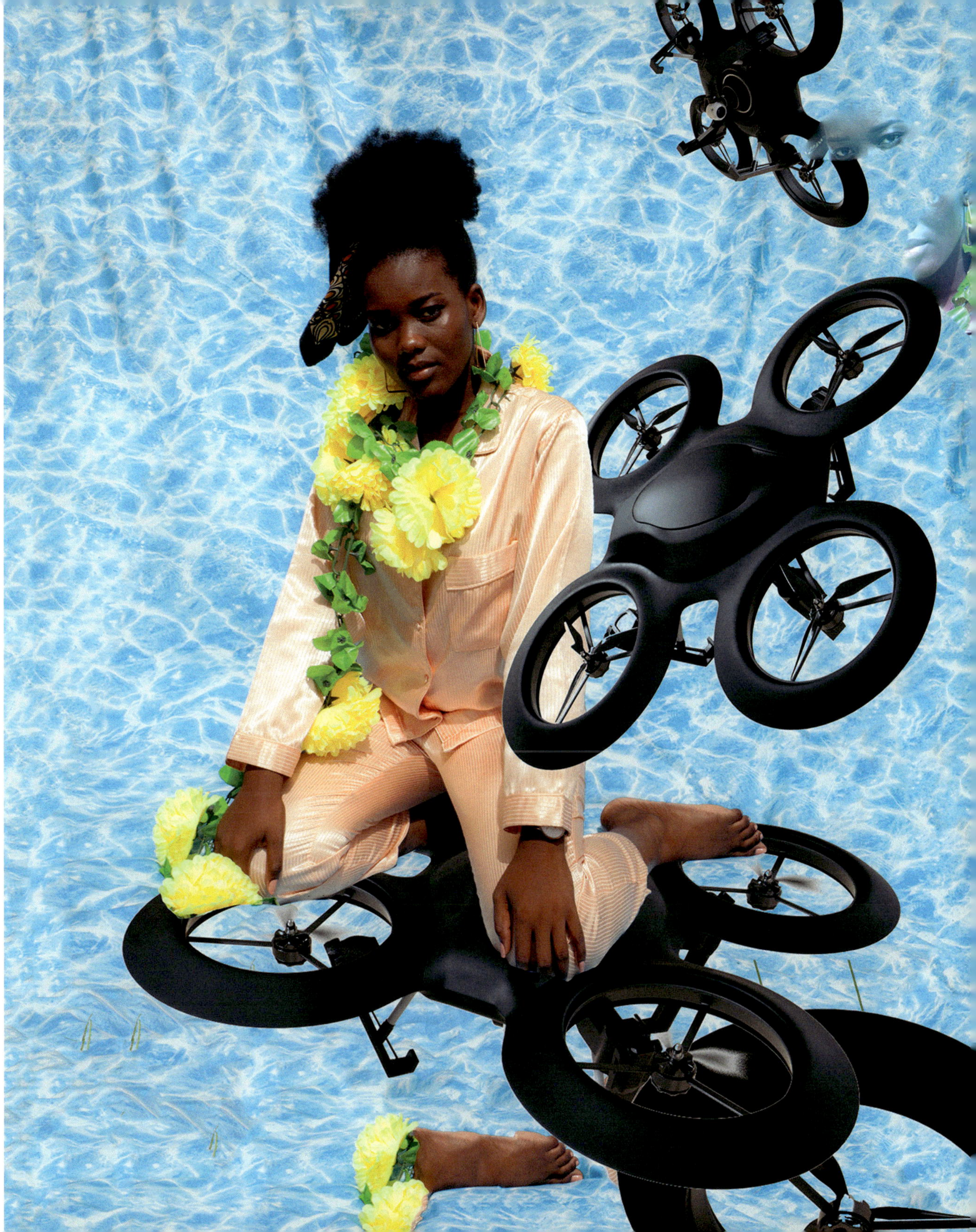

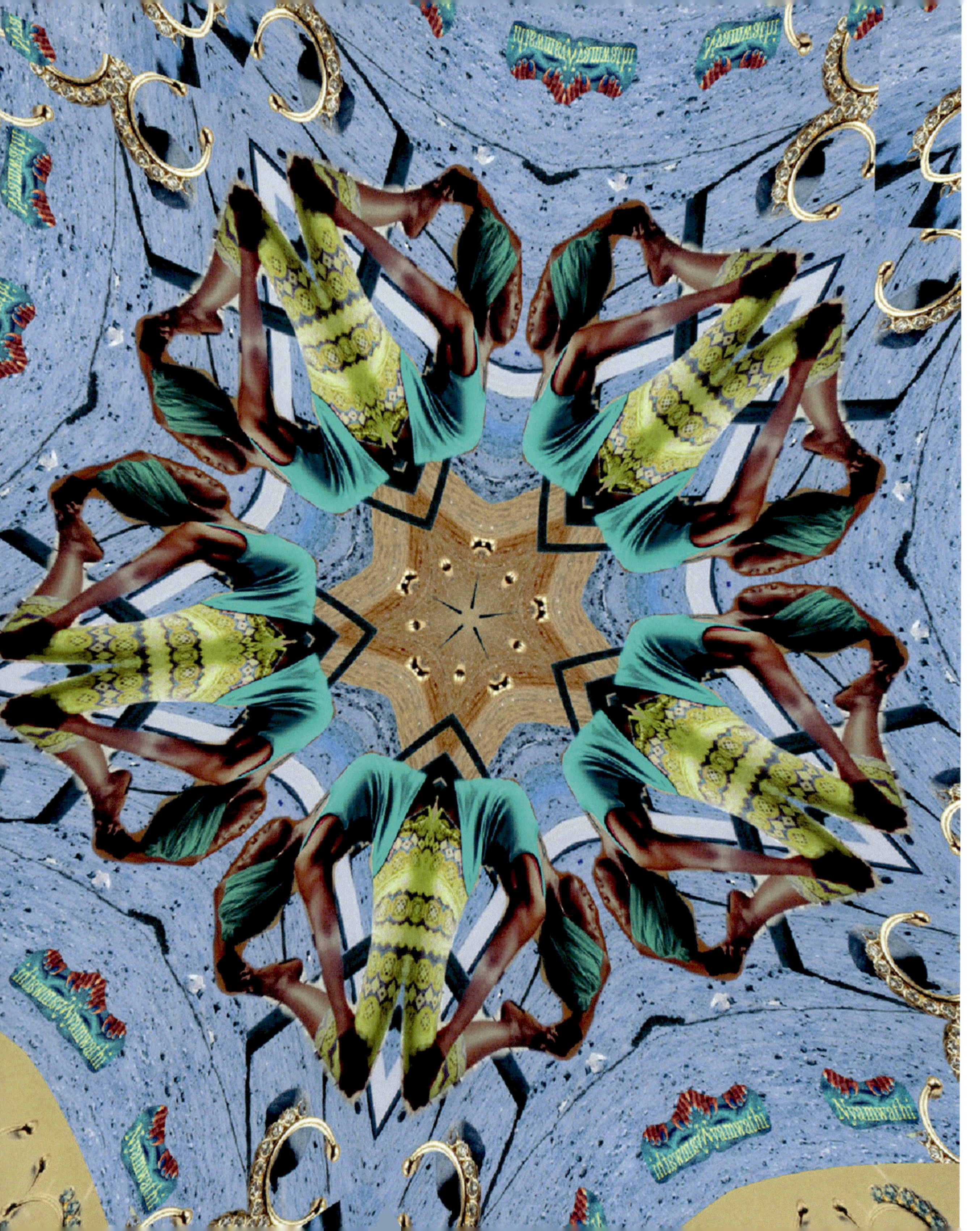

GROUP CHAT

Emily Watlington mit Anna Ehrenstein und Saliou Ba, Donkafele (Mandé Mory Bah und Thibaut Houssou), Nyamwathi Gichau, Lydia Likibi und Awa Seck

Im Juni 2020 stellte ich dem Team hinter *Tools for Conviviality* in einem Google-Dokument einige Fragen. Die Datei wurde für uns zu einem digitalen Raum, um uns trotz Reisebeschränkungen und Corona-Abstandsregeln und unabhängig von Ort und Zeitzone auszutauschen. Wir mussten uns auf technische Werkzeuge – ebenso wie aufeinander – verlassen, und unsere Beiträge in verschiedene Sprachen übersetzen, da die Beteiligten aus dem Senegal, Belgien, den Vereinigten Staaten, Deutschland, Albanien, Benin, Kenia, der Republik Kongo, Gambia und Guinea kommen oder dort leben.

Koproduzent*innen, bitte stellt euch in wenigen Sätzen vor!
SALIOU 2020-07-11　Ich bin Mamadou Saliou Ba. Ich habe American Studies studiert und einen Master in Englisch. Ich arbeite als Übersetzer und Dolmetscher, außerdem habe ich einen Autohandel und bin Gastgeber auf Airbnb. Ich bin ein offener Mensch und interessiere mich für alle Aspekte des Multikulturalismus und des Wohls des Einzelnen in der Gesellschaft.
AWA 2020-06-26　Ich heiße Awa Seck und bin die Gründerin des Kopfschmuck-Labels Les Moussors de Awa.
LYDIA 2020-06-24　Mein Name ist Lydia Likibi. Ich komme aus dem Kongo und lebe seit 2011 im Senegal. Ich bin die Gründerin und Kreativdirektorin des Labels Lyds Design, das Handtaschen entwirft und in Afrika handfertigen lässt.
MANDEN 2020-06-21　Ich bin Mandé Mory Bah und 28 Jahre alt. Ich stamme aus Guinea und lebe seit mehr als zehn Jahren im Senegal, wo ich als User Experience Designer arbeite. Daneben betreibe ich ein kleines Unternehmen, das Second-Hand-Artikel sucht und anbietet, Donkafele.com.
ANNA 2020-06-21　Ich übersetze mit Google für mich und Emily, *oui? Merci trop,* Manden <3 Sag bitte Bescheid, wenn ich und Google danebenliegen!
THIBAUT 2020-06-26　Hi! Mein Name ist S. Thibaut Houssou. Ich bin 26 Jahre alt und komme aus Benin. Seit knapp elf Jahren lebe ich in Dakar, und ich studiere Medizin. Aus Rebellion gegen die gesellschaftlichen Diktate habe ich mich schon früh auch mit Dingen beschäftigt, die als unvereinbar mit meinem Studium gelten. So habe ich unter anderem ein experimentelles Modelabel ins Leben gerufen und bin einer der Gründer des kleinen Unternehmens Donkafele, das sich dem Vertrieb von Produkten zum Wohle von Gemeinschaft und Umwelt verschrieben hat.
ANNA 2020-07-12　Ich habe mit Nyamwathi gesprochen, und sie hat im Moment ziemlich viel zu tun, dennoch soll sie hier nicht übergangen werden: Sie hat Psychologie studiert, arbeitet als Yogalehrerin, Kinästhetik-Trainerin, Reiki-Lehrerin, Schamanin und Autorin. Nach mehreren Jahren in Dakar lebt sie aktuell wieder in ihrer Heimatstadt Nairobi.

Wie habt ihr die Fotos, die Anna von euch gemacht hat, für eure Arbeit genutzt? <Könntet ihr unten Screenshots von eurer Webseite oder aus den sozialen Medien anhängen? Ich würde sie gern sehen!>

Emily Watlington, with Anna Ehrenstein and Saliou Ba, Donkafele (Mandé Mory Bah and Thibaut Houssou), Nyamwathi Gichau, Lydia Likibi, and Awa Seck

In June 2020 I posed questions to the team behind *Tools for Conviviality* in a Google doc. The document became a digital space for us to commune despite travel restrictions and the coronavirus's quarantine imperatives, and across a range of geographies and time zones. We also relied on tools, and on one another, to translate our thoughts into various languages: the conversation included participants who are from or based in Senegal, Belgium, the United States, Germany, Albania, Benin, Kenya, Republic of Congo, the Gambia, and Guinea.

Collaborators, please introduce yourself in a couple of sentences!
SALIOU 2020-07-11　I am Mamadou Saliou Ba. I majored in American Studies and have a master's degree in English. I provide services in translation and interpretation besides my car dealership and hosting on Airbnb. I am open-minded and interested in all aspects of multiculturalism and the well-being of individuals in societies.
AWA 2020-06-26　My name is Awa Seck, and I am the creator of the head accessory brand Les Moussors de Awa.
LYDIA 2020-06-24　My name is Lydia Likibi. I'm from Congo, and I have lived in Senegal since 2011. I'm the founder and the creative director of Lyds Design, a brand specialized in the design and manufacturing of handbags that are handmade in Africa.
MANDEN 2020-06-21　I'm Mandé Mory Bah, twenty-eight years old. Originally from Guinea, I have lived for over ten years in Senegal, where I work as a user experience designer. In addition, I am responsible for a small company that finds and sells products from thrift stores: Donkafele.com.
ANNA 2020-06-21　I am translating with Google for me and Emily, *oui? Merci trop,* Manden <3 Let me know if there is something I and Google don't get right!
THIBAUT 2020-06-26　Hi! My name is S. Thibaut Houssou. I am twenty-six years old, and I am from Benin. I have been living in Dakar for almost eleven years now, and I'm studying medicine. Rebellious to the diktats of society, I started early to explore my interest in things deemed incompatible with my studies, among other things by creating an experimental clothing brand and then cofounding a small company, Donkafele, which specializes in the distribution of products with a significant community and environmental impact.
ANNA 2020-07-12　I spoke to Nyamwathi, and she's quite busy at the moment—but to not leave out her personal work here: she studied psychology, works as a yoga teacher, kinaesthetic and reiki therapist, shaman, and writer. She lived and worked in Dakar for a few years and is currently based in her hometown, Nairobi.

How did you guys use the photos that Anna took of you in your own work? <If you can paste screenshots from your website or social media below, I'd love to see them!>

LYDIA 2020-06-24   Wir haben die gemeinsam mit Anna entstandenen Fotos und Videos in den sozialen Medien gepostet. Hier sind die Links:
https://www.instagram.com/lydsdesign/
https://www.instagram.com/lydsdesign/channel/

MANDEN 2020-06-21   Zum einen haben wir einen Artikel über Annas Werk übernommen, der ursprünglich auf der Webseite von Unseen Platform [Emily: eine Amsterdamer Foto-Messe] erschienen ist, haben ihn ins Französische übersetzt und für unser französischsprachiges Publikum auf unseren Blog Donkafele.com/papers gestellt. Darüber hinaus haben wir gemeinsam mit Anna ihre Arbeiten in mobile Arbeiten verwandelt und T-Shirts und Stofftaschen damit bedruckt.

ANNA 2020-06-26   Großartig, diese Idee der mobilen Arbeiten, Manden. Als ihr von Donkafele mir vorgeschlagen habt, Stofftaschen, Aufnäher und Shirts zu bedrucken, war mir die Parallele gar nicht richtig klar – bis du eben von „mobil" sprachst. In Dakar gibt es so viele mobile Straßenhändler, die mit ihren Waren durch die Stadt ziehen. Diese Verbindung von Eroberung des Stadtraums, Fernweh und Poesie – tolle Vorstellung, dass durch die Shirts auch die Kunst auf diese Weise verbreitet wird!

SALIOU 2020-07-11   Ich habe Anna zum ersten Mal bei mir zu Hause getroffen. Ich biete meine Unterkunft auf Airbnb an, und sie hat bei mir gebucht. Sie hat mir erzählt, was sie macht, und einige wunderbare Fotos von meinem Loft geschossen. Die waren so großartig, dass ich sie statt meiner alten Airbnb-Bilder genommen habe. Hier sind ein paar davon!

In dem Video spürt man deutlich, dass ihr als Gruppe eine gute Zeit miteinander hattet. In einigen Szenen ist auch Anna zu sehen. In der Szene von der Modenschau übergibt ein Model die GoPro-Kamera an ein anderes, als sie auf dem Laufsteg aneinander vorbeilaufen. Könntet ihr den Prozess der Zusammenarbeit bei den Kunstwerken und dem Video schildern?

SALIOU 2020-07-11   Ich hatte die Gelegenheit, bei den Interviews auf dem Markt mit ihr zusammenzuarbeiten. Es war eine wunderbare Erfahrung. Ich habe auf Wolof gedolmetscht [Emily: die meistgesprochene Sprache im Senegal], und Anna war mit so viel Energie bei der Sache, dass ich gar nicht anders konnte, als voll konzentriert zu sein und dieselbe Energie einzubringen. Das war für mich einfach großartig, außerdem habe ich dabei auch noch die wahren Hintergründe des gambischen Stoffmarkts in Colobane erfahren.

THIBAUT 2020-06-26   Haha! Das stimmt. Wir hatten in der Tat eine gute Zeit. Bei der Arbeit mit Anna, oder auch einfach nur beim Kontakt mit ihr, ist immer so viel Herzlichkeit dabei.

Sie hat mir ihr Projekt vorgestellt, und dadurch habe ich Ivan Illichs Werk für mich entdeckt, insbesondere [Emily: Illichs Buch von 1973] *Tools for Conviviality*, eine Kritik der Industriegesellschaft mittels einer Analyse des Kapitalismus, die nicht von der Ausbeutung des Menschen durch den Menschen ausgeht, sondern von der Versklavung des Menschen durch „kontraproduktive Werkzeuge" unter dem Deckmantel des technischen Fortschritts. Mir wurde klar, dass Annas Ansatz, wenn auch auf abstrakte Weise, so etwas wie ein „Werkzeug der Konvivialität" darstellt: ein Werk-

LYDIA 2020-06-24   The photos and videos we made with Anna were posted on social media. Please find below the links:
https://www.instagram.com/lydsdesign/
https://www.instagram.com/lydsdesign/channel/

MANDEN 2020-06-21   First, we appropriated an article on Anna's work that was originally published on the Unseen Platform [Emily: a photography fair in Amsterdam] site by translating it into French and publishing it on our blog, Donkafele.com/papers, for our French-speaking public. Then, with Anna, we set out to make her works into ambulant works by printing them on T-shirts and tote bags.

ANNA 2020-06-26   I love that you use the idea of ambulant works, Manden. I did not fully grasp the parallels until you now said "ambulant"—when you from Donkafele suggested printing tote bags, patches, and shirts. There are so many ambulant vendors in Dakar who, together with the goods they decided to sell, stroll through the city. This combination of taking over urban space, wanderlust, and poetics—love to think of the shirts spreading art this way, too!

SALIOU 2020-07-11   The first time I met Anna was in my apartment. I am a host on Airbnb, and she booked with me. After explaining about what she was doing, she took some nice photos of my loft. They were so nice that I used them and changed the old ones on my Airbnb profile. Here are some of them!

There's a real sense in the video that the group of you is more or less hanging out. There are scenes in the video where we see Anna. In the fashion show scene, one model hands off the GoPro to another as they pass each other on the runway. Can you talk about the process of collaborating together on the artworks and video?

SALIOU 2020-07-11   I had the chance to work with her while she was interviewing people at the marketplace. It was a lovely experience. I was translating into Wolof [Emily: the most widely spoken language in Senegal] and Anna was putting a lot of energy in the work that I had no other choice than staying focused and putting back the same energy. That was the best experience for me, and I learned the real background of the Gambia textile market in Colobane.

THIBAUT 2020-06-26   Haha! This is true. We were really hanging out and having fun. Working with Anna, or merely interacting with her, is always a source of warmth.

When she introduced me to her project, I discovered Ivan Illich's work through [Emily: the 1973 book] *Tools for Conviviality*, a criticism of industrial society through an analysis of capitalism, not through the prism of the exploitation of man by man, but through the prism of the servitude of humans to "counterproductive tools" under the guise of technological progress. I found that Anna's approach, although abstract, resembled "a tool for conviviality": a tool that must not create inequality, which must strengthen the autonomy of each and increase the scope of each. The application of the teachings of the work that inspired her this project impressed me. It was for me a real proof of authenticity.

zeug, das keine Ungleichheit erschafft, das die Autonomie des*der Einzelnen stärkt und seinen*ihren Spielraum vergrößert. Es hat mich beeindruckt, wie sie sich bei dem Projekt von den Lehren des Buches hat inspirieren lassen und sie praktisch umgesetzt hat. Für mich war das ein echtes Zeichen der Authentizität.

Anna hatte eine vollkommen klare Vorstellung von dem, was sie von der Zusammenarbeit erwartete, und es war überhaupt kein Problem, ihr zu folgen, da wir ihre Ansichten teilen. Ihr war es wichtig, einen Arbeitsbereich zu erschaffen, in dem alle profitierten. Der erste Schritt war, unsere Interessen klar zu definieren, um zu sehen, wie sie sich zusammenbringen ließen. Alle Rollen wurden von allen übernommen, gleichzeitig waren wir uns bewusst, unter welchen Umständen und bei welcher Aufgabe wir in den Hintergrund treten und die*den andere*n machen lassen mussten.

Was zum Beispiel die Zusammenarbeit bei dem Video und den Fotos betraf, ging es uns von Donkafele darum, dass die Ergebnisse unseren Werten entsprachen. Der Prozess der Zusammenarbeit selbst glich einer strukturierten Improvisation. Bei mehreren Brainstorming-Sessions berieten wir über das Format der Produktion, ihre Ausrichtung und die Werkzeuge, die wir benötigen würden und die wir bei unseren gemeinsamen Streifzügen über die Märkte der Stadt sammelten. Auch die ideale, außerhalb der Stadt gelegene Film-Location haben wir gemeinsam gefunden, und dann haben wir mit den Models einen Ausflug dorthin gemacht, damit es sich wie bei einer „Clique von Freund*innen" anfühlte. Ein perfektes Beispiel für die Improvisation beim Filmen ist die Szene, in der die Models die GoPro-Kamera untereinander weitergeben.

ANNA 2020-07-12 Improvisation war in der Tat ein zentrales Element des Shooting-Prozesses in Dakar. Für mich persönlich war es am allerwichtigsten, nicht mit konkreten Plänen und Ideen an die Sache heranzugehen, sondern sie vor Ort gemeinsam mit allen Beteiligten zu entwickeln. Am Anfang des Projekts stand für mich, dass ich wegen verschiedener Dinge wütend war. Ich hatte genug davon, dass die westlichen Medien die Migration immer so darstellten, als gebe es nur eine Richtung. Immer nur nach Norden und Westen. Als ob es nur in den imperialistischen Zentren der NATO-Staaten multikulturelle Räume gäbe. Gleichzeitig war meine Hoffnung, dass ich durch eine prozessbasierte Arbeitsweise im Austausch mit Kulturproduzent*innen aus Dakar diese Themen in einer fröhlichen Form angehen könnte, voller positiver und konstruktiver Energie. Knapp 90 Prozent des Migrationsgeschehens in Afrika findet innerhalb des Kontinents statt. In Dakar kann man ohne Visum arbeiten. Die Stadt ist dank ihres kulturellen Reichtums ein bedeutendes kreatives Mekka. Und dann war es absolut verrückt für mich, dass ich – durch die Lektüre Paul Gilroys [Emily: ein Historiker, der zu Rassismus und Ethnizität arbeitet] – auf Illichs 50 Jahre alte Kritik an Werkzeugen gestoßen bin und wie sich seither alles noch zugespitzt hat. Die Digitalkonzerne wollen uns weismachen, es wäre der Preis für das Leben in einem digitalen Zeitalter, dass man unsere Daten sammelt und unser Verhalten verändert. Das Outsourcen unserer Entscheidungen an Algorithmen stärkt Unterdrückungssysteme wie ethnische Zugehörigkeit, Klasse und Gender und verschärft das Tempo und

Anna had a very clear vision of what she was expecting from this collaboration, and it wasn't hard to follow her since we fully shared it. It was meaningful for her to create a mutually beneficial workspace. The first step was to transparently define our interests, then to decide how to converge them. We shared the roles, while knowing under what circumstances and for what task we had to step back and give the keys.

Regarding our video-photographic collaboration, for example, our interest in Donkafele was to support a content creation in line with its values. The overall collaborative process was structured improvisation. We held brainstorming sessions several times on the format of the production, its direction, and the tools that we would need and had collected together by crisscrossing the markets of the city. Together we also found, for example, the ideal place for filming, outside the city, and we took a road trip with the models to get there in a "group of friends" atmosphere. As for the scene of the models who are giving the GoPro to each other, this is a perfect example of improvisation during filming.

ANNA 2020-07-12 It's true, improvisation was a central element of the shooting process in Dakar. And for me, it was even more important to not have concrete plans and ideas from the beginning, but to develop them on site together with everybody involved. You know, from my side the project started with multiple moments of fury. Being sick of Western media depicting migration as unipolar. Merely toward the north and west. As if only imperialist centers in the NATO states had multicultural spaces. At the same time I was hoping that working in a process-based way and in conversation with cultural producers in Dakar could support a joyous approach to speaking about these issues through positive and constructive energies. Almost ninety percent of migration on the African continent is within. You can work without a visa in Dakar. Its cultural richness makes it an important creative mecca. At the same time it was absolutely nuts for me, through reading [Emily: the historian and critical race theorist] Paul Gilroy, to come across Illich's fifty-year-old critique of tools and how things have escalated since then. Tech bros are trying to tell us that collecting our data and modifying our behavior is the price we pay for living in the digital age. Outsourcing our decision-making into algorithms reinforces systems of oppression like race, class, and gender, escalating the pace and density in which the global is structured through these systems. What happens when photographic technologies like 360-degree video or virtual reality become consumer technologies? Because Albanians have been historically racialized and rendered as peripheral or Middle Eastern savages and their suffering is currently sustained by the EU and the Othering of Muslim communities I cannot personally identify with whiteness. Still, we have the privilege of proximity to whiteness and power. Let's keep it real—in the West African context I am snow-white, "Caucasian." It was clear to me that I could only do a project in Dakar through conversation. How can we overcome divisions while acknowledging our differences? An attempt to challenge the power hierarchies that usually make documentary practices and build the foundation of so many "collaborative" contemporary art projects by people living in Europe, but

die Massivität, mit denen diese Systeme die Welt strukturieren. Was geschieht, wenn Fototechniken wie 360-Grad-Videos oder Virtual Reality zu Heimtechnologien werden? Aufgrund der historischen Rassifizierung der Albaner*innen, die bis heute als randständig oder als Balkan-Wilde dargestellt werden und deren Leid gegenwärtig durch die EU und das Othering muslimischer Gemeinschaften aufrechterhalten wird, kann ich mich nicht mit dem Weißsein identifizieren. Dennoch sind wir durch unsere Nähe zum Weißsein und zur Macht privilegiert. Seien wir ehrlich: In Westafrika bin ich schneeweiß, eine „Kaukasierin". Mir war klar, wenn ich in Dakar ein Projekt mache, dann geht das nur im Gespräch. Wie können wir das Trennende überwinden und zugleich unsere Unterschiede anerkennen? Es ging mir darum, die Machthierarchien infrage zu stellen, die üblicherweise in dokumentarischen Praktiken bestehen und die vielen zeitgenössischen „kollaborativen" Kunstprojekten zugrunde liegen, wenn die Leute in Europa leben und auf dem afrikanischen Kontinent arbeiten. Viele Projekte kritisieren Strukturen, die sie durch ihre Arbeitsweise letztlich noch verstärken.

In dem brutalen Kontext einer auf Extraktivismus, *weißer* Vorherrschaft und Kapitalbesitz basierenden Weltordnung und vor dem Hintergrund des kolonialen französischen Vermächtnisses, in dem Westafrika und seine jungen Kreativen gefangen sind, wollte ich derartige missbräuchliche Machtstrukturen des künstlerischen Schaffens unbedingt aufbrechen. Ich nahm Kontakt mit einigen Menschen auf, auf deren großartige Arbeit ich im Internet oder durch Mails gestoßen war. Wie gesagt war es mir wichtig, nicht mit einem festgelegten Konzept zu beginnen, sondern mich mit meinen Partner*innen zu treffen und mir ihre Ideen anzuhören, einzelne Teile gemeinsam zu entwickeln und herauszufinden, wie ich mit meiner Arbeit ihre jeweiligen Projekte unterstützen konnte. Alle Beteiligten verfolgen in ihrer Arbeit einen soziopolitischen Wandel und nutzen dafür auf höchst unterschiedliche Weise Werkzeuge, Kreativität, Lehre und Unternehmertum. Ich bin ihr größter Fan! Unsere Arbeitsfelder sind ebenso unterschiedlich wie unsere Hintergründe, und ich spreche noch nicht einmal Französisch. Da jede*r Migrant*in ist, bestehen Asymmetrien, Barrieren und Möglichkeiten zwischen uns allen. Obwohl unsere Unterschiede nicht verborgen werden, geht es bei dem Projekt nicht um die Beziehung zwischen Europa und Afrika. Der Fokus liegt auf Theorien zu Konvivialität und Technologie, den Ideen des Teams und ihrer kreativen Arbeit.

Die ersten Jahre als freie*r Künstler*in lebt man in prekären Verhältnissen, wenn man nicht gerade aus einem reichen Haus kommt, und das geht nur, wenn man in imperialistischen Ländern arbeitet. Für dieses Projekt hatte ich ein lächerliches Budget. Aber auch bei einem zwanzigmal höheren Budget ist es immer einfacher, sein Umfeld auszunutzen, um ein noch spektakuläreres Projekt umzusetzen. Und meine bewusst gewählte prekäre Situation ist an sich schon ein Riesenprivileg. Manche Leute jammern, dass sie so viele Formulare ausfüllen müssen, um ein Kunststipendium zu bekommen, dabei haben andere noch nicht mal sauberes Wasser. Es ist eine zweischneidige Sache: Wenn man mehr Macht erlangt, kann man auch mehr Macht teilen. Es ist ein ständiges Austarieren von Zugangsmöglichkeiten und Barrieren. Die Arbeit im Kunstkontext basiert stark auf

working on the African continent. Many projects critique structures that they actually reinforce by the way they work.

In the harsh context of a world order based on extractivism, white supremacy, and capital and situated in the dependent French colonial legacy in which West Africa and its young creatives are trapped—these abusive power structures of art production were something I really wanted to disrupt. I contacted a few people whose amazing work I saw online through social media or e-mail. As I said, it was important to not have a fixed concept from the beginning, but to just meet and listen to the ideas of the collaborators, develop parts together, and see how my work can also serve their personal projects. Everyone involved is engaged in enacting sociopolitical change in their personal work through a very diverse usage of tools, creativity, teaching, and entrepreneurship. I'm their biggest fangirl! We all come from multifaceted fields and backgrounds, and I don't even speak French. Since everyone is a migrant, asymmetries, barriers, and possibilities exist between all of us. Though not hiding our differences, the project is not about Europe-Africa relations. The focus is on theories of conviviality and technology, the team's ideas, and their creative work.

The first years of working as a visual artist are very precarious if you don't come from generational wealth and only possible when working in imperialist nations. I had a ridiculous budget for the project. Even if your budget is twenty times larger, it is much easier to exploit your surroundings to do an even more spectacular project. And my chosen precarity is in itself a massive privilege. Some people cry about having to fill out too many documents in the hope of getting arts funding, yet others don't have access to clean water. The duality is that generating power also means having more power to share. A constant navigation of access and barriers. Work within the arts is so based on hierarchies and heroes that trying to work fair in my young position leads to a balancing act, and everything is always far from perfect. With barriers of . . . living on this planet LOL . . . space, language, time, money, and while trying to be aware of how we are situated—it was central to prioritize having a good time together!! Instead of trying to hide the barriers make them visible within the work.

As for Nyamwathi, she and I haven't been in the same physical space yet—so she sent me to her favorite self-love places in Dakar, and it was magic. Saliou showed me the best *thiéboudienne* [Emily: Senegal's national dish: fish, rice, and tomato sauce] spot in Medina. The Donkafele team constantly reinvents our collaboration, celebrates life with me on FaceTime or by dancing on top of rental cars, Lydia introduced me to amazing young femmes in the city, and Awa and I had the best time when she worked in Berlin. I learned and unlearned loads while working with the team and had mad fun.

So you guys met during the Dakar Biennial. What's it like having this big art event in your city?
<u>*SALIOU 2020-07-11*</u> She came to my place during the Biennial, but it doesn't mean a lot to me if it is held in my city or not. I am sorry—I don't pay close attention to the Biennial.

Hierarchien und Heldenfiguren, und der Versuch, in meiner Position als junger Künstlerin fair zu arbeiten, ist ein Balanceakt und alles ist ständig alles andere als perfekt. Mit den Barrieren von … auf diesem Planeten zu leben LOL … Raum, Sprache, Zeit, Geld und in Hinblick auf unsere jeweiligen Umstände, die ich im Auge zu behalten versuchte, war es für mich das Wichtigste, dass wir eine gute Zeit zusammen hatten!! Anstatt die Barrieren verbergen zu wollen, sie in der Arbeit sichtbar zu machen. Was Nyamwathi betrifft, so konnten sie und ich noch nicht an einem Ort sein, also hat sie mich zu ihren Lieblingsorten in Dakar geschickt, und das war magisch. Saliou hat mir in Medina den besten Ort für *thiéboudienne* [Emily: Senegals Nationalgericht aus Fisch, Reis und Tomatensauce] gezeigt. Das Team von Donkafele erfindet unsere Zusammenarbeit ständig neu und feiert mit mir auf FaceTime oder tanzend auf Mietwagen das Leben, Lydia hat mir unglaubliche junge Frauen der Stadt vorgestellt, und Awa und ich hatten eine großartige Zeit, als sie in Berlin gearbeitet hat. Ich habe in der Arbeit mit dem Team unglaublich viel gelernt und verlernt, und ich hatte einen Höllenspaß.

Ihr habt euch ja bei der Dakar-Biennale kennengelernt. Wie ist es, ein solch großes Kunstevent in der Stadt zu haben?

SALIOU 2020-07-11 Sie hat während der Biennale bei mir gewohnt, aber mir ist es eher gleichgültig, ob die in meiner Stadt stattfindet oder nicht. Tut mir leid, aber ich schere mich nicht wirklich um die Biennale.

LYDIA 2020-06-24 Anna und ich haben uns vor zwei Jahren kennengelernt, als sie das erste Mal bei der Biennale war. Wir haben viele intensive Momente miteinander verbracht und über unsere Träume und unser Leben als Selbstständige gesprochen. Als sie 2019 das nächste Mal gekommen ist, war uns klar, dass wir noch mehr wundervolle Momente erleben wollen, indem wir in Dakars Straßen Fotoshootings durchführen. Die Biennale ist eine wunderbare Plattform für das lokale kreative Schaffen. Menschen aus unzähligen Ländern kommen hierher, um unsere wunderbaren Künstler* innen zu sehen.

THIBAUT 2020-06-26 Ich habe Anna vor zwei Jahren kennengelernt, als sie zur Biennale nach Dakar kam. Sie hatte mich in den sozialen Netzwerken wegen ihres Fotoprojekts kontaktiert. Wir haben uns sofort super verstanden und uns direkt über viele verschiedene Themen unterhalten (Unternehmertum, Geopolitik und internationale Beziehungen, Mode, Kunst und so weiter), uns über unseren Hintergrund ausgetauscht, über persönliche Erfahrungen, Meinungen und Analysen. Ich sehe diese geistige Offenheit als wesentlich für jede*n Künstler*in an. Durch Künstler*innen kann man sich wie von sonst niemandem einen unvoreingenommenen Blick auf die Welt erhoffen. Insofern ist dieses internationale Event, eines der bedeutendsten Schaufenster der zeitgenössischen afrikanischen Kunst, ausgesprochen positiv für die Emanzipation und Anerkennung des Kontinents. Ich bin dankbar, dass wir uns durch die Biennale kennengelernt haben … das war und ist äußerst bereichernd.

ANNA 2020-06-26 @Thibaut und Saliou. Es ist verrückt, aber ich verstehe euch beide. Ich muss sagen, Thibauts Vertrauen erstaunt und fasziniert mich auch ein wenig, gleichzeitig denke ich, dass man sich über

LYDIA 2020-06-24 Anna and I met two years ago when she came to Dakar for the first time for the Biennial. We spent a lot of quality time together, talking about our dreams and entrepreneur life. When she came again in 2019, we decided to create more fabulous moments by doing photo shoots in the streets of Dakar. The Biennial is such a great platform for local creativity. People come from so many countries to see our talented artists.

THIBAUT 2020-06-26 I met Anna two years ago when she came to Dakar for the Biennial. She had contacted me on social networks about her photographic project. We immediately hit it off and, even at that time, we were talking about various and varied subjects (entrepreneurship, geopolitics and international relations, fashion, art, . . .), sharing things about our background, personal experiences, opinions, and analyses. I think that open-mindedness is essential for an artist. That makes the artist an ideal person with whom we can hope to find the least biased view of the world. This is why having this international event, one of the main expressions of contemporary African art, is something very positive for the emancipation and the affirmation of the continent. I feel grateful that the Biennial allowed us to meet . . . it was very rewarding.

ANNA 2020-06-26 @Thibaut and Saliou. It's crazy, but I feel you both. I am actually surprised and a little mesmerized by Thibout's faith, and simultaneously it feels important to recognize the many good reasons why the world of biennials looks so dull and dry.

The Western / European art canon has constructed an elitist and Eurocentric narration of modernity and the arts. It makes it very difficult for many people to relate to something so elitist and whitewashed. The myth of the Western art canon ignores actual history and reciprocity. How things have been inspired and literally been stolen from cultures outside of the West. Even in many "progressive" art circles colonialism, for example, is always depicted as something of the past. Always someone else's fault. People act as if culture is something coming outright from the West to other places. One way. This is not true. That is not the way things circulate and culture disseminates. My people suffer similarly from systems of state-enforced racialization in Albania, but living in Berlin I profit from an imperialist, Western environment. Way too many people in Berlin who see themselves as liberal, leftist, or critical think that West Africans just do what people in New York do on the Gram. Culture as "imported magic." Many have never been on the African continent and do not actually listen to what people from the continent say. They do not understand that all along music, visual arts, or fashion from West Africa have been a central influence on what we perceive as "Western or Digital Aesthetics." For example, West Africans migrate to the UK. They make Grime music. Canadian rapper Drake steals Grime. British-Ghanaian Grime legend Stormzy says thanks; he sees the power of amplifying culture. The neocolonial mind thinks Insta aesthetics are "imported" to West Africa. They are not—they circulate and are informed by West African culture.

What is one unexpected tool you guys are using for conviviality—for joy and for living together?

die vielen Gründe klar sein sollte, aus denen die Welt der Biennalen so langweilig und verstaubt wirkt. Der westliche / europäische Kunstkanon hat eine elitäre und eurozentrische Erzählung der Moderne und der Künste konstruiert. Manche Menschen können sich mit etwas derart Elitärem und Weißgewaschenem nur sehr schwer identifizieren. Der Mythos des westlichen Kunstkanons ignoriert die tatsächliche Geschichte und die stattgefundenen Wechselwirkungen. Dass manche Dinge von Kulturen jenseits des Westens inspiriert oder sogar im wahrsten Sinne des Wortes gestohlen wurden. Selbst in manchen „progressiven" Kunstkreisen wird beispielsweise der Kolonialismus stets als eine Sache der Vergangenheit dargestellt. Es ist immer die Schuld von jemand anderem. Die Menschen tun so, als würde die Kultur ausschließlich vom Westen aus an andere Orte gelangen. Eine Einbahnstraße. Das stimmt nicht. Das entspricht nicht der Art und Weise, wie die Dinge zirkulieren und die Kultur sich ausbreitet. Mein Volk in Albanien leidet auf vergleichbare Weise unter Systemen der staatlich durchgesetzten Rassifizierung, doch da ich in Berlin lebe, profitiere ich von einem imperialistischen westlichen Umfeld. Viel zu viele Menschen in Berlin, die sich als liberal, links oder kritisch verstehen, denken, dass die Westafrikaner*innen auf Instagram einfach dasselbe machen wie die Menschen in New York. Kultur als „importierte Magie". Viele von ihnen waren noch nie auf dem afrikanischen Kontinent und hören nicht wirklich zu, was die Menschen auf dem Kontinent sagen. Sie begreifen nicht, dass Musik, Kunst und Mode aus Westafrika schon immer einen entscheidenden Einfluss hatten auf das, was wir als „westliche oder digitale Ästhetik" ansehen. So sind beispielsweise Westafrikaner*innen nach Großbritannien migriert und machen Grime-Musik. Der kanadische Rapper Drake klaut Grime. Und die britisch-ghanaische Grime-Legende Stormzy sagt Danke: Er sieht das Potenzial, die Kultur zu erweitern. Der neokoloniale Geist denkt, dass die Insta-Ästhetik nach Westafrika „importiert" würde. Das stimmt nicht – sie zirkuliert und wird von der westafrikanischen Kultur geprägt.

Was ist ein überraschendes Werkzeug, das ihr für Konvivialität nutzt – für Lebensfreude und Zusammensein?

SALIOU 2020-07-11   Mein Verständnis von Konvivialität ist vom Islam beeinflusst. Und wenn ich ein Werkzeug benennen soll, dann sind das die moralischen Lehren der Religion, die ich als Erwachsener umzusetzen begonnen habe. Zum Beispiel ist es meine größte Freude und mein größtes Glück, anderen zu helfen und sie glücklich zu sehen, insbesondere arme Menschen.

LYDIA 2020-07-11   Mein Showroom zu Hause. Ich liebe es, dort Menschen zu empfangen und zusammen *bissap* [Emily: Hibiskusblütengetränk] zu trinken, während wir darüber diskutieren, wie die Welt verändert werden kann ahhhh.

ANNA 2020-06-26   OMG @lydia, ich kann nicht glauben, wie lange ich schon kein *bissap* getrunken habe! Und danke für die Links, ich werde auch einen Screenshot posten.

MANDEN 2020-06-27   Mein Fahrrad (hahahaha)!!! Ja, mein Fahrrad! Das erstaunt meine Kolleg*innen am meisten, wenn ich zur Arbeit komme. In

SALIOU 2020-07-11   My sense of conviviality is influenced by the Muslim religion. And if I were to choose a tool, it would be just the moral teaching I learned from religion and started practicing in adult life. For instance, my greatest joy and happiness is helping others or seeing them happy, especially poor people.

LYDIA 2020-07-11   My at-home showroom. I love to receive people there and have a *bissap* [Emily: hibiscus flower drink] together while we are talking how to change the world ahhhh.

ANNA 2020-06-26   OMG @lydia I can't believe I haven't had a *bissap* in such a long time! And thanks for the links, I will also post a screenshot.

MANDEN 2020-06-27   My bike (hahahaha)!!! Yes, my bike! This is the thing that my colleagues least expect when I get to work. Dakar is a city where roads are difficult to cycle, so they are surprised to see me so carefree and let off steam with this machine in the streets when they are in their car. It must be said that cycling is often very practical.

THIBAUT 2020-06-26   I will answer as Manden, and it is not surprising haha. We use the bicycle in everyday life, so it is not surprising that we made it the delivery method of the Donkafele company.

ANNA 2020-06-25   @Emily, screens from photos I took with Lydia on her channels:

ANNA 2020-06-26   Haha, REALLY forgot about this photo of me with the bag you gave me as a present when we met the first time @lydia. It's in front of my old building in Berlin :) Also I love the first photo from the shoot we did at the Marché Tilène [Emily: a fabric market], I remember it was so much fun even though it was Ramadan—your muse and model was fasting properly in the heat, and I had to fly back the same evening!

Dakar sind die Straßen nicht besonders fahrradfreundlich, darum überrascht es sie, wie unbekümmert ich bin und dass ich mich in den Straßen abstrampele, während sie in ihrem Auto sitzen. Aber ich muss sagen, dass Fahrradfahren oft sehr praktisch ist.

THIBAUT 2020-06-26   Ich antworte wie Manden, und das ist nicht überraschend, haha. Wir nutzen das Fahrrad im Alltag, daher dürfte es nicht erstaunen, dass wir es auch bei unserer Firma Donkafele als Liefermethode gewählt haben.

ANNA 2020-06-25   @Emily, Screenshots von Lydias Kanälen mit Fotos, die wir zusammen gemacht haben:

ANNA 2020-06-26   Haha, @lydia, dieses Bild von mir mit der Tasche, die du mir geschenkt hast, als wir uns kennengelernt haben, hatte ich ABSOLUT vergessen. Das ist vor meinem früheren Haus in Berlin :) Ich liebe auch das erste Foto von unserem Shooting auf dem Marché Tilène [Emily: ein Stoffmarkt], ich weiß noch, wie viel Spaß wir hatten, auch wenn Ramadan war – deine Muse und Model hat ganz brav in der Hitze gefastet, und ich musste noch an dem Abend zurückfliegen!

Anna Ehrenstein (ALB/GER) erforscht den Austausch von Mensch und Objekt im digitalen Zeitalter. Sie hat Fotografie und Medienkunst an der Fachhochschule Dortmund studiert sowie ein Postgraduiertenprogramm für Medienkunst an der Kunsthochschule für Medien bei Mischa Kuball und Julia Scher durchlaufen. Ihre Arbeiten waren in internationalen Gruppenausstellungen zu sehen wie u. a. dem Format _Situations_ des Fotomuseum Winterthur, (2019) dem Fotofestival Les Recontres d'Arles (2018) und der Triennale für Fotografie in Hamburg (2018). Ehrenstein war u. a. für den Prix Pictet, den NRW.BANK Kunstpreis und das Karl Schmidt-Rottluff-Stipendium nominiert. 2020 erhielt sie ein DAAD Stipendium für ein Rechercheprojekt in Bogota, Kolumbien. Anna Ehrenstein lebt und arbeitet in Berlin, Köln und Tirana.

Tools for Conviviality entstand in Zusammenarbeit mit dem Übersetzer **Saliou Ba** (GIN/SEN), dem Modekollektiv „Donkafele", bestehend aus **Mandé Mory Bah** (GIN/SEN) und **Thibaut Houssou** (BEN/SEN), der Yogalehrerin **Nyamwathi Gichau** (KEN/SEN), der Taschendesignerin **Lydia Likibi** (COD/SEN) und der Kopfschmuckdesignerin **Awa Seck** (SEN/BEL).

Emily Watlington (USA) setzt sich mit aktueller Medienkunst und feministischer Ethik auseinander. Sie hat einen Abschluss in Kunstgeschichte (BFA) und einen Master of Science in Architecture Studies (SMArchS) im Programm History, Theory, and Critcism of Architecture and Art (HTC) am Massachusetts College of Art and Design absolviert. Watlington war 2018/2019 mit einem Fulbright Fellowship für Journalismus in Berlin und arbeitet derzeit als Assistant Editor bei der _Art in America._ Ihre Texte erschienen in Ausstellungskatalogen, Sammelbänden, Magazinen und Zeitschriften, u. a. in _Art in America, Hyperallergic, Haunt Journal of Art, Frieze, Another Gaze, Mousse, Art Review_ und im _Spike Art Magazine._ Emily Watlington lebt und arbeitet in New York.

Anna Ehrenstein (ALB/GER) explores the exchange between human and object in the digital age. She studied photography and media art at the University of Applied Sciences and Arts Dortmund and completed a postgraduate program in media art at the Academy of Media Arts with Mischa Kuball and Julia Scher. Her work has been shown in international group exhibitions including _Situations_ at Fotomuseum Winterthur (2019), the photo festival Les Recontres d'Arles (2018), and the Triennial of Photography in Hamburg (2018). C/O Berlin will present her first institutional solo exhibition. Ehrenstein has been nominated for grants including the Prix Pictet, the NRW:BANK Kunstpreis, and the Karl Schmidt-Rottluff Stipendium. In 2020 she received a DAAD grant for a research project in Bogota, Colombia. Anna Ehrenstein lives and works in Berlin, Cologne, and Tirana.

Tools for Conviviality was developed in collaboration with the translator **Saliou Ba** (GIN/SEN), the fashion duo "Donkafele," consisting of **Mandé Mory Bah** (GIN/SEN) and **Thibaut Houssou** (BEN/SEN), the yoga teacher **Nyamwathi Gichau** (KEN/SEN), the bag designer **Lydia Likibi** (COD/SEN), and the headwrap designer **Awa Seck** (SEN/BEL).

Emily Watlington (USA) writes about contemporary media art and feminist ethics. She holds a bachelor's degree in art history (BFA) and a master of science in architecture studies (SMArchS) in the History, Theory, and Criticism of Architecture and Art (HTC) program at the Massachusetts College of Art and Design. Watlington spent 2018–19 in Berlin as the holder of a Fulbright Fellowship for journalism and is currently working as an assistant editor at _Art in America._ Her essays have been published in exhibition catalogs, anthologies, magazines, and journals including _Art in America, Hyperallergic, Haunt Journal of Art, Frieze, Another Gaze, Mousse, Art Review,_ and _Spike Art Magazine._ Emily Watlington lives and works in New York.

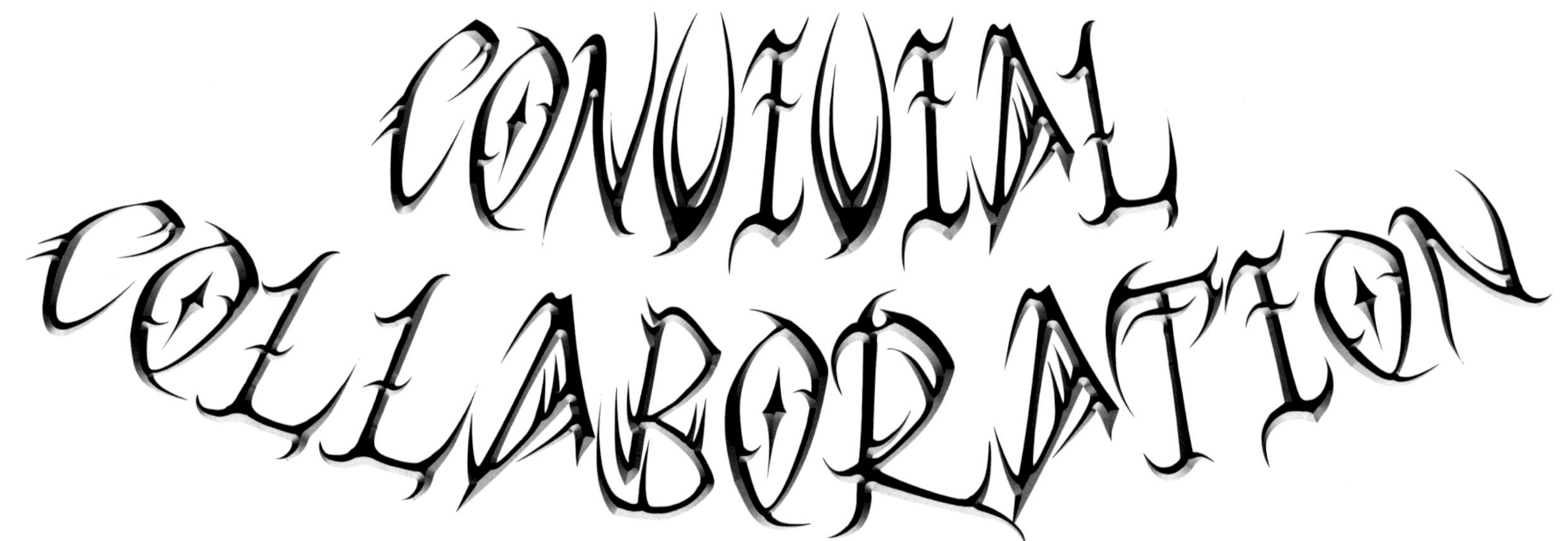

EMILY WATLINGTON

„Ich glaube nicht, dass man jemand anderen als sich selbst wahrhaft repräsentieren kann", sagte mir Anna Ehrenstein bei einem virtuellen Atelierbesuch mitten in der Pandemie.[1] Gleichwohl erfordert das von ihr gewählte Medium, die Fotografie, stets die Auseinandersetzung mit dem Verhältnis vom Ich zum Anderen und der damit einhergehenden Machtdynamik. Mit ihrer oftmals in Installationsform präsentierten künstlerischen Arbeit, an deren Beginn gleichwohl in der Regel eine Kamera steht, widmet sich die in Köln, Berlin und Tirana lebende und arbeitende Ehrenstein (*1993) der Dekolonisierung. Mit der Arbeit an *Tools for Conviviality* begann sie 2018, als sie die Dakar-Biennale im Senegal besuchte. Dort lernte sie über Internet-Plattformen wie Instagram und Airbnb einige Menschen kennen, mit denen sie in der Folge zusammenarbeitete: Saliou Ba, Nyamwathi Gichau, Lydia Likibi, Awa Seck und das Mode-Kollektiv Donkafele. Sie erkundigte sich bei ihnen, wie sie ihr Projektbudget und ihre Kamera als Werkzeuge einsetzen könne, so dass sie Spaß hätten und ihr jeweiliges Business gefördert werde. Sie selbst beschrieb ihr Projekt als „eine Sammlung visueller Ephemera zum Gebrauch von Werkzeugen für verschiedene Formen des menschlichen Zusammenseins"[2].

Ehrenstein suchte ausdrücklich nicht nach einer bestimmten Art von Bildern mit dem Projekt, an dessen Ende eine Reihe von Fotografien und Installationen sowie ein 360-Grad-Video standen. „Bei Auftrags-Fotoreportagen", erklärte sie mir, „hat man immer den Druck, etwas vorher Festgelegtes zu fotografieren; sonst killt die Zeitschrift deine Arbeit."[3] Die entsprechenden Konventionen lernte sie in ihrem Fotografie-Studium in Dortmund, bevor sie in Köln einen Masterabschluss in Medienkunst erwarb. Für ihr Projekt entwickelte sie eine neue Form dekolonialer Zusammenarbeit. *Tools for Conviviality* begegnet mit Skepsis der langen Tradition eines fotografischen Engagements, in dem die vermeintlich furchtbaren Lebensumstände der Marginalisierten vorgeführt wurden und werden. Allzu häufig wurde die Fotografie in ihrer Geschichte als ein Instrument des Otherings genutzt, insbesondere hinsichtlich ethnischer Zugehörigkeit, Gender, Kultur und Behinderung.

Die Fotografien von *Tools for Conviviality* umfassen Porträts der Projektpartner*innen sowie stilllebenartige Bilder. Für die Porträts posierten die Partner*innen vor dem Hintergrund eines kristallblauen Swimmingpools. Die mediale Berichterstattung über den Senegal ist geprägt von Darstellungen der Armut im Land oder seinem Image als tropisches Paradies. Nur selten bekommen die Menschen im Westen Bilder einer Realität zwischen diesen beiden Polen zu sehen. Ehrensteins Interesse an Dakar wurde geweckt, als sie für die 10. Berlin Biennale arbeitete und erfuhr, dass eine der Kurator*innen, Nomaduma Rosa Masilela, an einer Dissertation zu Dakars Performanceszene der 1980er-Jahre saß. Mit den poolartigen Hintergründen ihrer Porträts hebt Ehrenstein hervor, dass ihre Bilder – wie alle Bilder – Konstruktionen sind, keine objektiven Porträts. Ihre Koproduzent*innen – die teils aus dem Schmelztiegel Dakar stammen, teils aus Gambia, Guinea, der Republik Kongo, Kenia oder Benin dorthin kamen – sind ausnahmslos gut gekleidet. Ehrensteins Bilder rücken den Glamour der Modelle in den Mittelpunkt und erinnern damit in gewissem Maße an

"I don't think that it's ever possible to truly represent anyone other than yourself," Anna Ehrenstein told me in a mid-pandemic virtual studio visit.[1] Yet her chosen medium, photography, always necessitates negotiating the question of self versus other, which always involves a power dynamic. With her work, which usually begins with a camera, though is often shown in the form of installations, Ehrenstein (b. 1993)—who lives and works between Berlin, Cologne, and Tirana—is committed to decolonization. She began *Tools for Conviviality* in 2018, while visiting the Dakar Biennial in Senegal. There, she met collaborators—Saliou Ba, Nyamwathi Gichau, Lydia Likibi, Awa Seck, and the fashion duo Donkafele—online, via platforms including Instagram and Airbnb. She asked them how she might use her project budget and her camera as tools for having fun together and promoting their businesses, framing the project as "a collection of visual ephemera about the usage of tools for various modes of human togetherness."[2] Ehrenstein was decidedly not looking to capture a specific kind of image with the project, which resulted in a series of photographs and installations, as well as a 360-degree video. "With photojournalism assignments," she told me, "there's all this pressure to capture a predetermined thing; otherwise, the magazine kills your work."[3] She learned these conventions while studying photography in Dortmund. She later completed a master's in media art in Cologne and has devoted her project to creating a new method for decolonial collaboration. *Tools for Conviviality* expresses skepticism toward photography's long history of framing photographic activism as the process of exposing the supposedly horrid realities of the marginalized. Throughout its history, photography has often been used as a tool to otherize, especially across lines of race, gender, culture, and disability.

The photographs in *Tools for Conviviality* include both portraits of collaborators and images that more closely resemble still lifes. In the portraits, collaborators pose in front an image of a crystal-blue swimming pool's surface. Representations of Senegal in mass media typically emphasize either the nation's poverty or its reputation as a tropical paradise. Rarely do Westerners see images that show something in between. Ehrenstein first became interested in Dakar while working for the 10th Berlin Biennale: Nomaduma Rosa Masilela, one of the curators of that edition, was, at the time, working on a dissertation about the city's performance art scene in the 1980s. Ehrenstein's pool-like backgrounds emphasize the fact that these images—and all images—are constructed, rather than an objective portrayal. All of the collaborators—who are from or came to the melting pot of Dakar from the Gambia, Guinea, Republic of the Congo, Kenya, and Benin—are well-dressed. To a degree, Ehrenstein's images resemble fashion photography, in that they highlight the subjects' glamour. In fact, one of Ehrenstein's collaborators is Donkafele, a fashion collective that sells and upcycles clothes, then delivers them throughout Dakar via bicycle. Likewise, Lydia Likibi designs handbags among other things: both used photographs that Ehrenstein took of their designs to promote their work. When displayed in galleries, Ehrenstein often prints her photographs on large, flexible material, then drapes them over wardrobe racks, further emphasizing their relationship to fashion.

Modefotografien. Dazu passend gehört zu Ehrensteins Partner*innen das Modekollektiv Donkafele, das Kleidungsstücke upcycled, verkauft und in Dakar mit dem Fahrrad ausliefert. Auch Lydia Likibi ist als Designerin unter anderem für Taschen tätig, und wie Donkafele nutzte sie Ehrensteins Aufnahmen von ihren Entwürfen, um für sich zu werben. Ehrenstein streicht den Bezug ihrer Fotografien zur Mode noch heraus, indem sie manche auf große, flexible Materialien druckt und in Ausstellungen an Garderobenständern befestigt.

Wie Ehrenstein aus den Beteiligten Koproduzent*innen machte, statt sie einfach als Modelle zu betrachten, wird noch zu klären sein. Doch zunächst möchte ich mich der Schwarzen Lebensfreude widmen, die die Porträts von *Tools for Conviviality* ausstrahlen. In der Tradition zeitgenössischer Schwarzer Fotograf*innen wie Tyler Mitchell (*1995, Atlanta), Nadine Ijewere (*1992, London) und Arielle Bobb-Willis (*1995, New York) widersetzt sich Ehrenstein den in den Massenmedien allgegenwärtigen Bildern vom Leid der Schwarzen, von afrikanischem „poverty porn" („Armutspornografie") bis zu Videos rassistischer Polizeigewalt, die unaufhörlich zirkulieren. Derlei Bilder des Leidens sollen im Allgemeinen zum Handeln aufrufen, doch wie nicht zuletzt Zoé Samudzi festgestellt hat, instrumentalisieren sie letztlich die Schwarzen, indem sie aus dem weit verbreiteten *weißen,* westlichen Verlangen nach Bildern Schwarzen Leids Kapital schlagen und es weiter verstärken.⁴ Die Aufnahmen hungernder afrikanischer Kinder stehen beispielhaft für ein fotografisches Modell, das westliche Bilder vom afrikanischen Kontinent kontaminiert und das Maggie Nelson „Beschämen-um-uns-zum-Handeln-zu-bringen" genannt hat.⁵ Susan Sontag wiederum widmete sich in *Das Leiden anderer betrachten* (2003) den moralischen Vexierfragen, mit denen Bilder der Grausamkeit die Betrachter konfrontieren, und zwar anhand des seinerzeit aktuellen Beispiels der Aufnahmen von Kriegsgräueln auf dem Balkan, von wo Ehrensteins albanische Familie stammt.⁶ Wie Nelson und Sontag, aber auch eine zunehmende Zahl von Künstler*innen und Fotograf*innen, steht Ehrenstein derartigen realistischen und fotojournalistischen Konventionen kritisch gegenüber. Bilder von Armut, Gräueltaten und Elend zeigen niemals die ganze Wahrheit und sind häufig manipuliert, um die Auffassung vom „Anderen" als minderwertig oder zurückgeblieben zu rechtfertigen.

Stattdessen zeigte etwa Ijewere in ihrer *i-D*-Modestrecke mit dem Titel „Joy as an Act of Resistance" („Lebensfreude als Akt des Widerstands") modische Schwarze Frauen, die sich teils allein, teils miteinander am Strand vergnügen. Ein Bild zeigt das ausgelassen lachende Model Wayne Booth in einem leuchtend orangefarbenen Kleid mit ausladendem Tüllrock. Aus der Froschperspektive aufgenommen, erhebt sie sich über den*die Betrachter*innen und überwältigt sie mit ihrer Lebensfreude. Ijewere stellt entschieden fest, dass nicht nur das Leben der Schwarzen zählt, sondern ihnen auch zusteht, sich entfalten zu können und Freude und Erfolg zu haben. Auch Mitchell, der es mit seiner Aufnahme von Beyoncé mit Blütenkopfschmuck als erste*r Schwarze*r Fotograf*in auf das *Vogue*-Cover schaffte, widmet seine künstlerische Arbeit der Schwarzen Lebensfreude. Für seine Ausstellung *I Can Make You Feel Good* im International Center

Putting aside, for now, the process by which this cohort is made a collaborator and not simply a subject, I want to note that the portraits in *Tools for Conviviality* radiate Black joy. In the tradition of contemporary Black photographers including Tyler Mitchell (b. 1995, Atlanta), Nadine Ijewere (b. 1992, London), and Arielle Bobb-Willis (b. 1995, New York), Ehrenstein endeavors to counter widespread mass media images depicting Black suffering, ranging from African poverty porn to videos documenting anti-Black police brutality, both of which have circulated endlessly. Often these images of suffering are ostensibly intended to ignite action, but, as Zoé Samudzi and others have argued, they wind up instrumentalizing Black people, capitalizing upon and reinforcing the widespread white and Western eagerness to consume images of Black suffering.⁴ Photographs of malnourished African children are the quintessential example of the model of photography that has plagued Western images taken on the African continent. Maggie Nelson calls this model "shaming-us-into-action-by-unmasking-the-truth,"⁵ though when grappling with the moral conundrums that atrocity images impart upon their viewers in her 2003 book *Regarding the Pain of Others,* Susan Sontag used the contemporaneous example of photographs showing the horrors of war in the Balkans, where Ehrenstein, who is Albanian, has roots.⁶ Like Nelson and Sontag, as well as a growing group of artists and photographers, Ehrenstein is critical of such realist and photojournalistic conventions. Images exposing poverty, atrocities, and misery can never capture the whole story, and are often manipulated to justify views that the "other" is lesser or backward.

Instead, Ijewere's 2018 editorial for *i-D*, titled *Joy as an Act of Resistance,* shows fashionable Black women enjoying a day at the beach. They are photographed individually and also seen enjoying one another's company. In one photograph, we see the model Wayne Booth smiling exuberantly, wearing a bright orange dress with a swaying tulle skirt: she towers over us; her joy is powerful. Ijewere insists that Black lives not only matter, but deserve to thrive, experience joy, and prosper. Meanwhile Mitchell, whose photograph of Beyoncé in a floral headdress made him the first Black photographer to have his work grace the cover of *Vogue,* devotes his artistic practice to capturing Black joy. For his 2020 installation *Laundry Line,* which debuted in his exhibition *I Can Make You Feel Good* at the International Center of Photography in New York, he took inspiration from an image by Black American photographer Gordon Parks from the 1950s, showing two women at a fence used as a laundry line. This time, he hung portraits of models, influencers, and friends printed onto various textiles. Ehrenstein's work is indebted to such images of Black joy, which also merge fashion photography and fine art.⁷

Many artists working today have responded to ways in which photographers impart their biases onto their subjects by representing only, or at least primarily, those who belong to their "identity group"—a term Ehrenstein used in a July 2020 virtual performance lecture she gave for the opening of the PhotoIreland festival titled *On Decolonising Lens-Based Practices.* One cannot photograph another without projecting some of their own bias, and thinkers like Maurice Berger and Lauren Michele Jackson have cast

of Photography in New York schuf er die Installation *Laundry Line* (2020), inspiriert von einem Bild des Schwarzen US-amerikanischen Fotografen Gordon Parks aus den 1950er-Jahren, auf dem zwei Frauen ihre Wäsche zum Trocknen an einen Drahtzaun gehängt haben. Mitchell befestigte für seine Installation auf verschiedene Stoffe gedruckte Porträts von Models, Influencern und Freunden an Wäscheleinen. Derartigen Bildern Schwarzer Lebensfreude, in denen Modefotografie und Kunst verschmelzen, ist Ehrensteins Arbeit verpflichtet.[7]

Zahlreiche aktuelle Künstler*innen haben sich damit auseinandergesetzt, dass Fotograf*innen ihre jeweiligen Vorurteile in gewisser Weise auf ihre Modelle übertragen, indem sie ausschließlich oder zumindest vorrangig Menschen aus ihrer „Identitätsgruppe" darstellen, um einen Begriff aufzugreifen, den Ehrenstein im Juli 2020 bei der virtuellen Performance-Lecture *On Decolonising Lens-Based Practices* zur Eröffnung des Festivals Photo-Ireland verwendete. Man kann einen anderen Menschen nicht fotografieren, ohne zumindest teilweise die eigenen Vorurteile auf sie*ihn zu projizieren, und Theoretiker*innen wie Maurice Berger und Lauren Michele Jackson bezweifeln, dass man den eigenen Rassismus jemals vollständig verlernen kann.[8] Ehrenstein indes befolgt in *Tools for Conviviality* Desmond Tutus vielfach zitierte Feststellung: „Wer sich in einer Situation der Ungerechtigkeit neutral verhält, stellt sich auf die Seite der Unterdrücker."[9] Ausschließlich Menschen darzustellen, die einem selbst gleichen, stellt in Ehrensteins Augen eine Form der Segregation dar und bietet *weißen* und europäischen Künstler*innen die Möglichkeit, schwierigen Themen, an denen sie eine Mitschuld tragen, aus dem Weg zu gehen. Demgegenüber sucht sie nach einem Weg, um mit ihren afrikanischen Partner*innen zu sprechen, nicht für sie.

Ehrensteins Ansatz ist provokativ und setzt bei der Arbeit einer Handvoll europäischer und US-amerikanischer Künstler*innen an, die mit vorgeblich guten Absichten in der südlichen Hemisphäre tätig sind. Sie werden großteils als „weiße Retter" bezeichnet, nicht etwa, weil sie tatsächlich jemanden retten würden, sondern um auf ihren zweifelhaften Anspruch zu verweisen. Ein Beispiel dafür ist der problematische Film *Enjoy Poverty* (2008) des niederländischen Künstlers Renzo Martins (*1973), in dem er kongolesische Hochzeits- und Porträtfotograf*innen ermutigt, Fotografien zu produzieren, die die eigene Armut unterstreichen, und die sie teuer an westliche Medien verkaufen könnten. Martens will ihnen helfen, Geld zu verdienen, allerdings tut er das, indem er den Kongoles*innen nahelegt, schädliche Stereotypen aufzuwärmen und letztlich die Schwarzen Fotograf*innen für seine eigene Arbeit instrumentalisiert. Zudem unterstellt er ihnen gewisse Prioritäten und Werte und gibt vor zu wissen, was für sie am besten sei – Geld. Die US-amerikanische Fotografin Susan Meiselas (*1948) wurde vor allem für ihre Fotografie *Molotov Man* (1979) aus der Zeit der Nicaraguanischen Revolution 1978/1979 bekannt, ein Bild, das sich in der Folge Vertreter*innen gegensätzlicher Ideologien für ihre je eigenen Zwecke angeeignet haben. Nachdem Meiselas vor Augen geführt worden war, dass die Menschen sehen, was sie sehen wollen, widmete sie sich in ihrem nachfolgenden Schaffen explizit der unausweichlichen Subjektivität der Fotografie und den ihr innewohnenden Machtverhältnissen, um auf diese

doubt as to whether one can ever completely unlearn one's own racism.[8] Yet Ehrenstein, in *Tools for Conviviality,* maintains Desmond Tutu's oft-quoted wisdom: "If you are neutral in situations of injustice, you have chosen the side of the oppressor."[9] Ehrenstein believes that the predominant approach, of refusing to show those unlike yourself, is a form of segregation, and a way for white and European artists to avoid difficult subjects in which they are complicit. Instead, she seeks to create a method of speaking with and not for her African collaborators.

Ehrenstein's approach is provocative, one preceded by a handful of other European and American artists endeavoring to work in the southern hemisphere, ostensibly with good intentions. Many are labeled "white saviors"—which is not to say they actually save anyone but are problematic for assuming it is their job to do so. Take, for example, the troubling film *Enjoy Poverty* (2008) by the Dutch artist Renzo Martens (b. 1973), in which he instructs Congolese wedding and portrait photographers to take images emphasizing their own poverty, because they will sell for big bucks to Western media. Though Martens endeavors to help them earn money, he does so by encouraging Congolese people to rehash damaging stereotypes, thus instrumentalizing Black photographers for his own work. Moreover, he makes assumptions about their priorities and values, as if he knows what's best (money). American photographer Susan Meiselas (b. 1948) became best known for her 1979 photograph *Molotov Man,* taken during the 1978–79 Nicaraguan Revolution. The image was later used to support a wide range of conflicting ideologies. After witnessing how people see only what they want to see, Meiselas later devoted her practice to reflecting on, and taking ownership of, the inevitable subjectivity and power dynamics inherent to photography. Like Meiselas, Ehrenstein believes that Western artists *can* work in the southern hemisphere, but that it must be handled with extreme care. Whether or not one agrees that Western artists can or should ever make work in or about Africa, Ehrenstein's gesture is distinct from a practice like Martens's in that she asks how her collaborators can benefit from her photography, while acknowledging that her work benefits from their participation, too, treating the ordeal as transactional.

Yet though Ehrenstein and her collaborators differ along the lines of race and geography, they also share other "identity groups." First, as I mentioned, Ehrenstein is Albanian, so both she and her collaborators belong to a group known as the "global south." The term was first coined by the World Bank: it was intended as an alternative to the more derogatory "third world," and referred to countries in the southern hemisphere. Yet a growing group of scholars have reframed the term, arguing that the southern region of nearly any territory encompasses "peoples negatively impacted by globalization," including poorer regions within wealthier countries or continents.[10] Whether comparing Milan to Sicily, Europe to Africa, New York to Mississippi, or Germany to Albania, the North emerges as the wealthier and more industrialized region. The South is both poorer and often regarded as provincial, backward, or lazy in the eyes of the North. Ehrenstein first became compelled to work in the global south after a formative experience in photography school. She had been working on a project

Weise die Kontrolle darüber zu behalten. Wie Meiselas ist Ehrenstein über-
zeugt, dass westliche Künstler*innen in der südlichen Hemisphäre arbeiten *dürfen*, dass sie dabei jedoch äußerst umsichtig vorgehen müssen.
Ob man nun der Auffassung ist, dass westliche Künstler* innen in oder
über Afrika arbeiten dürfen und sollten oder nicht: Ehrensteins Vorgehen
unterscheidet sich unzweifelhaft von Martens' Ansatz, da sie sich bei ihren Partner*innen erkundigt, wie diese von ihren Fotografien profitieren
könnten, und zugleich bekennt, dass sie gleichfalls von der Zusammenarbeit profitiert und mithin den Prozess als Transaktion behandelt.
Bei allen ethnischen und geografischen Unterschieden zwischen Ehrenstein
und ihren Koproduzent*innen gehören sie zugleich gewissen gemeinsamen
„Identitätsgruppen" an. Erstens ist Ehrenstein durch ihre albanische Her-
kunft wie ihre Partner*innen Teil des „globalen Süden", eine begriffliche
Wendung, die von der Weltbank als Alternative zu der abwertenden Bezeich-
nung „Dritte Welt" geprägt wurde und die sich ursprünglich ausschließlich
auf die Länder der südlichen Hemisphäre bezog. Doch eine zunehmende
Zahl von Forscher*innen hat den Begriff neu gefasst, da im Süden so gut
wie jedes geografischen oder politischen Gebiets „von der Globalisierung
benachteiligte Menschen" leben würden – auch in Ländern und auf Konti-
nenten, die zu den wohlhabenden gehören.[10] Vergleicht man Mailand mit
Sizilien, Europa mit Afrika, New York mit dem Mississippi-Delta oder
Deutschland mit Albanien, so ist stets der Norden reicher und stärker indust-
rialisiert. Doch nicht nur, dass der Süden ärmer ist, zudem werden die Menschen dort vom Norden als provinziell, zurückgeblieben und faul abgewertet.
Für Ehrenstein gab ein Schlüsselerlebnis im Fotografiestudium den Aus-
schlag, sich mit ihrer Arbeit dem globalen Süden zuzuwenden. Als sie sich

in einem Projekt mit Weiblichkeit in
Albanien beschäftigte, wurde sie
ständig dafür kritisiert, die Armut in
Albanien nicht zu zeigen. In ihrer Serie
Tales of Lipstick and Virtue (2013–
2018) geht es ihr vielmehr um die
Konstruiertheit und Performativität
von Weiblichkeit – aber auch, in gewisser Hinsicht, von sozialer Klasse,
wenn sie etwa Designerfälschungen
wie limettengrüne Slipper mit auf-
genähtem Chanel-Logo oder eine
Torte mit Burberry-Karomuster zeigt.
Auf einem Bild ist ein weiblicher Un-
terleib zu sehen, bedeckt von einem
rosafarbenen Seiden-Tangaslip mit

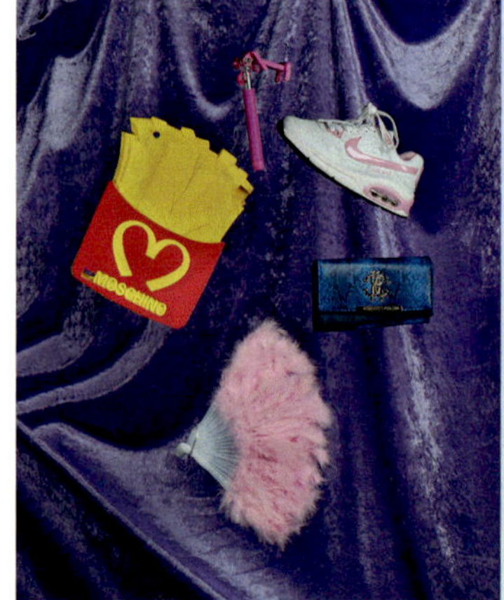

Kolonat is not McDonald
(Tales of Lipstick and Virtue), 2016

der grasgrünen, verschnörkelten Aufschrift „Western Girl". Die an den Rän-
dern des Slips hervorquellende Schambehaarung verdeutlicht, dass diese
Frau sich keinem Diktat unterwerfen kann oder will. Ein anderes Bild zeigt
auf den ersten Blick eine Pommes-Tüte von McDonalds, doch der genau-
ere Blick offenbart ein gelbes Moschino-M statt der goldenen Bögen: eine
bewusste und respektlose Verschmelzung von Alltags- und Luxussphäre.

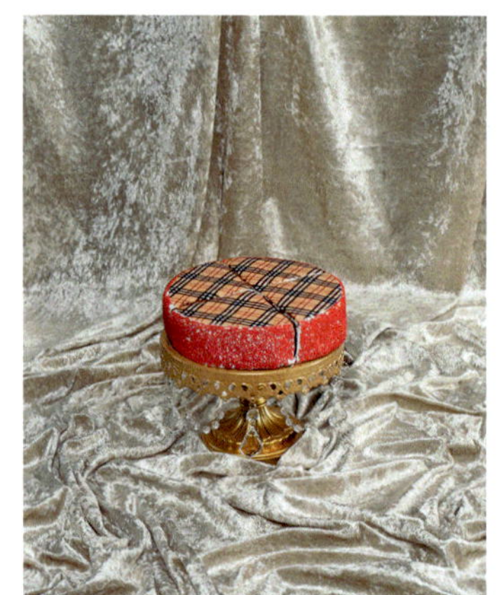

Piece of Cake (Tales of Lipstick and Virtue), 2015

about femininity in Albania and was constantly critiqued for not showing how poor
Albania is. Instead, her series *Tales of Lipstick and Virtue* (2013–18) confronts the
ways in which femininity is constructed and
performative. In some ways, class is, too:
she shows fake designer goods, such as
lime-green slip-on shoes with a Coco Chanel
logo sewn on top and a cake printed with
a Burberry-esque plaid. In one image, we
see a crotch adorned with a pink, silk thong

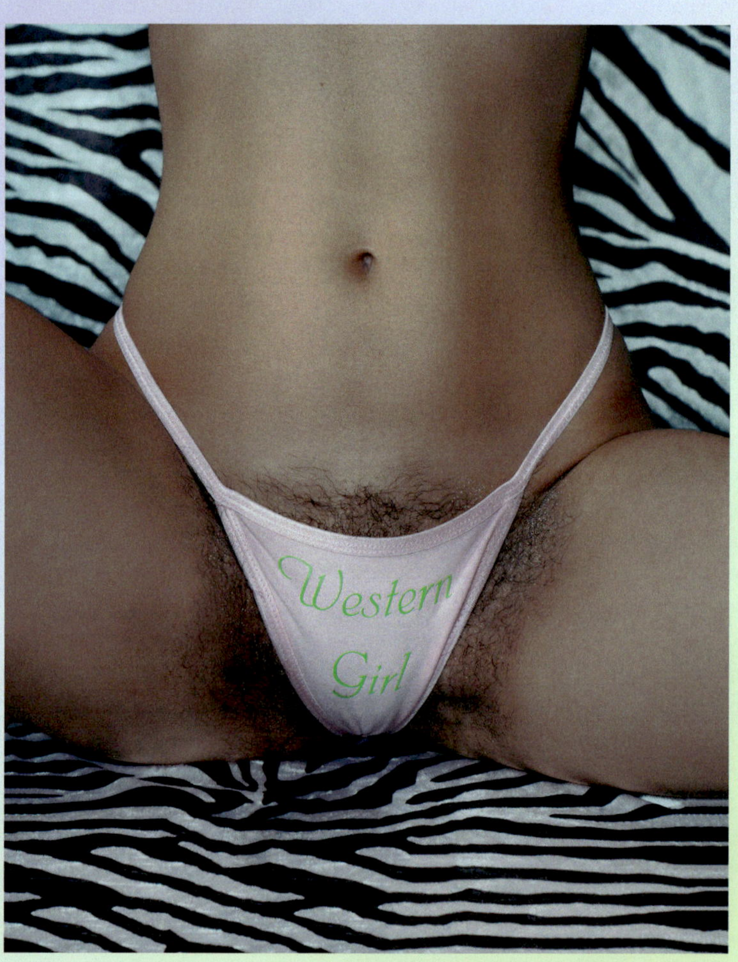

Western Girl (Tales of Lipstick and Virtue), 2016

that reads "WESTERN GIRL" in a curly, lime-green font. Pubic hair is very
visible beyond the garment's edges, suggesting this woman cannot or will
not conform to fit in. We see what looks like McDonald's French fries,

Anstatt die Armut hervorzuheben, stellt Ehrenstein die Werte infrage, die Geschmack und Reichtum definieren: Ebenso, wie Markenlogos oberflächliche Signifikanten sind, gilt das auch für Klasse und Geschlecht.

Das essentialistische Feedback auf ihre Arbeit brachte Ehrenstein zu Bewusstsein, dass negative Stereotype des globalen Südens in Fotografien aufscheinen und durch sie und ihre Verbreitung aufrechterhalten werden. Sie begann, die Fotografie als Schlüsselwerkzeug zu begreifen, mit dem sich diese Stereotype demontieren lassen. In *On Decolonising Lens-Based Practices* führte die Künstlerin vor, dass bei der Google-Bildersuche nach „Albania+person" 18 von 41 Treffern auf der ersten Seite Menschen in von ihr so genannter „ethnischer Kleidung" zeigten (zumeist ein weißes Kleidungsstück unter einem bestickten), sechs zeigten Kriminelle und sieben arme Menschen. Bei der Suche nach „Africa+person" erschienen auf der ersten Seite ausschließlich Bilder traditionellen Stammeslebens und unterernährter Menschen; nichts deutete auf ein modernes Leben auf dem Kontinent hin. Dagegen tauchten bei den Suchbegriffen „Germany+person" unter den 41 Ergebnissen nur zwei Menschen in traditioneller Kleidung auf. Fünf Bilder verwiesen auf die anhaltende Fremdenfeindlichkeit und den Rassismus im Land. Die Mehrzahl jedoch zeigte Menschen beim Biertrinken oder bei Klimademonstrationen.

Zweitens kommt Ehrenstein aus einer muslimischen Familie, und Albanien ist ein vorwiegend muslimisches Land. Unter den Fotografien von *Tools for Conviviality* befinden sich Hommagen an die islamische Ornamentik, eine Kultur und visuelle Sprache, die sie mit ihren Koproduzent*innen gemein hat.[11] Traditionell enthalten islamische Muster sich wiederholende und mosaikartige Motive, die vielfach einer komplexen Geometrie gehorchen. In einem von Ehrensteins Stillleben steht beispielsweise die Abbildung eines Stoffes neben Ausschnitten aus Bildern desselben Stoffes, die zu einem neuen mosaikartigen Muster zusammengesetzt wurden. Das Bild ist eine digitale Collage aus mehreren Fotografien und enthält am unteren Rand schwarze Plastiksandalen mit einem weißen Nike Swoosh und dem Apple-Logo. Andere Bilder zeigen wie bei dem Blick durch ein Kaleidoskop den fragmentierten Körper der Yoga treibenden Nyamwathi Gichau in mehrfacher Wiederholung. In beiden Fällen spielt Ehrenstein auf jahrhundertealte Traditionen und Techniken an, setzt diese in ihren digitalen Collagen jedoch mit zeitgenössischen Mitteln wie Photoshop um.

Doch nun zu dem oben bereits kurz erwähnten Prozess: Ehrenstein begreift die auf ihren Fotografien abgebildeten Menschen nicht als „Modelle" – dieser Begriff, der in Kunst und Fotografie die dargestellte Person bezeichnet, deutet zugleich ein Herrschaftsverhältnis an, insofern das Modell als passiv gedacht wird, als eine Person, mit dem*der etwas gemacht wird. Demgegenüber betrachtet Ehrenstein diese Menschen als ihre Koproduzent*innen. Für die Fotografien von Nyamwathi Gichau – mit der Ehrenstein nicht persönlich zusammentreffen konnte – schickte Gichau Ehrenstein an einige ihrer Lieblingsorte in Dakar, an die sie sich selbst zu einem Date ausführen würde. Ehrenstein machte Fotos der Orte und schickte sie an Gichau, die sie bearbeitete. Aus den entstehenden Vorlagen schuf Ehrenstein schließlich ihre Collagen. Die in den Bildern zu sehenden Stoffe hat

though on closer inspection, the packaging bears a yellow M, for Moschino, and not golden arches: a deliberate and irreverent conflation of high- and low-class items. Instead of emphasizing poverty, we see her questioning values that define taste and wealth: just as brand logos are superficial signifiers, so are class and gender.

After experiencing this essentialist feedback to her work, Ehrenstein concluded that negative stereotypes impacting the global south are both visible in and perpetuated by photographs and their circulation. She began treating photography as a crucial tool for undoing these stereotypes. In *On Decolonising Lens-Based Practices*, the artist demonstrated that, when she searched on Google images for "Albania+person," out of the forty-one images on the first page, eighteen of them showed people in what she called "ethnic wear" (usually a white garment underneath an embroidered one), six were images of criminals, and seven were images of people in poverty. When she searched "Africa+person," the first page of results showed only tribal life and malnourishment; there was no evidence of modernity on the continent. Yet for "Germany+person," of the forty-one images, only two people wore traditional German outfits. Five images illustrated ongoing xenophobia or racism in the country. The majority showed modern people drinking beer or attending climate strikes.

Second, Ehrenstein also comes from a Muslim family, and Albania is a predominantly Muslim country. Among the photographs in *Tools for Conviviality* are homages to Islamic patternmaking, a culture and visual language that she shares with her collaborators.[11] Traditionally, Islamic patterns involve repeating and tessellating motifs, often according to complex geometries. In one of the still lifes, for example, we see an image of a textile shown alongside fragments of images of that same textile, tessellated to form a new pattern. The image is a digital collage of a number of photographs, and at the bottom, we see black plastic sandals that bear both a white Nike Swoosh and an Apple logo. In other images, we see Nyamwathi Gichau doing yoga; her figure is repeated and refracted, almost as if seen through a kaleidoscope. Both allude to centuries-old traditions and techniques, yet are realized with contemporary tools as photoshopped, digital collages.

Now, about the process that I alluded to above: Ehrenstein sees the people in her photos not as her "subjects"—this word is used in art and photography to refer to the person in the picture, but it implies a kind of domination: it is also used by scientists to describe the person on whom they are experimenting. Rather, they are her collaborators. To create the photographs of Nyamwathi Gichau—with whom she was not able to share a physical space—Gichau sent Ehrenstein to some of her favorite places around Dakar, places Gichau would take herself on a date. Ehrenstein photographed those places, then sent them to Gichau, who edited them. Ehrenstein created the collages with the results. The textiles visible in her photographs were chosen in consultation with Donkafele, who took her to Dakar's market and worked with her to select fabric for the backgrounds, as well as objects for the still lives. Among these objects are colorful buckets; metal trays that appear almost holographic; Nike sneakers; plastic clothes hangers;

sie gemeinsam mit den Machern von Donkafele ausgesucht, die mit ihr in Dakar auf dem Markt gingen und die Textilien für den Hintergrund der Stillleben und die übrigen Requisiten wie farbenfrohe Eimer, beinahe holografisch anmutende Metalltabletts, Nike-Schuhe, Kunststoffbügel und karierte Plastiktaschen auswählten. Von diesen in Dakar auf dem Markt gekauften Objekten sind laut Ehrenstein insbesondere die Plastiktaschen als weit verbreitete Alltagswerkzeuge „auf Dakars Straßen allgegenwärtig".[12] Doch Ehrenstein wollte ihr Projektbudget auch zum Nutzen ihrer Koproduzent*innen einsetzen, zumal sie ihnen nichts bezahlen konnte. Also nahm sie Gegenstände aus dem Portfolio ihrer Partner*innen für deren Onlineshops auf. Die Fotografie ist per se ein transaktionales Medium, was in der englischen Wendung „to take someone's photograph" (wörtlich „die Fotografie eines anderen nehmen") deutlich wird. Im Gegenzug wollte Ehrenstein etwas zurückgeben. Mit einem Teil ihres Budgets mietete sie über Airbnb ein Apartment, das als großartiges Setting einer Modestrecke diente, dann heuerte sie Models an und organisierte und fotografierte eine Modenschau. Sie wollte nicht einfach Lebensfreude und Gemeinschaft darstellen, sondern sie tatsächlich *erschaffen*.

Die Künstlerin kann selbstverständlich nicht vermeiden, dass ihre eigene Perspektive und ihre eigene Ästhetik in die Bilder einfließen, und sie erhebt auch nicht diesen Anspruch: Mit gutem Grund geht sie nicht davon aus, dass die Fotografie jemals neutral oder objektiv zu sein vermag. Vielmehr gesteht sie ein, dass sie sich durch die Aufnahme einer anderen Person etwas von dieser zu ihrem eigenen Nutzen „nimmt", zugleich hofft sie, der oder dem anderen mit ihrem Projekt etwas zurückgeben zu können.

Ehrenstein strebt nicht allein mit ihrer kollaborativen Methode gleiche Machtverhältnisse an, sondern auch durch ihre formalen Mittel. In dem 360-Grad-Video verbringen sie und ihre Koproduzent*innen entspannt Zeit miteinander. Man sieht, wie Ehrenstein die Kamera hält, mithin sich nicht als allsehendes neutrales Auge geriert, sondern ihre subjektive Position transparent macht. Zudem sieht man, dass Ehrenstein keineswegs durchgängig die Kamera bedient; immer wieder übernehmen auch ihre Koproduzent*innen. In der Modenschau-Szene reichen die auf dem Laufsteg aneinander vorbeischreitenden Models die an einem Selfiestick befestigte GoPro-Kamera untereinander weiter, sodass die Perspektive aufgesplittet und das binäre Verhältnis von Betrachter*in zu Betrachtetem*r gekippt wird. Das soll nicht etwa heißen, dass das Machtgefälle vollkommen verschwinden oder Ehrensteins Perspektive eliminiert würde. Ganz im Gegenteil: Ihre unvermeidliche Subjektivität wird sichtbar gemacht und hervorgehoben, worin man ein Bekenntnis zu der eigenen unentrinnbaren Voreingenommenheit und eine Kritik an der vermeintlichen Neutralität des Bildjournalismus erkennen kann. Der 360-Grad-Bildbereich erschwert es, mittels Beschneidung oder Ausschnitt ein ausschließlich Ehrensteins eigenen Blickwinkel wiedergebendes Bild zu konstruieren, gleichwohl stellt sie die neue Technik nicht als Lösung der alten Probleme der Fotografie dar. Gelegentlich überblendet sie die von ihr produzierten Aufnahmen mit Found-Footage-Material. In einem Clip führt Facebook-Chef Mark Zuckerberg die neue 360-Technik seiner Plattform vor und „besucht" dafür von

and plaid, plastic bags. All of these items are things she bought in the market in Dakar; she described the bags, in particular, as "very visible in Dakar's urban life," common and everyday tools.[12] She also wanted to use the budget for her project to benefit those with whom she was working, especially since she was unable to pay them. And, she shot items her collaborators were selling for their online shops. Photography is inherently transactional: that's why we say we "took" someone's photograph. Ehrenstein wanted to give something in return. She used a part of her budget to rent out an Airbnb that served as a gorgeous backdrop for a fashion shoot, then hired models, and hosted and photographed a fashion show. She endeavored not simply to depict, but also *produce*, joy and conviviality.

The artist, of course, cannot refrain from incorporating her own perspective and aesthetic into her images, nor does she claim to: she rightly does not believe that photography can ever be neutral or objective. Rather she acknowledges that, in taking someone's photograph, she is taking something from them for her own benefit and hopes the project can give them something in return.

Ehrenstein endeavors to level the power dynamic not only by employing a collaborative method, but also in formal terms. In her 360-degree video, we see her hanging out among her collaborators. We can see her holding the camera: she does not pretend to be some all-seeing, neutral eye, but rather she quite literally reveals her subject position. And we see that it is not always Ehrenstein who wields the camera: sometimes her collaborators do as well. In the fashion show scene, models walk down the catwalk and hand off the Go Pro mounted on a selfie stick as they pass one another, further distributing the point of view and upending the binary between the gazer and the gazed upon. This does not mean the power dynamic disappears entirely or that her point of view is neutralized. Quite the contrary: her inevitable subjectivity is made visible and emphasized, which we might also think of as a way of taking accountability for her own inevitable biases and also as a criticism of photojournalism's supposed neutrality. Her 360-degree purview makes it more difficult to construct an image reflecting solely her own point of view via cropping or framing, though she does not suggest that this new technology is a solution to photography's old problems. She sometimes overlays her recorded footage with found footage. One clip shows Facebook CEO Mark Zuckerberg showing off his platform's latest 360 technology by "visiting" the flooded, hurricane-damaged Puerto Rico from the comfort of his office. His promotional video was criticized as both opportunistic and a flashy, unhelpful use of expensive technology.[13] Ehrenstein captures a conviviality that she juxtaposes with Zuckerberg's disaster tourism. And she captures her video with a relatively low-tech camera—a GoPro—then pushes the colors, so that we see lots of purples and greens. Though some, like Zuckerberg, claim that VR or 360 cameras can make it seem like you're really "there," Ehrenstein's non-naturalistic colors emphasize the artifice of the image, and the ease with which it can be manipulated. This inclusion of found footage also emphasizes that the video is edited: it is ultimately up to Ehrenstein to decide in the editing process which footage to include and which to omit: it is by no

seinem sicheren Büro aus das überflutete und von einem Hurrikan verwüstete Puerto Rico. Sein Werbevideo wurde als opportunistisch und als ebenso großspurige wie nutzlose Demonstration einer teuren Technik gegeißelt.[13] Zuckerbergs Katastrophentourismus stellt Ehrenstein die von ihr eingefangene Konvivialität gegenüber. Zudem nutzt sie für ihr Video eine eher einfache Kamera – eine GoPro – und verändert die Farben so, dass Lila und Grün dominant werden. Im Widerspruch zu Zuckerberg und anderen, laut denen VR-Kameras und 360-Grad-Kameras den Eindruck des „Dabei-Seins" vermitteln würden, hebt Ehrenstein durch ihre nicht naturalistische Farbgebung die Künstlichkeit der Bilder und ihre einfache Manipulierbarkeit hervor. Die Verwendung von Found Footage verdeutlicht zudem, dass das Video geschnitten wurde und letztlich Ehrenstein beim Schneiden entscheidet, welche Aufnahmen sie verwendet und welche sie fortlässt; es ist also keineswegs frei von Eingriffen durch sie oder gar restlos objektiv. Das Video entstand bei einem zweiten Besuch in Dakar 2019. Laut Ehrenstein ist es im Gegensatz zu den straffen Terminvorgaben im Fotojournalismus ein unabdingbarer Bestandteil ihres Arbeitsprozesses, sich bei einem Projekt mehrere Jahre Zeit zu lassen, um es zwischendurch immer wieder beiseitezulegen und darüber nachdenken zu können.

Der Begriff der „conviviality" im Titel der Arbeit bezieht sich nicht allein auf Schwarze Lebensfreude oder die Merriam-Webster-Definition des Begriffs als „Freude am Feiern, am Trinken und an Geselligkeit", wie sie in dem Video zu sehen und in dem zugehörigen Soundtrack mit fröhlicher Rave Musik der 1990er-Jahre zu hören ist, die von der englischen Band Opus III stammt und in einer kantonesischen Version in Berlin produziert wurde. Zudem zitiert Ehrenstein mit ihrem Titel das gleichnamige Buch des kroatisch-österreichischen Philosophen Ivan Illich von 1973. Illichs Familie kam wie die der Künstlerin vom Balkan, und wie sie ist er in der deutschsprachigen Welt aufgewachsen. Seine Eltern gingen aus Kroatien nach Wien, als er noch ein kleines Kind war, und sein Vater war Diplomat. Viele seiner Beobachtungen von 1973 zur Technik klingen auch heute noch aktuell: Illich beklagt den Trieb, neue Werkzeuge allein um des Erfindens willen zu erfinden, und erklärt mahnend, dass wir zwar hofften, neue Werkzeuge würden uns das Leben erleichtern, wir jedoch oftmals als ihre Sklaven endeten. Ehrensteins Projekt mag auf den ersten Blick technikbejahend wirken, denkt man an die Drohnen, Computer, VR-Headsets und iPhones in ihren Porträts und Stillleben und die Art und Weise, wie sie mittels Photoshop repetitive Muster erzeugt. Und der Titel *Tools for Conviviality* legt nahe, dass diese Werkzeuge im Dienst der Lebensfreude und Geselligkeit genutzt wurden. Doch wie Illichs Buch ist auch Ehrensteins Projekt kein Loblied auf die Werkzeuge. Illich warnt davor, dass die Werkzeuge zumeist keineswegs Konvivialität erzeugen: „Die Hypothese war, dass die Maschinen die Sklaven ersetzen könnten. [Doch] es ist offenbar, dass […] die Maschinen den Menschen versklaven."[14] Illich fährt fort: „Um die Krise zu lösen, müssen wir die gegenwärtige Grundstruktur der Werkzeuge umstülpen. Wir müssen dem Menschen Werkzeuge in die Hand geben, die ihr Recht gewährleisten, mit hoher, unabhängiger Wirksamkeit zu arbeiten, um so zugleich die Notwendigkeit von Sklaven und Herren zu

means free of her decisions or totally objective. The video was shot during a follow-up visit to Dakar, in 2019: Ehrenstein told me that having space to work on the project over a couple of years, and to go back and forth to allow time for reflection, was an important part of her process and distinct from the tight deadlines common in photojournalism.

The "conviviality" of her title is a reference not only to Black joy, or to what Merriam-Webster defines as "relating to, occupied with, or fond of feasting, drinking, and good company"—which we see in the video and hear in the soundtrack, which includes upbeat, 1990s rave music by the English band Opus III in a Cantonese version produced in Berlin. It is also a reference to a 1973 book by the Croatian-Austrian philosopher Ivan Illich, *Tools for Conviviality,* from which Ehrenstein borrowed her title. Like the artist, Illich has roots in the Balkans but grew up in the Germanic world: he was raised in Vienna by Croatian parents, and his father was a diplomat. Many of the observations about technology from his 1973 book ring true today: Illich laments the impulse to invent new tools for invention's sake, and warns that, though we ostensibly create new tools in the hopes that they will serve us better, we often end up enslaved to machines instead. At first glance, Ehrenstein's project might suggest a technopositivist bent: we see images of drones, computers, VR headsets, and iPhones in her portraits and still lifes, photoshopped and repeated to create patterns. And the title, *Tools for Conviviality,* suggests these tools were used to create their joy and togetherness. But like Illich's book, it is not a project in praise of tools. Illich warns that, most often, tools engender anything but conviviality. "The hypothesis was that machines could replace slaves," he wrote, "[but] the evidence shows that . . . machines enslave men."[14] He continues, "The crisis can be solved only if we learn to invert the present deep structure of tools; if we give people tools that guarantee their right to work with high, independent efficiency, thus simultaneously eliminating the need for either slaves or masters and enhancing each person's range of freedom. People need new tools to work with rather than tools that 'work' for them. They need technology to make the most of the energy and imagination each has, rather than more well-programmed energy slaves."[15]

Hacking existing tools, rather than creating new ones, is one approach Illich proposes. Similarly, Ehrenstein is deeply critical of the ways that photography captures damaging stereotypes, and algorithms circulate and reinforce them online. Yet instead of doing away with those tools and the power dynamics embedded deeply therein, she *re*-tools them, acknowledging that the camera inevitably sets up a power dynamic, but insisting that is not something to ignore: damaging, stereotypical images are already out there, and they need to be replaced. With *Tools for Conviviality,* she and her collaborators replace them.

1   Studio visit with the artist via Skype, May 25, 2020.

2   Anna Ehrenstein, "Tools for Conviviality," www.annaehrenstein.com/tools-for-conviviality.html.

3   Studio visit with the artist via Skype, May 25, 2020.

4   Zoé Samudzi, "Plantation Politics: The Congolese Plantation Workers Art League," *Art in America* (September 2020).

5   Maggie Nelson, *The Art of Cruelty: A Reckoning* (New York: W. W. Norton, 2011), 31.

überwinden und das Maß der individuellen Freiheit zu steigern. Der Mensch braucht neue Werkzeuge, um damit zu arbeiten, nicht aber Werkzeuge, die an seiner Statt ‚arbeiten‘. Er braucht eine Technologie, die den besten Nutzen aus der persönlichen Energie und Phantasie zu ziehen erlaubt, nicht aber mehr gut programmierte Sklaven der Energie.“[15]

Illich schlägt als eine Möglichkeit vor, die existierenden Werkzeuge zu hacken, statt neue zu erschaffen. Ähnlich geht Ehrenstein vor. Denn bei aller Kritik an den schädlichen, im Internet durch Algorithmen verbreiteten und verstärkten Stereotypen der Fotografie verwirft sie nicht etwa die beteiligten Werkzeuge mit den tief in ihnen eingeschriebenen Machtverhältnissen, sondern programmiert sie um. Ihr ist klar, dass durch die Kamera zwangsläufig ein Machtgefälle entsteht, und sie pocht darauf, dieses nicht zu ignorieren, da die schädlichen stereotypen Bilder bereits zirkulieren und ersetzt werden müssen. Eben das tun sie und ihre Koproduzent*innen in *Tools for Conviviality*.

1 Ateliergespräch mit der Künstlerin über Skype, 25. Mai 2020.

2 Anna Ehrenstein, „Tools for Conviviality“, www.annaehrenstein.com/tools-for-conviviality.html.

3 Ateliergespräch mit der Künstlerin über Skype, 25. Mai 2020.

4 Zoé Samudzi, „Plantation Politics: The Congolese Plantation Workers Art League“, *Art in America* 108, Nr. 9 (September 2020).

5 Maggie Nelson, *The Art of Cruelty: A Reckoning*, New York: W. W. Norton 2011, S. 31. Nelson setzt sich in ihrem Buch mit Bildern der Gewalt und Grausamkeit auseinander, doch ihr Modell lässt sich auf die Armutspornografie übertragen.

6 Sontag befasste sich mit den Jugoslawienkriegen von 1991 bis 2001, einer Reihe miteinander zusammenhängender Kriege infolge des Zerfalls des ehemaligen Jugoslawiens. Albanien selbst gehörte nicht zu Jugoslawien, doch die Kriege in den Nachbar-Republiken hatten spürbare Auswirkungen auf das Land.

7 Mehr zu dieser Generation Schwarzer Fotografen findet man in: Antwaun Sargent (Hg.), *The New Black Vanguard: Photography between Art and Fashion*, New York: Aperture 2019.

8 Maurice Berger, „Are Art Museums Racist?“, *Art in America* 78, Nr. 9 (September 1990), S. 68–77, www.artnews.com/art-in-america/features/maurice-berger-are-art-museums-racist-1202682524/; Lauren Michele Jackson, „What Is an Anti-Racist Reading List for?“, *New York Magazine* (June 2020), www.vulture.com/2020/06/anti-racist-reading-lists-what-are-they-for.html.

9 Auch Ehrenstein hat Tutu in ihrer Performance *On Decolonising Lens-Based Practices* zitiert.

10 Anne Garland Mahler, „Global South“, *Oxford Bibliographies in Literary and Critical Theory*, Oxford: Oxford University Press 2018, S. 32.

11 In dem Begleittext zu einem der Bilder aus *Tools for Conviviality* auf Instagram verweist Ehrenstein selbst auf islamische Ornamentik.

12 Ateliergespräch mit der Künstlerin über Skype, 25. Mai 2020.

13 Olivia Solon, „Mark Zuckerberg ‚Tours‘ Flooded Puerto Rico in Bizarre Virtual Reality Promo“, *The Guardian*, 10. Oktober 2017, www.theguardian.com/technology/2017/oct/09/mark-zuckerberg-facebook-puerto-rico-virtual-reality.

14 Ivan Illich, *Tools for Conviviality*, New York: Harper 1973, S. 33. Auf Deutsch unter dem Titel *Selbstbegrenzung. Eine politische Kritik der Technik* erschienen, allerdings lag der deutschen Übersetzung die vom Autor überarbeitete und erweiterte französische Ausgabe zugrunde. Da die Autorin die englischsprachige Originalausgabe zitiert, wurden die vorliegenden Ausschnitte unter Hinzuziehung der deutschen Buchausgabe neu übersetzt.

15 Die deutsche Neuübersetzung basiert auf Illich, *Tools for Conviviality*, S. 27.

Nelson was specifically writing about images of violence and cruelty, though her model applies to poverty porn as well.

6 Sontag was referring to the Yugoslav Wars, which lasted from 1991 to 2001 and comprised a series of related conflicts, primarily centered around dissolution of Yugoslavia. Though Albania was not a part of Yugoslavia, its surrounding nations were, and the conflicts impacted the nation.

7 For more on this generation of Black photographers, see *The New Black Vanguard: Photography between Art and Fashion*, ed. Antwaun Sargent (New York: Aperture, 2019).

8 Maurice Berger, "Are Art Museums Racist?," *Art in America* (September 1990), www.artnews.com/art-in-america/features/maurice-berger-are-art-museums-racist-1202682524/; Lauren Michele Jackson, "What Is an Anti-Racist Reading List for?," *New York Magazine* (June 2020), https://www.vulture.com/2020/06/anti-racist-reading-lists-what-are-they-for.html.

9 Ehrenstein quoted Tutu in her performance *On Decolonising Lens-Based Practices*.

10 Anne Garland Mahler, "Global South," *Oxford Bibliographies in Literary and Critical Theory* (Oxford: Oxford University Press, 2018): 32.

11 Ehrenstein referred to Islamic pattern making in an Instagram caption for one of the images for *Tools for Conviviality*.

12 Studio visit with the artist via Skype, May 25, 2020.

13 Olivia Solon, "Mark Zuckerberg 'Tours' Flooded Puerto Rico in Bizarre Virtual Reality Promo, *The Guardian*, October 10, 2017, https://www.theguardian.com/technology/2017/oct/09/mark-zuckerberg-facebook-puerto-rico-virtual-reality.

14 Ivan Illich, *Tools for Conviviality* (New York: Harper, 1973), 33.

15 Illich, *Tools for Conviviality*, 27.

Wir leben im sogenannten postfaktischen Zeitalter, in dem nicht Tatsachen, sondern Gefühle regieren. Als Folge der Informationsflut der digitalen Welt, in der zentrale Standards wie Objektivität verblassen, sind an die Stelle von Wahrheiten Emotionen gerückt. Was bedeutet diese Entwicklung für das Medium Fotografie, das seit seinem Aufkommen im 19. Jahrhundert mit der Abbildung der Wirklichkeit betraut war?

Der *C/O Berlin Talent Award* steht unter dem Thema „Neue dokumentarische Strategien". Damit ist eine mediale Erweiterung und kritische Befragung traditioneller dokumentarischer Narrative, Verfahren und Ästhetiken gemeint, die nicht mehr nur in Zeitungen und Magazinen anzutreffen sind, sondern verstärkt auch in Museen und Galerien. Auch als Medium der Dokumentation hing Fotografie immer von technischen Voraussetzungen, dem fotografierenden Subjekt und seiner Perspektive auf die Welt sowie dem Kontext ab, in dem sie gezeigt oder reproduziert wurde. Heute, da wir alle als Dokumentaristen unseres Alltags in den sozialen Netzwerken agieren, ist die traditionelle dokumentarische Fotografie in der Kunst aufgegangen und entfaltet dort ihr kritisches Potenzial: Künstler*innen der Gegenwart entwickeln mithilfe des Mediums Fotografie neue Erzählstrategien, um die gesellschaftlichen und politischen Ereignisse zu befragen, die die Welt um uns herum bestimmen. Ihrer Arbeit ist das Förderprogramm von C/O Berlin gewidmet, das sich zugleich an den künstlerischen und wissenschaftlichen Nachwuchs richtet.

Der *C/O Berlin Talent Award* wird einmal jährlich in den Kategorien Kunst und Theorie ausgelobt. Die Auszeichnung ist mit einem Preisgeld für beide Gewinner*innen, einer Einzelausstellung und einer individuell gestalteten Publikation verbunden, in der die prämierte künstlerische Arbeit zusammen mit Texten der ausgezeichneten Theoretiker*in erscheint. Im Förderprogramm von C/O Berlin wurden seit 2006 mehr als 80 junge Talente mit Ausstellungen und Publikationen unterstützt und auf ihrem Weg begleitet.

Dr. Kathrin Schönegg
Kuratorin
C/O Berlin

We are living in what has been termed the post-truth era, in which feelings, not facts, reign supreme. Emotions have supplanted certitudes as a result of the torrent of information available in the digital realm, a place where core principles such as objectivity have lost their force. How does this development affect the medium of photography, which has been entrusted with depicting reality since its invention in the nineteenth century?

New documentary strategies are the focus of the *C/O Berlin Talent Award*. The term indicates the increasing medial broadening and critical querying of traditional documentary narratives, processes, and aesthetics, more and more found in museums and galleries as well as in newspapers and magazines. Even when functioning as a means of documentation, photography has always been shaped by technological parameters, by the subjects depicted and their perspective on the world, as well as by the context in which the images are shown and reproduced. Now that we are all documentary makers, performing everyday moments on social networking sites, traditional documentary photography has become an art form, assuming a critical potentiality: contemporary artists use the medium of photography to develop new narrative strategies, attempting to question socio-political events that define the world around us. The C/O Berlin Talent Program is aimed at the next generation of artists and researchers alike, supporting their work.

Once a year, the *C/O Berlin Talent Award* is awarded to two individuals in the categories of art and theory. This honor carries a monetary award for the winners, as well as a solo exhibition and a custom-designed publication on the award-winning artistic work paired with texts by the winning researcher. Since 2006, C/O Berlin's Talent program has made exhibitions and publications possible for more than eighty emerging new talents.

Dr. Kathrin Schönegg
Curator
C/O Berlin

C/O BERLIN TALENT AWARD 2020

Danke / Thank you
A million thanks to Lydia Lykibi, Nyamwathi Gichau, Awa Seck, Thibaut Houssou, Mandé Mory Bah, Saliou et Madame, Franceline Lebrun, Abdourahmane Sety Diallo, Jordane Bakita, Etienne E. Moutekeee, Assane Diaw, Cheikh Sylla, Antoine Tempé, Azu Nwagbogu, and Rabiana, always.

Die Publikation erscheint im Rahmen des C/O Berlin Talent Award 2020, anlässlich der Ausstellung / This book is published as part of the C/O Berlin Talent Award 2020 on the occasion of the exhibition
Anna Ehrenstein . Tools for Conviviality
C/O Berlin Foundation . Amerika Haus . Hardenbergstraße 22 – 24 . 10623 Berlin

Konzept / Concept
C/O Berlin Foundation in Zusammenarbeit mit der Künstlerin und der Autorin / C/O Berlin Foundation in cooperation with the artist and the author

Projektleitung, Redaktion / Project Management, Editing
Dr. Kathrin Schönegg

Übersetzungen / Translations
Saliou Ba, Sylee Gore und / and Sven Scheer

Lektorat / Copyediting
Dr. Jan-Frederik Bandel, Emmanuel Faure, Dr. Tas Skorupa und / and Jan Wenzel

Gestaltung / Design
naroska.de, Marc Naroska und / and Bryndís Þ. Sigurjónsdóttir

© 2020 C/O Berlin Foundation und / and Spector Books, Leipzig.

Für die abgebildeten Werke / For the reproduced works
© Anna Ehrenstein . Courtesy Office Impart und / and KOW Berlin

Für die abgedruckten Texte / For the texts © Emily Watlington

Limitierte Auflage / Limited Edition 1.200 Exemplare / copies

Bibliografische Information der Deutschen Nationalbibliothek. Die Deutsche Nationalbibliothek verzeichnet diese Publikation in der Deutschen Nationalbibliografie; detaillierte bibliografische Daten sind im Internet über http://dnb.dnb.de abrufbar. /
Bibliographic information published by the Deutsche Nationalbibliothek. The Deutsche Nationalbibliothek lists this publication in the Deutsche Nationalbibliografie; detailed bibliographic data is available on the internet at http://dnb.dnb.de.

Erschienen im Verlag / Published by
Spector Books . Harkortstraße 10 . 04107 Leipzig . www.spectorbooks.com

Distribution
Germany, Austria:
GVA, Gemeinsame Verlagsauslieferung Göttingen GmbH&Co. KG, www.gva-verlage.de

Switzerland:
AVA Verlagsauslieferung AG, www.ava.ch

France, Belgium:
Interart Paris, www.interart.fr

UK:
Central Books Ltd, www.centralbooks.com

USA, Canada, Central and South America, Africa:
ARTBOOK | D.A.P. www.artbook.com

South Korea:
The Book Society, www.thebooksociety.org

Australia, New Zealand:
Perimeter Distribution, www.perimeterdistribution.com

Japan:
twelvebooks, www.twelve-books.com

1. Auflage / First edition

Printed and bound in Germany
ISBN 978-3-95905-428-7

Ermöglicht durch / Made possible by

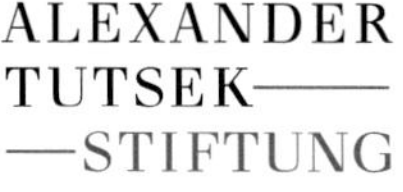